To Understand

To Understand

New Horizons in Reading Comprehension

Ellin Oliver Keene

Heinemann
Portsmouth, NH

Heinemann
361 Hanover Street
Portsmouth, NH 03801-3912
www.heinemann.com

Offices and agents throughout the world

The author and publisher wish to thank those who have generously given permission to reprint borrowed material:

"Early Sunday Morning" from *Renaming the Streets: Poems* by John Stone. Copyright © 1985 by John Stone. Reprinted by permission of Louisiana State University Press.

Excerpt from "Toward an Impure Poetry" from *Five Decades: Poems 1925–1970* by Pablo Neruda. Copyright © 1974 by Grove Press. Used by permission of Grove/Atlantic, Inc.

"Ode to the Spoon" from *Odes to Common Things* by Pablo Neruda. Copyright © 1994 by Pablo Neruda and Fundación Pablo Neruda (*Odes* in Spanish); Copyright © 1994 by Ken Krabbenhoft (*Odes* in English); Copyright © 1994 by Ferris Cook (Illustrations and Compilation). Reprinted by permission of Little, Brown and Co.

"Neruda" from *The Book of Embraces* by Eduardo Galeano, translated by Cedric Belfrage with Mark Schafer. Copyright © 1989 by Eduardo Galeano. English translation copyright © 1991 by Cedric Belfrage. Used by permission of the author and W. W. Norton & Company, Inc.

Appendices C and E–H originally appeared in *Mosaic of Thought*, Second Edition, by Ellin Oliver Keene and Susan Zimmermann. Copyright © 2007 by Ellin Oliver Keene and Susan Zimmermann. Published by Heinemann, Portsmouth, NH. All rights reserved.

Library of Congress Cataloging-in-Publication Data
Keene, Ellin Oliver.
   To understand : new horizons in reading comprehension / Ellin Oliver Keene.
      p. cm.
   Includes bibliographical references and index.
   ISBN-13: 978-0-325-00323-8 (alk. paper)
   ISBN-10: 0-325-00323-8 (alk. paper)
   1. Creative thinking in children.   2. Learning, Psychology of.
3. Comprehension.   4. Children with social disabilities—Education
(Elementary).   I. Title.
   LB1062.K415 2008
   370.15'7—dc22

                      2007044148

Editor: Thomas Newkirk
Production: Sarah V. Weaver
Production coordination: Abigail M. Heim
Typesetter: SPi Publisher Services
Cover and interior design: Joyce Weston Design
Manufacturing: Steve Bernier

Printed in the United States of America on acid-free paper
12 11 10 09 08 VP   3 4 5

For Jamika,
and those like her who ask questions that must be answered.

For Bruce,
as ever.

Contents

Foreword

SOME THINGS ARE WORTH THE WAIT. Think chocolate chip cookies baking in the oven, flowers peeking their heads out of the snow in spring, that first day back at the beach after a long, cold winter. And just like fresh-out-of-the-oven chocolate chip cookies, bright yellow daffodils, and warm sand sifting between fingers and toes, Ellin's insightful and thought-provoking book *To Understand* is worth the wait, too.

You may know Ellin from *Mosaic of Thought*, the groundbreaking book on comprehension she coauthored with Susan Zimmermann. Because of their book and others that followed, teachers across the country now teach their students strategies for enhancing understanding and constructing meaning.

But it was a chance encounter with a brilliant little girl named Jamika that propelled Ellin to think more deeply about her earlier work. When Jamika looked Ellin straight in the eye and asked her, "What does 'make sense' mean?" Ellin didn't know what to say; she wasn't really sure. But if you know Ellin like I know Ellin, you know she wouldn't let Jamika's question go unanswered.

Through research and study, introspection and reflection, sleepless nights and countless days in classrooms working with teachers and their students, Ellin crafted a substantive answer to the question, What does "make sense" mean? What does it mean to understand?

To Understand is not a sequel to *Mosaic of Thought*. *To Understand* challenges us to think beyond comprehension strategies; it invites us to ask what these strategies are for. Why should readers use them? What's our ultimate goal? Once our goal is defined, what are its characteristics? What mentors might we turn to?

To tackle these questions, Ellin has developed three powerful models. In the first, Dimensions and Outcomes of Understanding, she identifies, names, and explains key indicators of intellectual engagement, among them dwelling in ideas, revising our thoughts, and creating emotional connections. As always, Ellin aims high, encouraging us to think of all our children as intellectuals and scholars.

But to create space for this kind of engagement, she urges us to cut through the clutter, slow down, determine what's essential, and teach those things deeply and well. Where to begin? Fortunately, Ellin has developed another powerful model that she aptly calls What's Essential for Literacy Learning? It's here that she lays out the key features of literacy learning. Based on mountains of research, Ellin has synthesized it for us in a practical, easy-to-use format.

Along with the Literacy Studio, the reader's/writer's workshop model first described in the second edition of *Mosaic of Thought*, Ellin brings these models to life through compelling vignettes of her work in some of the most economically distressed schools in this country. You'll fall in love with Jamika and Kevin. You'll want to transport yourself to Kathy Francescani's and Jodi Snyder's amazing classroom in Cleveland. And most of all, you'll be inspired to consider the implications for you and the children you teach. *To Understand* is the perfect book to read and discuss with colleagues. It will make you think. It just might keep you up at night. And that's just what Ellin would love to hear!

Happy reading,

Debbie Miller

Acknowledgments

THIS BOOK IS THE RESULT OF A VERY LONG "labor and delivery"! It might never have been born without the support of dear family, friends, and colleagues.

My little family—David, Elizabeth, my nephew Eddie, my uncle Randy, and my sweet daddy—never succumbed to asking, "Is there really a book at all?" Instead, they always said, "How's the book coming?" and to them I am grateful for their patience that extended beyond all reason. David and Elizabeth, in particular, tempted me with nights out at our favorite sushi restaurant if I would finish just one more chapter, and when I did, celebrated as if I'd finished the book.

My dear friends Barb Emerson, Laura Michaels, Bruce Morgan, and Mary Vockrodt routinely put their own lives and concerns on the back burner to commiserate, read drafts, and express confidence that this book would see the light of day. Occasionally they suggested that I might want to take a little break, perhaps seek refuge on a desert island or in five days per week of psychotherapy! Through what must have been excruciating tests of these friendships, they persevered. I wonder if anyone has ever been so blessed as I to have friends like these.

Debbie Miller, long-time friend and colleague (and the author of *Reading with Meaning*) wrote a very generous foreword for *To Understand*, but her contributions didn't stop there. Debbie has read more drafts more times than anyone and with her warm laugh and sweet manner, asked questions that simply had to be asked. No one else can challenge me to rethink an idea with such tenderness. Her ideas and support reverberate in every chapter, and I look forward to many more "writing mornings" where we cozy up with coffee, talk about everything in our respective worlds, laugh, read, and converse about each other's work.

My career took an important turn when I left a school district and went to the Public Education & Business Coalition (PEBC) in Denver. For twenty-five years, the PEBC has given me the freedom to explore ideas and experiment in all kinds of classrooms. I owe the PEBC and its people—past and present—everything. It was and is the sanctuary for my ideas and the home of colleagues who challenge me and provide essential colleagueship.

In particular, I wish to thank Rosann Ward, Suzanne Plaut, Lori Conrad, and Judy Hendricks. Without the latter, who is kind enough to serve as my assistant, I would never get anywhere on time, never have a rental car, and would always be double-booked.

I remain deeply grateful to Tom Newkirk, my editor and dear friend who read twenty-six different versions of Chapter 1 before saying, "Ellin, I think we're ready for Chapter 2 now!" He understood and indulged my overwhelming desire to write something original and challenging for the field when a sequel to *Mosaic of Thought* may have been enough. He supported my need to take the less worn path and to explore ideas even I didn't understand. In addition to countless phone calls and emails in which he provided incisive, potent feedback, Tom traveled to Denver and interviewed me for two days about what I wanted to accomplish with the book. That trip provided the jump start I sorely needed.

I am indebted to all of my colleagues at the Cornerstone Initiative, my professional home for four years. The teachers with whom we worked in some of this country's lowest income schools taught me everything I now know and believe about what the concept "high expectations" really means in America's schools. Heartfelt thanks to Steve Prigohzy, Kevan Collins, Edna Varner, Becky McKay, Lu Lewis, Sara Schwabacher, Mary Jean Whitelaw, Johnnie Tankersley, Kathy Francescani, and Jodi Snyder. I loved working with you all and miss you very much.

When the manuscript was "done," I asked some of my most trusted colleagues at Heinemann to read it, beginning with Vicki Boyd, Director of Professional Development. She loved the book, but asked key questions that led to major revisions. I thank her for her clarity of thought and for being savvy enough to say, "It's good, but it could be great." Leigh Peake, Editorial Director, was unfailingly patient, supportive, and helpful. Stephanie Colado tackled the Herculean task of obtaining permissions for the art and excerpts from other authors with her characteristic good cheer. Abby Heim, with her extraordinary design sense, indulged me in finding just the right cover.

Smokey Daniels, author of some of the most useful books I read in our field, gave the manuscript a very careful read and made invaluable suggestions. That guy has a razor-sharp eye, and I'm just glad I bugged him to train it on this book. Patrick Allen, a superb teacher in Douglas County, Colorado, did the same. I trust Patrick's insights implicitly.

Sarah Weaver, who edited this book, not only found the discrepancies, goofs, blunders and inconsistencies, she made important, substantive contributions to its clarity. Until Sarah, I had no idea the role a truly great editor can play and I've not yet met her, but when I do, I intend to fall to the floor and kiss the hem of her garment!

Finally and most importantly, I thank you, the teachers, literacy coaches, principals, and curriculum directors who will read this book. Your willingness to take important risks in a policy climate that is not always conducive to uncommon thinking and your thirst for new ways of thinking about literacy learning inspire and drive me more than I will ever be able to express. I only want to say, it's worth it. The risks you take, the battles you may be called upon to fight, the unacknowledged contributions you make to children, the investment you make in their intellectual development—it's all worth it. You are showing them the way to understand.

Prelude

*I*CAN FIND 110,000 THINGS TO DO instead of writing: another load of laundry to throw in, a bathroom that could use a fresh coat of paint, emails to which I really should respond, plans for upcoming speeches and workshops, errands to run. Once seated at the keyboard, as I am now with a little music in the background and December sun reflecting off the snow and streaming into my little office, I actually relish the physical sensation of my mind speaking through my fingers as they fly across the keys. I rarely have to wait for ideas to come; as soon as I sit down, my fingers begin to move. It's that sitting-down thing . . .

My long-suffering friend, editor, and mentor, Tom Newkirk, professor of English at the University of New Hampshire and author of numerous important books for teachers (including *Misreading Masculinity*, 2002), drew the short straw and was asked to shepherd this book from conceptualization through publication. Tom worked with me and Susan Zimmermann while we were writing *Mosaic of Thought* (1997, 2007). I trust his judgment, respect his work, and am a huge fan of his writing, so I was thrilled, but I doubt he knew what he was in for.

One afternoon when Tom was in Denver to work with teachers in the area, I was chauffeuring him around town and mentioned how surprised I was that *Mosaic of Thought* had been so successful. I said I had hoped it would sell in the double digits (i.e., more than nine!) and that if it needed a little help, I figured I could talk my dad into buying five or six more copies. The conversation led to my difficulty in getting started on a second book, and then I made a comment Tom will never, ever, ever let me forget. It was something along the lines of, "You know, I feel a bit like John Elway [superstar quarterback for the Denver Broncos football team], who had to make a decision about whether to retire after winning the [1998 and 1999] Super Bowl. Shouldn't you quit while you're on top? *Mosaic* did well; maybe I'm a one-hit wonder!"

I thought I had made a wonderful analogy that would explain why I was struggling so much to get started on a second book, but Tom laughed so hard he nearly split open. He doubled over in the car seat next to me and gasped for air, trying to get some words out between howls of laughter.

"John Elway? John Elway?" I began to wonder if he was going to choke or have some kind of a seizure. "You have the audacity to compare yourself to John Elway?" This was followed by more shrieking laughter from the distinguished professor. "You think you're John Elway? That's the funniest thing I've ever heard. Way to take yourself too seriously, Ellin. John Elway, ahhhh haaaa, haaaa, haaaa." Tom takes his sports seriously. "You're talking about writing a book, not winning the Super Bowl!" Peals of laughter.

A little shot of humility does wonders every once in a while. The truth is that Tom has tried to work with me in every conceivable way to move this book forward, and the bottom line is that it has been a tough one to write. I was uncertain during the writing, as most writers are, whether the ideas would be useful for anyone outside my immediate circle of colleagues. I wondered if readers would question the use of vignettes about artists and writers with which I begin most chapters. I wondered if I could make the "What's Essential" model clear enough to truly help teachers focus literacy instruction on what matters most. I lay awake at night imagining exasperated readers wondering when I would just get to the heart of the matter—the classroom applications. I wondered if state standards and testing requirements would restrict teachers to such a degree that they would question whether they had the time to probe the limits of understanding with their students. I wondered if it was even worthwhile to talk about the nature of comprehension with students in a country that appears to value test scores over lasting understanding. I wondered if there was any real purpose for the book.

The worrying was familiar territory. I had similar concerns when we were writing *Mosaic* and eventually discovered that they were groundless. In the last ten years, teachers have taken the concepts we presented and used them in masterful and innovative ways; I could never have imagined how much learning was possible with strategy instruction. Teachers have discovered new facets in each strategy, experimented with different teaching sequences, manipulated the timing for instruction on particular strategies, used new language to define and describe strategies to children, and discovered new ways for children to capture and record their thinking and become truly masterful in thinking aloud about the strategies. Teachers have engaged in thoughtful and provocative debate in conferences, publications, listservs, and study groups in schools throughout the country. As I review the program for this year's International Reading Association conference, I notice dozens of sessions on comprehension strategy instruction. The energy, creativity, and intelligence teachers have applied to their understanding and implementation of the strategies has been nothing short of a phenomenon, and I have been privileged to observe it all in a state that might only be described as awe.

And oh, the stories I've heard of children's learning. Every week for nearly ten years, teachers have shared the stories of children whose insights about the texts they read and the concepts they learn are surprising and brilliant. Using strategies as tools to leverage deeper understanding, students from preschool through college have come to understand subtleties and themes that previously eluded them. They have used the strategies to write more persuasive college entrance essays, to engage in lively conversation with other students, and to share alternative points of view that cause other students to rethink their own interpretations. Children around the country and beyond have experienced, some for the first time, the joy that comes from creating meaning for themselves, rather than being dependent on a teacher's interpretation or a summary in Cliff's Notes. In so doing, these children have shown educators how gratifying it is to contribute to students' independence and how rewarding it is to teach children to think rather than to recall, retell, and answer endless "comprehension" questions. I've learned about the limitless power of children's minds—they have moved me to tears, laughter, and shock; they have reenergized those of us on the cusp of burnout; they have reminded us why we teach. I guess I needn't have worried.

In 2007, Susan Zimmermann and I dug back in and created the second edition of *Mosaic of Thought*, which was published on its tenth anniversary. We wanted to update readers about innovations we've observed in classrooms and to tell the stories of children who are more potent and efficacious learners because of comprehension strategy instruction. We brought readers up to speed on the research in reading comprehension, provided more teaching tactics, and discussed comprehension strategy instruction across the curriculum.

In partial defense of the time it took to write this book, I must say that a few other things have been going on in the last ten years. I left the Public Education & Business Coalition (PEBC) in Denver and began work as deputy director for Cornerstone, a national literacy initiative working in some of this country's lowest-income schools. I traveled to nearly every state and three foreign countries to work with teachers interested in teaching comprehension, and I celebrated as my colleagues from PEBC in Denver followed *Mosaic* with ten books focused on teaching comprehension and other aspects of literacy and professional learning. In a moment ten years have flown by. My daughter, Elizabeth, has found her way to college; Noodle the cocker spaniel died; and Chaucer and Toby, the basset hounds, have taken up residence with the

Keenes. Sadly, an old friend or two has faded from sight, and family and friends have endured great suffering and sorrow. New and wonderful friends have become air and water in my life, and I have met teachers in every place I've visited who inspire me more than I'll ever be able to describe.

Maybe the worry about this book was needless. Or maybe worry is just focused thinking—working to solve problems, trying to write clearly, crafting something with staying power, giving oneself time to reinvent and strengthen the ideas. It may be that I needed these ten years to percolate and observe, learn from colleagues, and revise my own thinking. It may be that I needed to test these ideas in schools where children who have very little could teach me about boundless intellectual strength. I suspect John Elway worried, too. Maybe, Dr. Newkirk, that is the connection that makes my analogy work—just a little!

Working with Cornerstone schools fundamentally changed the way I view children. Through the initiative's efforts in some of this country's neediest schools and districts, I had to come face-to-face with some fundamental beliefs. Do I believe that *all* children—not just those who come from two-parent households, aren't identified for special education, hold a library card, go to preschool, and live with someone who reads to them—can comprehend deeply, retain and reapply complex concepts, and live an intellectual life, if they so choose? I would have quickly answered that question in the affirmative before, but Cornerstone kids dramatically expanded my thinking. They made me want to move beyond the cliché language we all use and emblazon on tee shirts and tote bags—"all kids can learn at high levels"—to a discourse we can use in classrooms that defines "high expectations" more precisely and moves children toward their nearly unlimited capacity for understanding.

Working with Cornerstone children, my expectations came into clear focus; they became more specific. I came to believe that *any* child who has the intellectual capacity to develop oral language in the first five years of life is capable of becoming one of the leading original thinkers of the future. I began to believe that any child could surely find herself taking the podium of the U.S. Senate, or conducting groundbreaking research on leukemia, composing original symphonic music, delivering babies, writing a policy paper on starting small businesses in developing countries, counseling young mothers trying to work their way out of poverty, or leading a movement in postmodern painting. Listening to the originality of their thinking, getting beyond their sometimes limited oral language to the exquisite ideas that lie beneath, I realized that existing beliefs about high levels of academic achievement are utterly inadequate if we want children, particularly those in poverty, to realize their intellectual potential.

I know that many educators reading this book *do* go beyond the rhetoric, do see their students as powerful thinkers capable of growing into scholars and leaders—but we have colleagues for whom the last paragraph may have caused a moment of discomfort, maybe even a laugh. Some of these colleagues are well respected and do good things for children. I have no doubt that even those who chuckle at the prospect of their students serving as U.S. senators would characterize themselves as teachers with high expectations for their students. What, then, does it mean to have high expectations for children's learning? How can we alter the ingrained beliefs that limit children's options? How can we move beyond that cliché—all kids can learn at high levels—to a language of expectation that opens doors for all children?

I will argue in this book that when we rethink what we mean by comprehension, when we redefine what it means to understand, we can reshape our beliefs about children's learning potential; we can come closer to making real the promise that all children can make lasting contributions to the society in which they live. I believe that we can extinguish the notion that some kids are going to make it intellectually and other kids just aren't. We can begin to see that all children can be responsible for private or public greatness. We can become certain that the vast majority, regardless of their present performance level and life situation, have the wherewithal to live intellectually engaged lives.

A principal said to a colleague of mine recently, "Someone has to man the gas stations, flip the burgers, and drive the taxis." We're shocked by this statement because one can only surmise that his attitude spills over into decisions he makes as a school leader. Yet as a society we apparently adhere to his notion, consciously or otherwise. The evidence abounds in schools and beyond. Adults sort children physically and academically, making silent but potent decisions that some will live lives in which they use the power of their minds to make a contribution to the world, and others will provide backup for those who think. Are we at ease with that view? If not, how can we transform entrenched beliefs that have been quietly reinforced by people who believe that someone has to flip the burgers? These are the questions I wish to explore in this book.

In *To Understand*, I want to walk on untouched snow. When I first started to work on the ideas we wrote about in *Mosaic of Thought*,

I realized I had to write in order to figure out why I thought comprehension strategy instruction was so useful and important to American literacy education. When I finally got down to the writing, I discovered that I was figuring out some of the complexities of comprehension strategy instruction *because* I was writing about them. *Writing to learn* is a phrase that took on a very personal meaning.

I struggled for months—okay, years—with this project, knowing that I could write a "how-to" book filled with lesson ideas that would be relatively easy to write and that teachers would appreciate and find useful. I knew I could write a book that would affirm what great teachers were already doing and perhaps give some the strength to continue. Why couldn't I work up the enthusiasm to do that? I was mindful of *Mosaic*'s success and realized that, like certain unnamed sports stars in certain unnamed sporting contests, it's tough to repeat a big success. I worried about the loneliness of writing alone, knowing how much Susan Zimmermann brought to the experience of writing *Mosaic of Thought*. I had bathrooms to paint, laundry to do, dogs to groom . . .

I came to realize that my interest lay in writing another book in which I didn't fully understand all that I was writing about. I wanted to write about concepts I was struggling with; I wanted to write a book that would give readers the delicious opportunity to sort out for themselves (rather than having me prescribe) what it all means for children's learning. I wanted to write a book in which I would learn more than teach, in which I could pose big questions; I wanted to write a book that would challenge me intellectually in the process; a book in which I could field-test ideas that *might* be provocative, *might* be useful; a book in which I could write to learn—again.

Chapter 1

Rethinking Understanding

Jamika's Story

The classroom was crowded with adults, and the second graders—thirty-two of them—were noticeably fidgety, hyperaware of our presence as well as the colder-than-usual late-fall temperatures outside. There had even been talk of a snowflake or two mixed in with the persistent Jackson, Mississippi, rain. Not that anyone could see snowflakes if they appeared; there was a kind of film over the classroom windows that blurred the shapes beyond and allowed only a dingy light.

I was visiting the schools in Jackson for the first time, accompanied by several of my colleagues from the Cornerstone Initiative, a University of Pennsylvania–based literacy staff development project working in extremely low income schools around the country. We were thinking together about the best staff development strategies, hoping to develop and refine tactics for working with teachers and children in nearly thirty schools—schools where many programs had been launched and abandoned and where teachers had learned to keep their heads down, do the best they could for children, and weather the next "program du jour" that someone decided was worth a try.

I had suggested to my colleagues that we begin in these schools by getting into classrooms immediately. We should get a sense for the books kids were reading and the kinds of writing they were doing—we could confer with children to begin to understand their oral language and reading fluency as well as gain insights and ideas about the stories they were reading and writing. The conferences would yield records we could then discuss with classroom teachers. We would begin our work not by "training" teachers in some program we were bringing to them, but in discussion about their students' actual strengths and needs.

I was ready to show my colleagues what I meant as we began our work in the second-grade classroom on that chilly morning. I pulled a stool next to Jamika and flipped my notebook to a clean page.

"Jamika, my name is Mrs. Keene, and I'm very interested in what you're reading this morning." Wordlessly, she showed me her book and glanced over my shoulder to the dozen or so adults looking on. I thought about what I could do to help her relax a little. "Honey, when did you start this book?"

"This morning." She seemed timid and utterly overwhelmed by the crowd of adults around her.

"Okay, what do you think about it so far? Do you feel like you understand it? Does this book make sense to you, Jamika?"

These are questions I must have asked thirty thousand times in my twenty-seven years in education. I ask them almost as if I'm on automatic pilot—they just come out at the beginning of a conference with a child I don't know. I ask them almost subconsciously—my mind could be anywhere—they're a sort of reflexive way to get the conference going. But those three innocuous questions unleashed a torrent for which I was utterly unprepared. Jamika was anything but timid. Jamika's response became the driving force behind this book.

"All my life," she began in a very determined voice and at relatively high volume. It crossed my mind that she was all of seven years old, and I stifled a giggle. For this tiny girl, I was obviously the straw that had broken the camel's back. "All my life, there's just one thing I don't ever understand. Y'all always say that—does this book make sense? Ms. McKin, she always says that, too. She say, 'Jamika, does that book make sense to you, you feel like y'all are understanding that book, because you know the most important thing about books is they got to make sense to you.' She tell the whole class that, she tell me that, she always sayin', you make sure if you reading a book that don't make sense, you get another book because it got to make sense when you reading.'"

Jamika hardly drew a breath and was picking up speed and volume a bit like an airplane rolling down the runway for takeoff. "Then it's the same at home. My mama's always saying to me, 'Jamika, you know you better be reading books that make sense to you. The whole thing about reading is that books have to make sense to you and if they don't, you tell me and I read it to y'all or we get you another book, 'cause you gotta remember that the most important thing about reading is that books, they got to make sense to you.' And then I come back here to school and they always asking me, 'Jamika, that book make sense to you? You sure? Because you know the most important thing about reading is it got to make sense to you.'"

I took a quick glance at Jamika's teacher, who was squatting nearby listening in on the conference—make that monologue. From the look on her face, the president of the United States might have just opened the door holding a bouquet of flowers. She was flabbergasted—think deer in headlights—and while she was still being flabbergasted, Jamika was still talking about how every adult in her long life had emphasized the need to read books that make sense.

Jamika finally took a breath. It was a dramatic pause long enough for me to wonder if she may well *become* the president of the United States some day. I was thinking that the sooner that happened, the better, when she let her final salvo fly.

"But, none a y'all ever say what make sense mean." She looked at me defiantly.

While I staggered under the weight of that statement, I glanced around me at the rest of the adults, all of whom had that deer-in-headlights look going on. I could almost read their minds, "Okay, Keene, let's see you deal with *this* firecracker! You sure had a bright idea—start in a new school by conferring with kids in the classroom. Wonder what you think of that now!" And I could almost hear the teacher thinking, "I thought this one was supposed to have written a book on comprehension. She doesn't look too smart to me." Their perceptions were undoubtedly strengthened when I replied to Jamika's query, "Ah, well, ah, you know, hmm, you see, ah . . . I'll have to get back to you, Jamika!"

Well, what was I going to say after a diatribe like that? I guess I could have said, "Jamika, comprehension occurs when the reader constructs meaning in a way that combines his or her schemata with the author's intended message, deriving a unique interpretation." Somehow, I don't think it was the graduate school definition she was looking for. I staggered away to another child, hoping to recover and focus on some of the objectives I had for the day, but Jamika's question haunted me.

I lay awake that night in my less-than-ideal hotel-room bed with Jamika's words resonating. "None a y'all ever say what make sense mean." I tried to recall whether, in the first edition of *Mosaic of Thought*, we had ever really defined comprehension. (We had not.) I tried to think of a way I'd like to talk to kids about what it means to understand. (I came up short.) I resolved to return to Jamika's classroom the next day and to examine how she would have answered her own question, just by being a member of the class. In other words, if Jamika had not asked me what it means to understand that day, what conclusions would she have drawn, if left to her own devices?

I met with Jamika's teacher to inquire about a typical day in her classroom. What would Jamika have done if we hadn't visited the day before?

What did her normal classroom routine entail? The teacher pulled out the teacher's edition from the basal anthology and opened it to a little story she had intended to use with Jamika's guided reading group the day before. The story had a simple plot involving a stray cat that wanders into an elderly woman's garden and is adopted by her, but is prone to stealing food from her table. The woman teaches the cat a lesson by sprinkling hot chile peppers in and around the food.

The story was a typical leveled text we would expect to use in early second grade. When I looked at the teacher's edition, however, I was struck by the publisher's suggestions for teachers. This little story was not only intended to help children with word learning and fluency practice (a very appropriate use for a leveled text); the teacher was also directed to ask comprehension questions. And not just a few questions—sixty-eight of them!

Now, let's say that you're Jamika. You want to know what "make sense" means. You are part of the group that reads this story, and you and your peers respond to the comprehension questions your teacher asks. Let's imagine that the teacher cuts—by half—the number of questions she asks, reasoning that children do not need that many questions to lead them through a story so simple it is comprehensible even if the reader only looks at the pictures! You're still responding to thirty-four questions! You're Jamika. What does "make sense" mean?

After the story is read, the teacher's edition suggests that children be invited to retell the story, in the order it is written. Children are encouraged to use words such as *then* and *next* in their retellings. Finally, a few vocabulary words are thrown into the postreading discussion, and that constitutes the group's reading instruction for the day. You're Jamika. What does "make sense" mean?

If, like Jamika, this scenario describes your daily comprehension instruction, "make sense" must mean you read a story, answer questions, retell, and learn a few new vocabulary words.

I began to wonder about the children on whose behalf Jamika asked her question. Surely other children who hear us emphasize the importance of understanding what they're reading must also wonder "what make sense means." The answer is the same in the vast majority of classrooms I have visited. If we consider the way in which we use materials (reading short pieces and asking children to retell, learn new vocabulary, and answer comprehension questions) and how we spend time in the name of comprehension (asking children to answer questions, keep journals, and create projects about the books they read, all of which are just more elaborate retelling), we actually do have an answer for Jamika. In this country, our de facto definition of comprehension is that we want children to:

- retell
- answer questions
- learn new vocabulary

I certainly have no problem with asking children to retell, answer questions, and learn new vocabulary words. As a matter of fact, I believe those skills are terribly important and recognize that they will be useful in a number of contexts throughout children's lives, not the least of which is when they take high-stakes tests.

My concern is this: Is this enough? Is this definition worthy of our students' considerable intellectual capacity? Isn't it possible that they can do much more when working to understand?

As I considered Jamika's question, I also had to ask: Do students even need comprehension strategy instruction if all they're expected to do is retell, learn a few new vocabulary words, and answer questions? My conclusion was not a good one if you happen to be the coauthor of a book on comprehension strategies, but it was unavoidable. Our students *don't* need comprehension strategies if our only objectives are answering questions, retelling, and learning new vocabulary. These were certainly the objectives toward which our own teachers taught. We can all remember book reports, endless written responses to comprehension questions, and vocabulary exercises in which we were asked to reveal the meaning of the word within a sentence we wrote. We didn't have comprehension strategy instruction as children—we didn't need it! Our kids don't need it either unless we change our objectives for comprehension—unless we create a definition more worthy of their intellectual development. Comprehension strategies are the *tools* with which we leverage deeper understanding. But what is deeper understanding?

Finally, I realized that Jamika's daily experience in comprehension wasn't actually improving her comprehension. When we ask questions, have the children retell stories, and help them learn new words, we aren't necessarily *teaching* comprehension, we're actually *assessing* comprehension! We're checking to see if they "got it," which in and of itself, does little to help students improve their comprehension. We wring our hands about how little time we have to actually teach in contemporary classrooms, but a great deal of time that might be devoted to teaching is instead being spent *testing* comprehension. And the one thing we definitely need to do more of in this country is assessment, right?

It became clear to me that we need a new definition for comprehension, a definition more worthy of our children's intellectual potential. We need to define and describe our objectives—our teaching intentions—in comprehension. When we teach comprehension strategies, what do we hope they lead to in children's thinking? What do we expect to see and hear when children understand? What indicators and outcomes are we likely to observe? What constitutes deep understanding?

Understanding and the Development of the Intellect

When I began to write about Jamika's question, I realized that to understand is, in some ways, synonymous with the development of the intellect. When we work hard to understand any concept or idea—whether a theme in a novel or a scientific or mathematical concept—we are building intellectual muscle. We experience the intellectual gratification that comes from struggling with an idea until we understand it. We begin to feel efficacious, capable of deep understanding. We experience the capacity of our own mind. When we truly understand a concept, we are able to remember it, revise it, and reapply it later. When we retain and reuse an idea in a new context, we create new knowledge, new thinking for ourselves and for others. When we create new knowledge, we often find ourselves curious about more subtle facets of the problem or concept. When we're curious, we are building upon a uniquely human trait—the need to pose questions and seek answers. Curiosity becomes insatiable, seeking to understand becomes intoxicating, and we find the life of the mind deeply pleasurable. We want more. The cycle repeats (see Figure 1.1).

One of my first recollections of an intellectual experience may help to illustrate this connection between understanding and intellectual development. I was asked to do a research project on the death penalty for my honors U.S. history course in high school. I used dozens of resources, interviewed people of widely varying backgrounds and ages, studied laws in various states, and probed my own values and beliefs until I was exhausted. I woke up in the middle of the night filled with questions and images, forced my friends and family into lengthy conversations, and changed my mind repeatedly. I had to present and defend my ideas to my classmates, who peppered me with questions and challenges. When my presentation was over and the paper submitted, I still couldn't shake the topic. I continued to flail in my mind, struggling with the complexity of the problem, the unanswerable questions. I don't remember what grade I was given, but I had discovered the elation of intellectual enterprise. My gratification was born of an

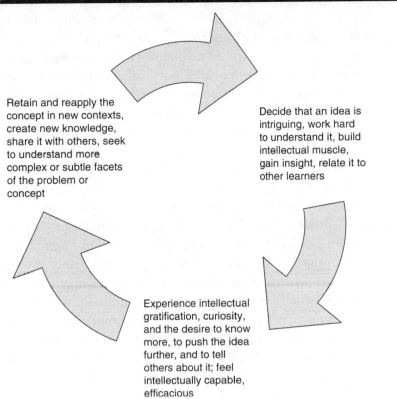

Fig. 1.1. Understanding and the Development of the Intellect

Decide that an idea is intriguing, work hard to understand it, build intellectual muscle, gain insight, relate it to other learners

Experience intellectual gratification, curiosity, and the desire to know more, to push the idea further, and to tell others about it; feel intellectually capable, efficacious

Retain and reapply the concept in new contexts, create new knowledge, share it with others, seek to understand more complex or subtle facets of the problem or concept

internal source. No external reward could ever supplant the excitement I felt as I gradually pieced that puzzle together. Coming to understand this complex issue made me want more. It opened my mind to learning for learning's sake. The project was a powerful introduction to an intellectual life, one that had not been part of my early education.

Remembering My Intellectual Roots, Hoping for More

I was fortunate to grow up in a family where education was valued. There was never any doubt I would go to college. I was praised and sometimes rewarded for good grades. My mother read to me as a child, took me to the library for summer reading programs, and made sure there was always a book or two under the Christmas tree.

However, mine was not a home in which children were asked to discuss ideas at the dinner table (except when my grandfathers were present—more on that in Chapter 8). My parents did not bring my brother and me into their conversations about the events of those volatile Vietnam and Watergate-era days. My mother did take us to the Greeley Philharmonic concerts, but we whined about sitting through what felt like endless nights in the University of Northern Colorado gymnasium listening to music that seemed meaningless. We traveled frequently, but often missed the intensive learning that can accompany the discovery of new places. We begged to forgo another cathedral or museum, and my parents relented. They must have reconciled themselves to our lack of interest by assuming that kids don't really want to spend time out of school engaged in intense discussion and more learning. I don't think it occurred to them to include us in more intellectual discussions.

Were they right? I certainly didn't lose myself in thought or find myself tempted to delve more deeply into my learning (with the exception of the death penalty research) during high school. I got decent grades, participated in student government, and talked to friends on the phone for hours—that's what we did before "texting" and IM'ing! I liked some teachers and worked hard for them, abhorred algebra, and ditched class to go to Winchell's donuts on Friday mornings—until my mom caught me (it was a small town). I skated by with minimal effort, far more interested in social pursuits than academic ones. I didn't consider myself particularly smart, and few in my life tried to disavow me of that notion. I was above average, but not intellectually engaged, and I don't recall being bothered by that. I suppose, if I gave it much thought at all, I assumed I would go to college, teach elementary school as my mother and her mother had, during which time I would marry, have a family, nurture great friendships, and travel as much as I could. I didn't even consider what kind of intellectual life lay ahead of me.

I hadn't experienced intellectual engagement—I didn't know what it meant to truly understand—until that project in honors U.S. history. The trend shifted in college. I was fortunate to attend a university where classes were small and discussion was encouraged. I found the readings in most classes intriguing and learned to build an argument based on my evolving understanding of the content and of my values, beliefs, and opinions. I found real joy in writing and, for the first time, received feedback that my writing was good. I read authors whose writing I deeply admired and longed to hone my skills.

I began to savor a life of learning. I prioritized my time to include intellectual pursuits. I discovered museums, theater, opera, and classic literature. I sought relationships with people who talked about ideas. I enjoyed political banter and loved the feeling of pushing a feisty conversation to a new place. I started to understand concepts I thought were beyond my intellectual reach. I got involved in political causes. I wrote letters to the editor. I volunteered to assist professors in their research. I read. And read and read and read.

I am one of the lucky ones. In my family, you went to college. If I hadn't, it is quite possible I never would have fallen in love with learning. I suspect many Americans—and many teachers—had similar experiences.

Some Troubling Questions

If it is true that many of us first experienced the joy of living an intellectually engaged life while in college, I can't help but wonder—are we comfortable waiting for our students to reach college before they view themselves as intellectually powerful? What about the kids who never get there? When will they be introduced to the life of the mind? Is it possible to create for much younger children the kinds of intellectual engagement most of us first experienced in college? Can we avoid the all-too-common scenario in which children plod through our classrooms completing assignments, reading the required books, sitting through endless state and local assessments—getting by, but rarely engaging? When we say we're working to raise student achievement or narrow the achievement gap, does that mean we are trying to raise test scores, or does it mean we're working to ensure that students really learn—retain and reapply—important concepts? How do we know if students truly understand? Why do students fail to remember and reapply what we have so carefully taught? What about the students who struggle? Is their academic diet of more-of-the-same-each-year-only-louder acceptable?

These are the questions I believe we need to address if we are to make a profound impact on our children's intellectual lives. If, as I argued earlier, intellectual development is closely tied to understanding, and if understanding relates to the ability to retain and reapply concepts we have been taught, then the way we define and describe understanding takes on a new level of import. The way we talk to children about the *experience* of understanding—in their minds and in their lives—becomes paramount.

Into the Classroom

I knew that to answer Jamika's provocative question and all the questions to which it led, I had to experiment in the classroom. I wanted to *purposefully* introduce children to deeper understanding and intellectually engaging experiences much earlier, but in a manner appropriate to their age and development. I reasoned that I could begin by teaching the comprehension strategies we described in *Mosaic of Thought* (see Appendix A, "Comprehension Stategies Defined"). But I wanted to go further. I wanted to extend comprehension strategy instruction—having kids share their connections, images, and inferences—by asking them to describe the *outcomes* of using strategies. What did they come to understand when they used strategies? What was their experience, cognitively and behaviorally, when they were in the process of understanding? If comprehension strategies are the tools we use to leverage deeper understanding, what *is* deeper understanding? What does "make sense" really mean?

In dozens of classrooms with kids of all ages and "ability levels," I read aloud and invited children to use the comprehension strategies, but I went to the next step—I asked them to define and describe what they understood after using the strategies that they might have missed if they hadn't used them. I asked them to describe what it is like when they truly understand. I wanted to hear about their insights into texts, but also their *experiences* in the process of understanding. I wanted to use their descriptions to define and describe the comprehension process—in terms of both cognitive and behavioral experiences—to others.

I was astonished to find that when I asked them to push their thinking further, almost without exception, children expressed insights, views, opinions, and understandings that dramatically exceeded my expectations— they understood and articulated far more than I had imagined they could. I found that when I extended the teaching of a comprehension strategy and asked children to describe what they understood and how they experienced the comprehension process, kids could define and describe their thinking at unprecedented levels.

I decided to experiment with this new dimension in a demonstration lesson I was scheduled to give during a summer workshop for a large group of teachers. It was a somewhat risky decision, but I wanted a large group of teachers to witness what I had been seeing in classrooms around the country.

Eight upper-elementary students in Alief, Texas, were literally yanked out of the swimming pool across the street from the workshop site and led, dripping, into the school cafeteria to sit on a hard linoleum floor and discuss a picture book read to them by a total stranger in front of a hundred teachers. Not the most ideal learning environment, but these kids were not only engaged, they dazzled the observing teachers (whom they seemed to completely forget).

When I read *The Other Side* by Jacqueline Woodson, any nervousness they had felt evaporated, and they posed questions—the comprehension strategy I taught that day—that drew us into subtleties of meaning I had never imagined. When I pushed them further and asked them to describe what their questions helped them to understand, the responses exploded into a spirited conversation. They discussed issues related to how young children develop racial stereotypes, the role of parents in shaping children's racial perspectives, and their own experiences as black and Hispanic students in settings where the majority of children were white. The teachers couldn't take notes fast enough; some cried. When we announced that the kids could return to the pool, they groaned. They were nowhere near ready to leave.

These and dozens of other experiences with children representing the entire grade spectrum led me to believe that introducing children to the life of the mind is a largely untapped and rich area into which we can push our comprehension teaching. I began to realize that by building intellectual engagement and discussing the nature of deep understanding, we could indeed empower children to retain and reapply ideas.

Working with children and teachers helped me narrow the focus of this book to four key questions:

1. What does it mean to understand?
2. How do we define and teach toward high expectations and high levels of understanding?
3. What matters most in literacy learning?
4. In what ways can we live our adult lives as intellectually curious models for our students and our colleagues?

I address these four questions in four corresponding sections throughout Chapters 3–9. These four questions—explored in sections called Mentors, Dimension, Literacy Essentials, and Dwelling in the Mind—form the structure of most of the book. (I'll also introduce three descriptive models to help us recognize true understanding and discover how to teach it. But more about those in Chapter 2.) First, though, I want to provide a few introductory thoughts about each of these questions and explain how the sections of *To Understand* are structured around them.

What Does It Mean to Understand?

If *Mosaic of Thought* was about teaching children to use strategies to understand text more completely, this book must focus on Jamika's profound question—*what does it mean to understand?* When children tell us they have a text-to-self connection, does that necessarily mean they understand? When a child plasters his book with a flurry of yellow sticky notes describing his mental images, does he comprehend? If a child can generate inferences to share with her peers in a book club conversation, does she truly grasp the book's point? Comprehension strategies are taught for one reason—so that readers can understand more deeply. What, then, does that mean? In literacy education, we are told that reading and writing for understanding are of paramount importance. We teach children to decode and pronounce words so they can understand what they read. We teach children to write so their readers can understand them. We ask innumerable questions about books to assess whether children understand. We tell kids like Jamika that understanding is important. But when do we talk about what it means—what it looks like, feels like—to understand?

When I speculated about how Jamika might define comprehension based on her classroom experience, I imagined that she would probably deduce that "to understand" means to answer questions, retell, and learn new vocabulary words. When I examined state standards and documents created by teachers to define understanding, I found that we do use some common descriptors. We want children to:

- retell what they've read
- answer literal and inferential questions
- learn new vocabulary words from the text they read
- retain and reapply concepts from nonfiction
- appreciate poetry and literature
- read for pleasure and become lifelong readers

The same questions flooded back into my mind: Is that really what we mean by understanding? If these descriptors comprise our definition of comprehension, is it not likely that they will become our teaching objectives? And, if those definitions become our explicit or even implicit teaching objectives, is it not likely that those are exactly the targets toward which children will strive? Are we comfortable with those targets when we've glimpsed children doing so much more?

It is possible to use the comprehension strategies we described in *Mosaic of Thought* to help students not only to make connections or visualize, to synthesize or question, but also to *think* more effectively and with greater depth and insight, in a wider variety of books and genres, across disciplines, and in all aspects of their lives. It is possible that the comprehension strategies can be used as tools for *understanding and intellectual development* rather than simply tools for reading comprehension. It is possible that, when we define comprehension differently, children will transform their thinking accordingly, and aim for the new targets we define. It is possible, when we set higher targets for comprehending, that our children will rise to the occasion.

How can we begin to redefine understanding? As I pondered this question, it struck me that there are many who have come before us—artists and writers, for example—whose lives have been a testament to the urge to understand. I became intrigued with the idea that we might study these mentors—evaluate what moved and motivated them, examine what characterized their creative and intellectual lives, scrutinize the forces that drove them to understand, and translate those insights into the world of schools. By studying the lives and work of those whose work reflects deep understanding, we can help children adopt similar thinking traits and qualities earlier in their lives. In other words, people whose lives have been devoted to understanding the world can serve as examples for teachers who value deep and lasting understanding for their students.

The Structure of To Understand

Starting with Chapter 3, I begin each chapter with a short vignette in which I connect the lives of writers and artists who, I believe, have much to reveal to us about teaching and learning. I call this section **Mentors** and, through these vignettes, seek to redefine what it means to understand.

How Do We Define and Teach Toward High Expectations and High Levels of Understanding?

Often, especially in schools that serve low-income students, I see banners announcing, "We are all life-long learners!" or "Everyone in this school is a reader" or "We've read 10,000 books this year!" I hear of "incentive" programs in which the principal agrees to shave his head or wear her pajamas to school if the children read a certain number of pages or titles, and I've seen posters advertising parties and other rewards for children who meet particular goals during the school year.

I understand the benevolent intentions behind each of these efforts. Yet I must ask—do these efforts truly represent what it means to have high expectations? In fact, are we teaching children that learning is rewarded extrinsically and that learning for learning's sake may not be adequate? Are we teaching children that quantity of pages read matters more than the quality of their reading experiences—the degree to which they find themselves caught up in the adventures of Harry Potter or driven to learn more about the rain forest?

Few among us would say we harbor anything less than the highest expectations for children. But in what ways do those expectations manifest themselves, particularly in literacy learning? Do we demonstrate our lofty goals by asking the children to fly through hundreds of books, with little expectation that they dwell in the ideas or learn more? And an even more important question: Do we truly believe that what is expressed on the banners is true for *all* children? Do we weave the highest expectations into our daily communications with all children, overtly and subtly? Do we demonstrate our belief that they can think at high levels every day?

The power of constant high expectations came home to me following several demonstrations like the one in Alief, Texas. I began to realize that the only reason children weren't thinking at consistently high levels was that I hadn't consistently *asked and expected* them to. I hadn't modeled for them how people go about the process of understanding and what they can expect when they do. I was satisfied when I heard that they generated questions, for example, or had an inference or an image in their minds as they read. I was pleased when they became metacognitive—showed that they were thinking about their own thinking—but I rarely asked for, or got, much more. When I did, it felt like a happy accident.

It was almost as if the very manner in which I had previously asked children to define and describe their thinking had actually *limited* their thinking. For example, I had been asking children to "see if you can think of a question about the story" or "tell me if you can think of anything from your life that reminds you of this story" or "tell me if you can visualize anything as I read." I discovered that even subtle changes in my language promoted huge leaps in their thinking.

If instead I recast my language—"think about all the questions you have as I read and then pick one or two you think will best help us understand more about the story" or "what are all the things you already know, believe, or feel that will help you understand this piece" or "stop and create a vivid, detailed image in your mind that will help you to understand more than even the author put in this story"—the children responded with far more relevant questions, insightful connections, and detailed images, all of which helped them do far more than just use a comprehension strategy. If, when children did share a question or connection, an inference or synthesis, I pushed them to say more, to develop their ideas, they almost always did so.

I began to realize that showing high expectations for literacy learning is a far more subtle and precise process and requires far more consistent attention to the ways in which we interact with children than any contest, award, or banner, or any comprehension strategy. The degree to which children understand deeply is very dependent on the language we use to define, describe, and encourage higher levels of understanding.

The Structure of To Understand

The second section of each chapter explores ways to define and demonstrate higher levels of understanding; it is devoted to ideas for helping children discover what happens in their minds and in their lives when they understand. I call this section **Dimension**, as each chapter focuses on a particular dimension, or aspect, of understanding.

What Matters Most in Literacy Learning?

How can we teachers create the time in our demand-laden, curriculum-cluttered days to focus on the highest levels of understanding? In what ways can we transform ordinary literacy lessons into intellectually memorable experiences? How can we create a classroom culture conducive to those goals?

For nearly a decade I have struggled to respond when teachers say, "Kindly explain, Ellin, how I'm supposed to teach to a higher level of comprehension—one that is far more challenging for my children—when I can't begin to cover the prescribed curriculum? Isn't redefining comprehension and all the instruction and discussion it implies going to take a whole lot of time?" Of course it is—it would be dishonest to suggest otherwise. But it's time well spent, because teaching for deep levels of understanding dramatically increases the likelihood that children will retain and reapply what they learn.

I am acutely aware that we need to explore real, workable ways to manage a bloated curriculum and directly address the questions, What gets left out? and How do I know it's okay to emphasize certain areas in the literacy curriculum over others? These may well be the most important questions we can ask.

Wherever I go, I see teachers operating at high speed trying to teach "a little bit of this, a little bit of that" and hoping to "cover" what they're supposed to in time for the next assessment. Meanwhile, the kids observe this frenzy of activity like they're watching a great tennis match, as their teachers run back and forth trying to keep the ball in the air. They might as well be following a long volley—looking first this way and then that—as their teachers frantically try to get everything done. I can almost hear them say, "Wow, look at her go!"

It seems to me that our field has been avoiding one very important question—what matters most? Where should we focus our precious instructional attention so children have the opportunity to truly learn—retain and reapply—the literacy concepts they need? We know from decades of research that humans learn best when concepts are

- introduced a few at a time
- important to the learner
- taught in depth
- taught over a long period of time
- applied in a variety of texts and contexts

How can we reconcile this basic premise about human learning with the enormous curricula we're charged with teaching? If we can answer that question, and I believe we can, we can find the time to teach children to a higher standard—a different level of comprehension.

Once I understood that we need to overhaul our definition of comprehension and that the most overt expressions of high expectations aren't necessarily the most potent, I had to face the fact that we must learn to teach fewer concepts in greater depth over a longer period of time. But what does that look like in the classroom? How can teachers make informed decisions about what curricula to emphasize, what to put on the back burner, and what to leave out altogether? Clearly it is difficult for teachers, with their heavy workloads, to do the research that would identify which elements of the curriculum are most important and which matter less.

The Structure of To Understand

Answering this question—what is essential to teach—is tackled in the third section of each chapter, which I call **Literacy Essentials**. In it, I define and describe the K–12 literacy objectives that are most essential for children's literacy learning. I suggest specific ways teachers can focus on the key literacy skills and strategies that matter most, deemphasizing or eliminating skills and strategies that matter less, thereby creating time to teach for deeper levels of comprehension and greater retention and reapplication of concepts.

I also propose specific strategies teachers can use to transform daily literacy instruction into richer, more memorable learning experiences that simultaneously introduce children to the world of the intellect and equip them with the comprehension skills they need to manage a wide range of texts and concepts. I describe how teachers who work in some of this country's most diverse and challenging schools have found ways to overcome perceived and real obstacles and transform their classrooms into intellectual havens for children; I detail the improvements in the children's thinking and learning and outline the content these teachers focused on to help their students realize these gains. In this section I also argue that our traditional notions of how to structure literacy workshops may not be the most conducive to understanding at high levels, and offer an alternative— a new conceptualization for the daily reader's/writer's workshop.

In What Ways Can We Live Our Adult Lives as Intellectually Curious Leaders for Our Students and Our Colleagues?

I began my teaching career in a suburban Denver school district that valued not so much what we educators knew, but what we might become. Our leaders, in particular the superintendent of schools, Richard O'Connell, saw diamonds in the rough in young teachers and principals. Rick recognized leadership when he saw it and worked to promote not just the development of our teaching skills, but also our intellectual selves. He valued teacher's learning lives outside of school and found ways to encourage and support their growth. He understood the value of investing in teachers' graduate learning (my own included) so that we could come back to colleagues and share new insights and understandings. Professional development was based on a teacher-to-teacher model much more than on an expert-to-teacher model. Rick took considerable risks in placing people (myself included) in positions that were just beyond our reach, knowing somehow that interested, curious people would work hard and learn quickly in order to meet his expectations. He valued the struggle. He knew that it was important to *learn* to be good. I discovered that I was capable of working in leadership roles far earlier than I would have had he not pushed me. He sought to make people uncomfortable, somehow applying Piaget's concept of cognitive dissonance (we learn most effectively when we are slightly uncomfortable with an idea and not sure we understand it) at a district level. He understood that we learn when we are in just a bit over our heads. I attempted professional undertakings because he inspired me, challenged me, irritated me, fought back at me, and indulged my passionate tirades about directions the district was taking.

Part of my learning in those days in the early to mid 1980s was in graduate courses at the University of Denver, where literacy educators like Shelley Harwayne, Lucy Calkins, Don Graves, and Mary Ellen Giacobbe were brought in to conduct summer institutes. I vividly remember offering to make the coffee, clean up, and drive visitors to and from the airport so that I could sit in on the seminars and soak up every drop. The message, so consistently communicated in those days, was that to be the best teachers, we have to be avid learners ourselves. If we want to teach reading well, we must first read widely and voraciously. If we want to teach writing well, we must write frequently and take risks in our own writing. If we want to serve as credible intellectual mentors, we must live intellectual lives.

How lucky I feel to have had a leader like Rick, enjoyed regular exposure to nationally known literacy experts, and worked alongside people who provoked and inspired me. How lucky I was to be surrounded by interesting, intellectually engaged colleagues who kindled in me a need to know—through professional pursuits as well as a textured life outside school. I had superb models—partly the luck of the draw, partly because I chose to study them—whose leadership I could analyze and whose suggestions I considered carefully.

Now, in my twenty-fifth year in education, I have to ask how we can provide similar leadership for our colleagues. Do we live the intellectually engaged life from which our colleagues, as well as our children, can learn? Do we make the time to develop our intellectual lives outside of school? What good will living richly textured lives of the mind do for our students and our colleagues?

The Structure of To Understand

In the fourth section of each chapter, entitled **Dwelling in the Mind**, I ask the reader to consider his or her intellectual life. I suggest that if we remain cognizant of the dimensions and outcomes of understanding—the indicators and effects of understanding in our minds and in our lives—we can live the intellectual lives we may have forgotten or left untended for years. I suggest ways in which we can integrate insights from our intellectual lives into classroom conversations that will prove memorable and prophetic for students. I argue that by observing a teacher who not only *says* she loves learning, but also reveals the ways in which she intellectually organizes and experiences the world, her students and her colleagues will be drawn to the life of the mind.

A Tip for Reading This Book

I designed the book so that teachers reading together in a study group might approach the book in a couple of different ways. You may wish to read this book "horizontally"—that is, read all the Mentors sections first, followed by the Dimension sections, then the Literacy Essentials and Dwelling in the Mind sections. Or you may wish to read "vertically," as we traditionally read a chapter, progressing through all four sections in sequence.

This is a book about what it means to understand. It is about how we use books and language to discover, alongside children, the power of the human intellect. It is about focusing on what matters most in literacy teaching rather than teaching a little of this, a little of that, until we've squandered every opportunity for children to explore ideas in depth. It is about learning from intellectual mentors whose lives provide insight and direction for a nation of young scholars. This book is about capturing the essence of understanding and bringing it to life in our own and our children's hearts and minds. This book is about what it means to understand.

Chapter 2

Seeking Understanding in Our Minds, in Our Lives

WHEN I WAS TEACHING, my fifth and sixth graders would occasionally have conversations in class that astounded me. The depth of their insights into books is memorable to this day: Katie Fetter reading *Julie of the Wolves* and commenting on the parallels between physical and emotional courage; Carl Ramer reading *The Lion, The Witch and the Wardrobe* for the fourth time, probing the symbolism of the characters and noticing details I had missed; Gina Thompson reading *The Great Gilly Hopkins*, telling us about her experiences in foster care placements and pointing out where Katherine Paterson had it wrong.

I remember going home with great enthusiasm and telling my husband, David, "These kids were unbelievable in their book clubs today. They were able to probe a single idea to extraordinary depth. It's like they were holding a diamond up to the light to examine its facets—only the diamond was an idea. They could have talked for hours. I am so blown away by these kids. They can really surprise you, you know? I'm so lucky to be a teacher—these are the moments, I tell you. They are so smart. This is why I teach!" I could really get on a roll.

He looked at me with more than a little skepticism—eye rolling, even. I think he expected me to burst into the first verse of "God Bless America." My idealism at a fever pitch, I took myself a bit too seriously. I intoned something about how I touch the future and shook my head with feigned sadness for him, saying, "You poor thing—consigned to practice law for the rest of your life." He listened to this dramatic drivel for months before asking drily, "Why don't they do that *every day*?"

That question annoyed me more than I can say. I was quick to respond to it, though. "David, you just don't get it. They can't do that every day. They are ten and eleven. Geez, they get squirrelly every time a big storm rolls through—barometric pressure changes really throw them. They don't concentrate long enough to have discussions like that every day; someone is always pulling them out of class to go to this or that special ed class or band; some of them have hormones raging; they usually want to talk about who is going out with whom and who got new skis. If there is an assembly, they take forever to refocus and . . ."

I had a million excuses to explain the norm, the average day in my classroom, but no way to explain the exception. Why, on some days, did they tussle with each other, with me, or on paper until they really understood an idea, a character's motivation, a conflict from literature, or a concept in science? How did they reach such insights on those occasions? Why did they enter study in such a fervent manner, every once in a while? Why, on those days, were they willing to work hard to understand? Why did they find some ideas worthy of the time and effort it took to really comprehend? David's question haunted me. Why didn't they do that every day?

As David suggested; if they could think at high levels some of the time, they were capable of doing so all of the time. The truth is that they didn't think at high levels every day because I didn't expect them to. I hadn't defined and described what it looks, sounds, feels, tastes, and smells like to think at high levels every day. I accepted as a happy accident the times when they were most engaged and did little to ensure that they happened more consistently.

I couldn't figure out how to convert those happy accidents to de rigueur events, but I did know how the kids felt in those all-too-rare moments. By revisiting my own memories of intellectual engagement—such as my high school death penalty project—I understood what my fifth and sixth graders were thinking and feeling when they found themselves deeply engaged in a complex, intellectually challenging problem. I began to understand that what happened for them in those moments was nothing short of an introduction to the capacity of their own minds. They were experiencing their intellect. They were discovering the joy of understanding. How could I make that occasional experience habitual?

I began to consider how I could respond to David's question with something other than an excuse. Why didn't they do that every day and, more important, what chance did I, as their teacher, have to improve the odds? Could I make their moments of intellectual rigor and genuine understanding something more than accidental? Was there a way, in my own classroom, to better the odds that great conversations—whether spoken, written, or invisible and private—would be the norm rather than the exception? Could I recreate for young children the kinds of intellectual experience I didn't have until late high school and college?

From Questions to Models

How could I begin to answer those questions? Now, understand that I'm a bit of a research junkie. I love to struggle my way through the research journals each month, and I devour the latest books about promising class-room practices. I try to detect trends and patterns in studies about children's literacy learning. I'm not a researcher in the traditional, academic sense, but I am fascinated by what others have written and I love to speculate about how findings might translate into the classroom. I try to capture the essence of studies in models teachers can use to improve everyday instruction. I'm not interested in just reading research and colleagues' books, however. I believe that those of us who no longer work in a class-room every day owe it to all the teachers who do to stay current and to synthesize research findings, particularly when numerous studies point to the same conclusions. I consider it a responsibility to read research and scholarly writing from a wide range of perspectives and to *create models* (syntheses that attempt to condense a tremendous amount of information in a clear and manageable way) that will help my classroom colleagues better understand patterns and trends in the research. The truth is, *I* need models to make better sense of all the research and theory in our field!

I have read a huge number of studies, syntheses of studies, and books about literacy over the last twenty years and find that certain patterns and trends emerge so consistently, they lead me to the formulation of a model. Models based on research are critical to practitioners—in effect, they can help us answer David's question—how can we, through revisions in our practice, increase the consistency of desirable outcomes for students? Models show us how we can go from an occasional "happy accident" to far more predictable and productive learning behaviors. Models also help us to synthesize and make manageable an enormous amount of information about promising practices in teaching and learning.

Throughout *To Understand,* I'll share three models I've created and found helpful in my work with students and colleagues. I call these models:

• Dimensions and Outcomes of Understanding

• What's Essential for Literacy Learning

• Literacy Studio

I've developed and refined these models to help answer the four key questions I posed in Chapter 1. I show how the models relate to the four questions (and thus the chapter sections) in Figure 2.1.

First, a word or two about the way I devised the three models: They

Fig. 2.1. Organization of Key Questions, Chapters, and Models

Question	Corresponding Chapter Section	Relevant Models
What does it mean to understand?	Mentors	Dimensions and Outcomes of Understanding
How do we define and teach toward high expectations and high levels of understanding?	Dimension	Dimensions and Outcomes of Understanding
What matters most in literacy learning?	Literacy Essentials	What's Essential for Literacy Learning Literacy Studio
In what ways can we live our adult lives as intellectually curious leaders for our students and our colleagues?	Dwelling in the Mind	Dimensions and Outcomes of Understanding

are more descriptive than prescriptive; they show rather than tell. You'll find, for example, that in the upcoming chapters I show through the Dimensions and Outcomes model what "make sense" might mean rather than dictate a series of steps for teachers to follow. The What's Essential model describes the most essential literacy content so that each teacher can decide for herself where to focus instruction and what in the existing curricula to leave out in favor of teaching fewer concepts in greater depth. And, in the Literacy Studio model, I propose a structure for the literacy block that teachers can adapt for their own circumstances.

Like all theoretical models, these three models are meant to cull a vast amount of knowledge from observations, experience, research, and theoretical writing and make it manageable and useable. I try to describe sometimes nebulous goals in tangible, realizable terms. I don't promise that the models will provide definitive answers to the questions I've posed, but I do promise that, in discussing the questions and models with colleagues and trying some of the ideas in your classroom and school, you'll experience thoughtful, practice-changing conversation that will improve the likelihood that kids will think at levels you may have thought impossible.

Dimensions and Outcomes of Understanding Model

The first model, **Dimensions and Outcomes of Understanding** (Figures 2.2a and b), is less a product of reviewing research than it is a summary of

Fig. 2.2a. The Outcomes of Understanding
What Happens in Our Minds

We gain deeper understanding of text through the use of cognitive strategies:

- Monitoring
- Asking questions
- Determining importance
- Synthesizing
- Using prior knowledge (schema)
- Inferring
- Creating sensory and emotional images

Cognitive strategies may lead us to experience the following outcomes:

In Fiction/Narrative/Poetry:	In Expository Text:
Insights for writing—the ability to learn from great narrative writers, to read their work with a writer's eye and to incorporate writer's tools into our own writing	**Insights for writing**—the ability to learn from great expository writers, to read their work with a writer's eye and to incorporate writer's tools into our own writing
General empathy—a belief that the reader is actually a part of the setting, knows the characters, stands alongside them in their trials, brings something of himself to the events and resolution; emotions are aroused	**A sense of importance**—a clear idea of what matters most, what is worth remembering
Character empathy—the sense that we are feeling and believing what the character feels and believes	**New applications**—the ability to retain and reapply newly learned concepts in new settings and circumstances
Setting empathy—a feeling of actually being there, of experiencing the time, place, and conditions	**Connections**—the realization that newly learned concepts "fit" with and extend existing background knowledge, and make sense in relation to what is already known; they affirm our existing knowledge
Conflict empathy—a sense of experiencing a similar conflict such that the reader can relate to the internal and/or external struggle the characters endure	**Clarity about the problem and possible solution(s)**—a sense of the elements that make a situation problematic and what steps might be taken to solve the problem, perhaps in a particular order
Author empathy—understanding why/how one's interpretations have been shaped in the way they have and what literary tools (diction, foreshadowing, imagery, voice, plot structures) the author used to shape the reader's interpretation	**Author's intent**—understanding what the author thinks is important and is trying to communicate; an ability to cull key ideas from interesting details or long descriptions

Fig. 2.2a. The Outcomes of Understanding *(continued)*

Cognitive strategies may lead us to experience the following outcomes:

In Fiction/Narrative/Poetry:	In Expository Text:
A sense of what's next—the ability to anticipate what might be forthcoming and to predict events	**A sense of the general order or chronology**—understanding the order or progression of a series of events; the ability to predict with some accuracy what is likely to occur or be described next
A sense of what makes a text distinct—understanding how this text is similar to and different from others, perhaps those by the same author or in the same genre	**The ability to compare and contrast**—developing a sense of how concepts presented in text are alike or different and why that contrast matters to the overall text
Confidence—the ability and propensity to discuss and contribute to others' ideas about the narrative	**Confidence**—the ability and propensity to discuss and contribute to others' knowledge about a concept
A sense of the aesthetic—a desire to linger with portions of the text we find beautiful or moving; the desire to experience it again	**A sense of the aesthetic**—a developing sense of wonder about the complexities and inherent subtleties related to a concept
A need to pause and ponder—the desire to reread or pause to consider new facets and twists in the text, and to discuss or share ideas in some way	**A need to reread and revise thinking**—the desire to revisit, reread, or explore other texts in order to learn more about a concept
A desire to advocate—the feeling of being "behind" the character(s) or narrator, wanting events to evolve in a particular way, believing it is right that the plot moves in a certain way	**A desire to advocate**—a growing conviction of what is "right" related to a concept; a desire to support, learn more about, and convince others of an idea
Believability—a sense that "this is real and I believe it"; a sense of satisfaction with the way the events evolved	**Fascination**—a growing sense of wanting to know more, a developing passionate interest in a particular topic or idea
A gradual recognition of patterns and symbols—the ability to use literary tools to recognize motifs, themes, and patterns; the ability to examine one facet of the text and extrapolate to a larger meaning	**A sense of cause and effect**—knowledge of how events relate to each other and how new events are likely to relate; a sense of the effect or impact of one force, factor, or event on another
A revision of one's thinking—changing one's mind, revising, rethinking, and reshaping understanding	**A revision of one's knowledge**—forgoing previously held knowledge/beliefs in favor of updated factual information

Fig. 2.2a continues on next page

Fig. 2.2a. The Outcomes of Understanding *(continued)*

Cognitive strategies may lead us to experience the following outcomes:

In Fiction/Narrative/Poetry:	In Expository Text:
An affirmation of beliefs/values/opinions—reaffirmation of existing beliefs/values/opinions and/or developing new ones because of what we've read	**An affirmation of beliefs/values/opinions**—reaffirmation of existing beliefs/values/opinions and/or developing new ones because of what we've read
An increase in cognitive stamina—the willingness to sustain interest and attention and to exclude competing or distracting interests	**An increase in cognitive stamina**—the willingness to sustain interest and attention and to exclude competing or distracting interests
Clear recollection—the sense of permanence that comes with deeply understanding something; the ability to reapply that understanding in a new situation	**Clear recollection**—the sense of permanence that comes with deeply understanding something; the ability to reapply that understanding in a new situation

observations of children and teachers following Jamika's provocative question. In the weeks and months after my unsatisfactory response to her question, I was determined to observe myself, my colleagues, and their students in the *process* of understanding in order to better define and describe that process. In classrooms and workshops and curled up in my cozy office with great books and research, I resolved to become an observer of the process of comprehension with one driving question: What does it mean to understand? What is characteristic of children and adults when they are intellectually engaged and understanding deeply? What is the outcome when a reader uses comprehension strategies as tools to help deepen understanding? What outcomes are common when children and adults comprehend what they read and are able to retain and reapply what they have understood?

I wanted to be able to name and describe, for Jamika and all those who never asked, what happens *in our minds* and what happens *in our lives* when we understand. I reasoned that if I could define and describe patterns of cognitive and behavioral activity observable when people are in the process of understanding, I could use those descriptions to *increase the likelihood* that children would engage in those behaviors more consistently. And, I just might be closer to answering that haunting question: Why don't they do that every day?

Fig. 2.2b. The Dimensions of Understanding

What Happens in Our Lives

- We are **fervent**—we concentrate intensively, we lose ourselves in the experience of thought, the world disappears, and we work hard to learn more. We choose to challenge ourselves.

- We **dwell in ideas**—we take time to listen to our own thinking, time to reflect purposefully on an idea. We rehearse and repeat to perfect our ideas; we need time to be silent and time to discuss our ideas with others. We **create models** to help us remember.

- We **struggle for insight**; we savor and learn from the struggle itself; we venture into new learning territory and fight the debilitating influence of judgment.

- We manipulate our own thoughts to understand more completely—we **revise our thinking** by incorporating new knowledge, beliefs, and opinions. We can describe how our thinking has changed over time, how books and other learning experiences have changed us. We **take action** to mitigate or resolve conflicts in our world.

- We become **Renaissance learners**—we're driven to explore a wide range of topics and interests, texts and genres. We work to understand how ideas are related, to see patterns. We become **passionately interested** in particular topics and ideas and are willing to expend considerable time and energy in seeking to understand them; we dig deeply to discover previously unknown facets of an idea.

- We engage in rigorous **discourse about ideas** and find we have more to say than we thought. We consider the perspectives of others and challenge them until we understand our own and others' opinions and principles; we surprise ourselves with the clarity of our own thinking.

- Our understanding is enriched when we have **emotional connections**. We love to reexperience what we find beautiful, and we understand better when learning includes aesthetic journeys. In our own creative endeavors, we seek to craft something luminous and memorable, something that matters to others.

- Ultimately, our insights become potent and lasting—and **we remember**.

In workshops around the country and in discussions with students in grades K–12, I began to keep a series of simple lists in my notebooks. Eventually, the lists coalesced into two descriptions: what happens in our minds (outcomes) and what we experience in our lives (dimensions) when we understand. The first portion of this two-part model is presented in Figure 2.2a. It describes the desired outcomes—what happens in our minds—when we deeply understand something (described separately for fiction/narrative/poetry and nonfiction) and also highlights the comprehension strategies that help produce those outcomes.

The second part of this model (Figure 2.2b) seeks to define and describe what we experience *in our lives* when we are intellectually engaged—the behaviors and reactions we may exhibit when in the process of understanding. The language in the model may sound unlike any language you've used with children before, but as you reflect on and define this type of intellectual experience for yourself and your students, you'll find such terms indeed convey the nature of true understanding. I use this language throughout the book, not only to define understanding in a clear and consistent way, but also to model how we might help our students think at high levels more consistently. When we talk about fervent learning, for example, we can use that term when describing children's learning efforts or when studying great thinkers. Whether you use this language or a set of terms you create with your students, it's crucial to use consistent vocabulary in the classroom so that concepts, strategies, and behaviors become familiar, natural, expected, and describable.

Eventually my simple lists began to take shape, and I became very interested in what would happen if I explicitly shared the dimensions and outcomes with children. As I went into classrooms to experiment, the teachers with whom I worked had questions: Why should teachers bother to name and discuss the dimensions and outcomes? What purpose could it possibly serve to use the dimensions and outcomes in our discourse with children about books? Will talking about enhance comprehension?

The chapters that follow will explore those questions. I have found that when we recall the qualities and characteristics associated with the intellectual experiences we (or our students) have had, we can extract something more lasting than a recollection of the challenge itself. We can examine what happens in our minds and in our lives in new settings or learning contexts, when we are in the process of understanding. And *what we can define and describe, we can increase, both in frequency and quality*. We can, in response to David's question, increase the likelihood that children will think at high levels every day. And if students learn to consistently think at high levels, they will retain and reapply what they learn, not only in the context of literacy, but also across the disciplines of thought in which they engage every day—math, science, social studies, art, music, and athletics.

There are other benefits to reflecting on our intellectual experiences. By articulating the behaviors and changes that characterize understanding, we develop a vocabulary for classroom discourse about the nature of learning. We have a common language, a way to anchor a sometimes elusive concept and make it more tangible, a base from which students may discover their own dimensions of understanding. Moreover, such descriptions give us a barometer for gauging the degree of student engagement and their understanding of concepts and content.

Using the opportunities schools and districts give me to work with children, I began to experiment with the dimensions and outcomes of understanding as I taught comprehension strategies. Instead of merely teaching children to activate schema or infer to understand more deeply, I used my evolving list of dimensions and outcomes to talk about what happens, *exactly*, when we comprehend—in literacy experiences and beyond. I attempted to convert typical reading lessons into more intellectually memorable events by infusing their own experiences, their own dimensions and outcomes of using comprehension strategies, into the discussion. For example, when teaching children to question in order to better understand what they read (one of the seven comprehension strategies we described in *Mosaic of Thought*), I found that if I defined and modeled what happens when a reader does question—when I showed the children what they can *expect to experience* when they understand deeply (such as the desire to dwell in an idea for a long time [dimension] or the feeling of empathy for a character [outcome]—they tended to ask more relevant and penetrating questions and to do so much earlier in the process of learning a comprehension strategy.

These are the ideas I will discuss in Chapters 3–9. I'll explore (and model) the dimensions and outcomes of understanding in the first two sections (Mentors and Dimension) of each forthcoming chapter.

What's Essential for Literacy Learning Model

Imagine for a moment that you return to school next fall to find that you have a new colleague, Tracy, teaching in your grade level. She is at work well before she is required to report back, eager to set up her classroom, plan carefully, do the right thing for her students, and comply with your school and district policies and curricula. You meet and assure her that you're available to help should she need anything, and she says, well, yes, as a matter of fact there is something you can help her think through. She has only a few years of teaching experience and she is so overwhelmed she hardly knows what to focus on first. Your curriculum is very different from the one in her former district and she wants to ensure that she is teaching the right literacy content. She feels she would like to be much more focused on essential literacy content rather than trying to teach a little bit of everything. She felt too scattered in her first two years of teaching—she was trying to fit everything in and it seemed that she didn't teach anything as well as she knew she could. Could you just tell her—what is most essential for students' literacy learning?

"Well, Tracy," you laugh with her, "I'm sorry you don't have any important questions!" How will you begin to respond? Perhaps you have some of the same questions. At least you have a new colleague with whom you can share ideas, if not answers.

With most issues of great complexity, the most elegant and effective answers are usually the simplest. If we know that humans learn best when we learn a few important concepts at a time, taught in depth over a long period, then as teachers, we must understand clearly what concepts matter most. If we believe it's important to teach kids to understand, to weave the dimensions and outcomes of understanding into our classrooms, we must focus on the most essential elements of reading and writing instruction.

Fortunately, our colleagues in the research community have done us a great service. They have studied those few important concepts that we need to teach in depth over a long period of time. Given all the horror stories about how contentious our field is, how professionals engage in life-long battles over pedagogy, I was surprised to discover that there is far more agreement—yes, I said agreement—than disagreement about what matters most for literacy learning in grades K–12. The only true argument is the *emphasis* given to certain skills and strategies.

Unfortunately, I found few workable models that synthesize this research in a way that helps teachers decide what to teach. So, by building on a career of reading research, reading popular books on literacy, consulting with colleagues, and attending conferences where researchers and practitioners discussed this dilemma, I've created a model that I hope can give teachers that clear focus—what matters most for literacy learning, K–12.

The list is surprisingly brief, compared to the hundreds of pages that comprise typical district curricula and state standards. The four parts of the What's Essential model (Figures 2.3a–d) outline the essential K–12 content and instruction in four major categories:

1. A **Climate of Rigor, Inquiry, and Intimacy** represents the findings from research and practice that suggest how literacy classrooms might be set up, how rituals and routines might be handled, and how the seen (and unseen) environment of schools and classrooms can be created to support in-depth literacy learning.

2. **Cognitive Strategies** represents the research about what content matters most for literacy learning—in what areas we should focus our lessons and units.

3. **Text and Genre** lays out the varieties of text, genre, and level in which children should be engaged to maximize their literacy learning.

4. **Text Structures** summarizes the data we have from research and practice about how children's knowledge of text structures can help them predict and better understand.

I chose these four categories because they are areas in which we have substantial research as well as lots of classroom experiences to show they're essential. Appendix B, "What's Essential," further defines each of these categories. I'll discuss the What's Essential model in each Literacy Essentials section of the forthcoming chapters—the section in which I strive to answer the third set of key questions I raised in Chapter 1: What matters most in literacy learning? How can teachers focus on the most essential elements of literacy learning in a context of growing curriculum and assessment demands? How can we transform ordinary literacy lessons into intellectually memorable experiences?

In your conversation with your new colleague, Tracy, you realize that you have a place to start. You can spread the What's Essential model on a table and begin to discuss what the various elements mean and what they look like in the context of daily instruction and learning. You can imagine together what it would be like to provide more focused instruction. You imagine the confidence you would feel if you applied your focused instruction to these, the most essential elements of literacy content. You begin to realize that your instruction will become clearer and children's learning more lasting. You realize that you will be able to show students how the skills and strategies we teach relate to one another and still have time to explore the dimensions and outcomes of understanding—what we experience when we truly understand. You realize that if you know what's most essential, you are ready to follow the proven strategy for effective learning: teach a *few concepts of great import* (what's essential), teach them *in depth over a long period of time*, and apply them in a *variety of texts and contexts*. You agree to try together to make this the most focused year of instruction you've ever provided.

Literacy Studio Model

School appearances can be tricky; it's unwise to allow ourselves to form first-impression judgments. I recall visiting an elementary school in a mid-sized Northeastern city and being delighted by the vivid colors in the hallways, the brightly colored tiles made by children, and the inviting spaces for learning and conversation sprinkled around the school. What a difference a child-friendly environment makes, I remember thinking. I was visiting to get

Fig. 2.3a. What's Essential for Literacy Learning
A Climate of Rigor, Inquiry, and Intimacy

Teachers	Students
Create a predictable daily workshop that ensures abundant time for independent reading and writing—a literacy studio	Read and write independently for extended and growing periods of time each day; actively engage in all four components of the literacy studio
Create a culture conducive to in-depth study of a variety of books, genres, topics, authors, writer's tools, and comprehension strategies	Select books, topics, and authors appropriate for level, challenge, interest; engage in book discussions; share recommendations and insights with other readers; seek to understand the insights of others
Create a climate that visibly encourages serious but joyful work on authentic tasks through the use of several different types of learning spaces (use alternative lighting, room configuration, rugs, bookshelves, and decorative items to create intimate spaces)	Fully utilize the resources available and move independently in the classroom; work within the classroom with the knowledge that it is an honored place of scholarship and inquiry, a place to indulge learning passions and curiosity
Focus on helping children practice ways to share their thinking—display student work and anchor charts that describe the group's thinking about topics recently taught	Understand and use options for oral, artistic, dramatic, and written means to show thinking and respond to texts
Teach and respond with civility and respect, modeling sophisticated and scholarly oral language for children	Use oral language precisely to describe their thinking during reading and writing; use that language to apply strategies and writer's tools independently
Create an unseen culture of rigor, inquiry, and intimacy by continually expecting more, probing ideas further, and pressing children to explore their intellects	Understand and engage in the processes, procedures, and rituals of a learning community
Teach a few important concepts in depth over a long period of time	Apply important concepts in a wide variety of texts and contexts
Use five key instructional strategies— thinking aloud, modeling, conferring, demonstration, and sharing—to ensure retention and reapplication of concepts learned; use the strategies to focus simultaneously on essential deep and surface structure systems, K–12	Become independent, flexible, and adaptive in using surface and deep structure systems, including word identification, fluent reading, comprehension strategies, writer's tools, syntax, text structure, and conventions; share these skills with and teach other readers and writers

Fig. 2.3b. What's Essential for Literacy Learning

Cognitive Strategies

Surface Structure Systems	Deep Structure Systems
Sets of skills that help readers/writers identify words and read fluently	Sets of skills and strategies that help readers/writers comprehend literally to grasp plot, comprehend deeply to probe ideas, and extend and apply their understanding
Graphophonic System: Letter/sound knowledge, alphabetic principle, phonemic awareness, decoding	**Semantic System:** Understanding word meanings from literal to subtle; discussing or writing about associations related to words; precision and word choice in writing
Lexical System: Visual word recognition based on frequent visual exposure to words; visual memory for *all* words	**Schematic System:** Constructing meaning at the whole-text level (can be literal or inferential understanding of themes, ideas, and concepts); storing and retrieving relevant knowledge; connecting the new to the known
Syntactic System: Understanding (usually auditory) and use of language structures at the word, sentence, paragraph, and whole-text levels (see Figure 2.3d, Text Structures)	**Pragmatic System:** Multiple experiences with ideas we've read or learned; sharing and applying meaning; constructing meaning through oral, written, artistic, and dramatic means; writing for specific purposes and audiences; revising thinking based on interactions with others; adopting the habits and mores of readers and writers
What children know and are able to do when using surface structure systems	**What children know and are able to do when using deep structure systems**
Use decoding strategies such as identifying word families, chunking, point and slide, cross-check across systems (does the word make sense, sound like language, do the letters match the sounds), etc.	Monitor for meaning
	Activate and/or create relevant background knowledge (schema)
Recognize sight words and other words in environment visually; use recognized words repeatedly	Infer
	Create sensory and emotional images
	Determine importance
Use word analysis strategies such as identifying affixes, compound words, and derivations	Question
	Synthesize
Use text-management strategies such as rereading/reading ahead, deep reading, skimming/scanning, using text features like boldface and italics	

Fig. 2.3c. What's Essential for Literacy Learning
Text and Genre

Distinguish Among Genres	Use Different Level Texts for Different Purposes
Study genre characteristics; read and write in that genre	Vary the text difficulty depending on the task

Biography
Historical fiction
Textbooks
Reference texts
Web sites
Persuasion
Realistic fiction
Poetry
Memoir/autobiography
Science fiction
Mystery
Journalism
Opinion/editorial
Tests
Expository texts—narrative
Picture books
Photo essay
Promotional materials/advertising
Fantasy/science fiction

Work in instructional level text for:

- practice in decoding
- practice in word recognition
- practice in oral reading fluency
- practice in word analysis

Work in more challenging texts (including read-alouds, wordless picture books, and texts that have been read aloud multiple times) for:

- application of comprehension strategies
- study of writer's tools
- analysis of text structures
- book club discussions
- reading with a partner
- learning new content (especially when there are text features such as graphs, charts, bold print, and/or familiar text structures)

a sense of the faculty's needs and concerns prior to their work in Cornerstone, the professional development initiative I described in Chapter 1. I was relieved, frankly, to be in a newer school building with bright light flooding through the windows and abundant books in the library and in each classroom. Though this was a school that served a very impoverished area, it was clear that, with respect to materials and physical spaces, great care had been directed toward ensuring that children's needs were addressed. As I peeked through the windows in classroom doors, I saw new area rugs, easels, some comfortable seating for children and teachers, and books displayed throughout the rooms in an inviting way. Why, I wondered, can't we figure out a way to make all schools look and work this way?

I was thrilled to find that the school faculty had worked together to set aside a two-and-a-half-hour literacy block for each grade level for grades 1–5. What a pleasure it would be to go into a school where the time bat-

Fig. 2.3d. What's Essential for Literacy Learning
Text Structures

**Students Can Recognize and Use
Narrative Text Structures (whole text)**

Character
Setting
Conflict
Plot structure

- character, setting, conflict, rising action, climax, sequence of events, resolution

Narrative Writing Technique

Develop characters, setting, and conflict through:

- exposition
- action
- dialogue

Create believable characters, settings, conflicts, and events through use of writer's tools and voice, including

- foreshadowing
- parallel plot structures
- flashback and fast forward

Effective use of:

- word choice
- diction
- phrasing

**Students Can Recognize and Use
Expository Text Structures (paragraph/section)**

Cause/effect
Compare/contrast
Chronological
Problem/solution
Descriptive
Enumerative

Hurdles for Readers of Expository Texts

Word hurdles

- anaphora
- vocabulary load

Text hurdles

- insufficient schema for content and/or text structures
- inefficient predicting
- naïve conceptions
- staccato reading
- concept load
- pacing demands

Expository Writing Technique

Elaborate/develop and group ideas/themes
Organize ideas with a discernable, but not blatant, structure
Lay out and defend a position based on fact and/or opinion
Write to persuade based on fact and/or opinion
Write compelling leads and conclusions

tle had already been fought and won! I was starting to wonder why this school needed us for in-depth professional learning when I began to linger and observe instruction in the large, sunny classrooms during the literacy block. The teachers were warm and friendly to children, clearly devoted to them, but slowly I sensed that the children weren't responding in the way I had expected. I began to notice that they were passive during instruction. They were certainly well-behaved, even compliant, but there was very little talking among children, or even between the teachers and children. The hundreds of books neatly gathered in baskets around the room looked untouched, and when I began to ask children to talk about their favorite books, they were uncertain. Some could name a book, but few could talk about the ideas they found compelling in the text. When I asked if they had read some texts many times, they looked at me like I was crazy! In classroom after classroom, there was a detachment on the part of the children that was chilling. Why weren't they engaged and invigorated by this obviously well-crafted learning environment?

As I inquired further, I learned that in the primary classrooms, the students adhered to a tightly controlled schedule in which the following elements were rather rigidly imposed:

- The whole class gathered on the floor for a brief read-aloud.

- Children returned to their desks to read books designated at their "level" and selected by the teacher.

- When they were not reading their leveled books, the younger children worked their way through centers that included listening to books on tape and completing "extension projects" loosely related to the books on tape—creating artistic renderings of the books, writing in reading journals, completing sentence starters related to the books, and so forth.

- When they were not reading or in a center, each child met for over twenty minutes with the teacher and a small, homogenous group during which the teacher focused on particular skills the children were asked to demonstrate through reading orally.

- The whole class had a sharing session in which two or three children read aloud from their independent books.

Intermediate classrooms differed only in that most were reading the same novel and, instead of centers, students were working, sometimes in groups of three or four, on "novel units" that related to the books their reading group was reading. Charts on the wall showed how many books (or in some cases, pages) individual students had read and promised rewards like pizza parties if the number of books or pages read totaled some predetermined number. Teachers met less frequently with small groups, but it was evident that the small groups were identified based on autumn assessments and remained fixed throughout the year.

How appearances can be deceiving! When I looked below the surface, I saw kids (and teachers) who were going through the motions, taking part in the various standard workshop components ("We're doing shared reading, we're doing guided reading"), but with limited passion, little engagement, no fervency. It wasn't until I had visited several schools like this one—everything looks great on the surface, but little in-depth learning is taking place—that I realized we may need to rethink the ways in which we construct the time block we call reader's and writer's workshop. We need to move away from prescribing activities and groupings that may or may not meet students' needs, and move toward maximizing the time students have to be apprentices to more proficient readers and writers, to practice their skills and strategies, and to receive individualized guidance in their learning. Workshop components aren't doing the teaching—teachers are! We need to think about how the literacy workshop can be structured to facilitate thought and in-depth understanding, not how we can get all the components "done" each day.

I thought back to a model I had created years earlier to help my students at the University of Denver understand what a reader's and writer's workshop entailed and knew it was a model I could reshape to address the misinterpretations and rather unimaginative use of the literacy workshop I had observed (see Figure 2.4, Literacy Studio). I didn't use terms like shared reading or large-group instruction, independent reading, or small-group or guided reading, as those terms have been misinterpreted and laden with less-than-useful connotations. I created four fresh titles for the components I wanted to include in the workshop and emphasized that all apply to reading as well as writing. Large-group instruction, or shared reading and writing, was renamed *crafting*, independent reading and writing was called *composing*, small-group or guided reading and writing instruction changed to *invitational groups*, and sharing became *reflecting*. It wasn't just that I wanted to rename the traditional components or activities; I wanted to transform the way we use time and the level of student engagement in the literacy block. I wanted kids and teachers to think differently about the quality of their interactions and the degree to which they could (and did) engage in in-depth thought during the literacy block, not as a happy accident, but every day.

What characterizes the finest, most engaging large-group instruction, for example? How can we define and describe the best conferences we've ever witnessed and make them a daily occurrence? How can we transform the often deadly "sharing time" into a vibrant and dynamic opportunity for kids to teach other kids? Clearly more than a set of new titles for the workshop components was needed, but renaming and giving more time to particular components was a good place to start.

I will further define and describe each component of the Literacy Studio model in Chapter 3, and will refer to it throughout the book in the third section of each chapter, Literacy Essentials. For an overview, however, refer to Figure 2.4.

Fig. 2.4. Literacy Studio			
Description	**Teaching Tactics**	**Focus**	**Frequency**
Crafting: Reading			
Large-group, heterogenous, typically deep-structure instruction	Thinking aloud, some modeling; students turn and talk or share thinking with whole group	Strategies and skills in which all students need instruction, though they will apply what has been taught in different level texts	At least three times a week
Crafting: Writing			
Large-group, heterogeneous, typically deep-structure instruction	"Writing aloud" on an overhead projector or document camera; thinking aloud about the decisions a writer makes, the strategies and tools he/she uses	Writer's tools and tactics in which all students need instruction	At least three times a week
Composing: Reading			
Independent reading	Students apply what has been taught in the crafting session or invitational group	Teachers confer to assess present performance level and press students to higher levels of application	Every day
Composing: Writing			
Independent writing	Students apply what has been taught in the crafting session or invitational group	Teachers confer to assess current performance level and press students to higher levels of application	Every day

Description	Teaching Tactics	Focus	Frequency
Fig. 2.4. Literacy Studio *(continued)*			
Invitational Groups: Reading			
Small, needs-based groups, homogenous by need, not by level	Thinking aloud and modeling with frequent opportunities for students to practice and apply the skill or strategy in the context of the group with immediate reinforcement and instruction	Often surface structure needs	As needed
Invitational Groups: Writing			
Small, needs-based groups, homogenous by need, not by level	Thinking aloud and modeling, with frequent opportunities for students to apply the skill or strategy in the context of the group and receive immediate reinforcement and instruction	Often surface structure needs	As needed
Reflection Sessions			
Reflecting on what has been learned in a way that will instruct others; can be done as a whole class, in pairs, trios, or quads, or with students from other classrooms	Demonstrating a variety of ways for students to share what they have learned, particularly new applications of recently learned skills or strategies	Children share their applications of recently learned strategies—they do the "teaching" and plan for their learners' needs to ensure that learners understand	Each child "reflects" once or twice a month in this context

What's Ahead

In the rest of the book, I'll use all three of these models—Dimensions and Outcomes of Understanding, What's Essential for Literacy Learning, and Literacy Studio—to argue for schools that are determined to teach to high expectations, and to provide the practical details needed to reach that goal. I will propose, using the Dimensions and Outcomes model, that we can pin down those nebulous qualities associated with the most engaged learning, with intellectual energy, and ask children to use them in their daily literacy experiences. I'll show how concepts become more memorable when learners simply *expect* to understand. I'll explore the mental moves we may take for granted in our own lives and suggest that we define and describe them so that children can become as captivated by living an intellectual life as they are by television, video games, and music.

These three models are designed to provide a manageable structure to answer Jamika's all-important question—what does it mean to understand? They will help us explore ways we can use books and writing to discover, alongside children, the power of human intellect. Ultimately, the models are designed to help us better our odds, to increase the likelihood that our students think at high levels every day. I believe that we practitioners have the power to affect children's understanding. We can help students make deep understanding and critical thinking a habit rather than a happy accident.

Knowing how we must focus our precious instructional time with children and exploring the dimensions and outcomes of understanding raises the stakes for us and for our profession. We must ourselves rise to the occasion, think at high levels, explore the potency of our own intellect, and focus on what's most essential in our own lives. Once we have defined what it means to understand, once we focus, there's no turning back.

Chapter 3

Driven to Understand

MENTOR: VINCENT VAN GOGH

> I should like to do portraits which will appear as revelations to people in a hundred years' time.
>
> —*Vincent Van Gogh*

Elizabeth and I stand in line at the National Gallery holding our 12:10 p.m. tickets to the Van Gogh exhibit. We each have a notebook and we're planning our approach. She wants to go it alone, wander around the exhibit at her pace, not mine, and sketch as she roams. I want to linger for long periods with the paintings that are most magnetic to me, recording thoughts I hope will later evoke images of the paintings. I want to guard against forgetting.

We agree on a time to meet and begin our game. Toward the end of our visit, I will have written about several paintings; she will have sketched a half dozen. We will trade notebooks and search for the paintings depicted in our tablets, write the title next to the entry, and reconvene to see if we found the painting the other wrote about or sketched. Her drawings make the pieces easier to identify than the notes I take. I know I begin this challenge with a strong advantage.

She ventures out and I suppress a fleeting moment of worry. Will my nine-year-old be safe wandering around the exhibit on her own? My worry dissipates quickly as I'm

VINCENT VAN GOGH (1853–1890), *AN OLD WOMAN OF ARLES*, 1888. *Oil on canvas, 48 × 52 cm. Reprinted by permission of the Van Gogh Museum Amsterdam/Vincent Van Gogh Foundation.*

drawn in to the paintings. I wait until one of the few seating spots in the room opens and squeeze in next to two French visitors speaking so rapidly my high school French doesn't permit me to eavesdrop. I pull out my notebook and write, "The intensity of his eyes in *Self Portrait* (1886) is haunting. They follow me around the gallery and stare as if there is no one else in the room. Van Gogh's demons are, in this painting, clearly visible, painfully obvious to anyone who pauses long enough to let their own heart beat in tandem with the artist. The pipe between his teeth is too loosely held, given the suffering intensity of his eyes. Would someone with that kind of psychological intensity bother with a pipe, something I think of as a languorous pastime?"

I catch a glimpse of Elizabeth, but she doesn't see me. I love observing her from a distance, studying to see who she is when she believes no one is watching. She's standing before one of Van Gogh's final paintings, completed when he returned to the outskirts of Paris following his time in southern France. She is sketching with her right hand, holding the notebook a bit precariously with her left. A couple stands right in front of her, blocking her view, and she moves to the side, I think rather impatiently, but without taking her eyes off the painting. Her view still seems to be obscured and she finally sits down, cross-legged, in front of the painting. I hope a museum guard won't shoo her away. The fervency with which she continues her sketching despite the crowds surprises me. She seems utterly unconcerned about the other museum patrons, except for their occasional intrusion into her space, and absolutely determined to complete her sketch. I try to remember when—if—I've ever seen her concentrating with such intensity and decide to withdraw in case she should feel my eyes on her and allow me to break the spell.

An hour and a half later, I stand and close my notebook, searching among the crush of visitors for Elizabeth. I find her, again seated on the floor, this time sketching *The Courtesan* (1887), a painting that depicts a Japanese woman in a kimono—back turned, but looking at the viewer over her shoulder with a face that appears to me old and angry. I wonder why Elizabeth chose

VINCENT VAN GOGH (1853–1890),
SELF PORTRAIT (WITH PIPE),
PARIS, 1886. (F 0180).
*Oil on canvas, 38 × 46 cm. Reprinted by
permission of the Van Gogh Museum
Amsterdam/Vincent Van Gogh Foundation.*

this painting to sketch, but when she sees me she slams her notebook shut as if I were a peer attempting to look at her paper or cheat on a test. I motion toward the exit.

It is early November in Washington, D.C. When we emerge the air is cool and dry, and the light drains over the Potomac, highlighting the sky in pale orange. Planes lift out of National Airport with staggering frequency. I hope this is one of those times Elizabeth just wants to walk along in silence. The exhibit is still too overwhelming to talk about. I take her hand. She still permits this gesture. We have almost reached the Metro station when I ask her what she thought of the exhibit. Beauty and pathos, color and movement, an encompassing sense of loss—or was it madness—I can't find words, but feel sure she will.

VINCENT VAN GOGH (1853–1890),
THE COURTESAN (AFTER EISEN), 1887.
(F 373). Oil on canvas, 105.5 × 60.5 cm.
*Reprinted by permission of the Van Gogh Museum
Amsterdam/Vincent Van Gogh Foundation.*

She asks, "Mom, did you see the quote where Van Gogh said 'I want to get to the point where people say of my work: that man feels deeply'?"

"It's amazing you should say that! I'll show you something in a minute." In the crush of rush hour, we are lucky enough to find seats on the Metro. I rustle in my bag and pull out my notebook to show her where I recorded the same quote.

"I liked that because it made Van Gogh seem like a regular person. When he said that, it was like I could understand him even though he was a famous artist. I just want to understand him, but he's dead, so we can't really."

Her words roll out as a question. It's hard for me to respond. I, too, want to feel that I understand some small part of his work, some part of who he was. But dare I presume to understand what he felt or how he used his brush to define those emotions?

We humans long to understand, and we did our best that day. Elizabeth used her sketches to better understand the paintings she was most attracted to; I used my pen to make sense of others. I'm not sure we fully understood this complex man, but I can remember to this moment the urgent *desire* to understand, the longing to make sense of the paintings that drew me the most. We may not have succeeded, but I am certain we tried and, for us, therein lay the pleasure.

I turn the pages in the notebook I take along to art museums. Under the title, *An Old Woman of Arles,* I had written:

> Another woman of no historical import. Van Gogh confronts us from close range, his subject stares directly at us. She is cloaked in faded blue. Her scarf is knotted tightly about her head. She has tied it exactly the same way for how many days of her long life? Some color remains in her cheeks but it is doing open battle with her mortality. The bed, only a corner of headboard and a triangle of white linen in the left center, reminds us of her age. Is she an invalid? Is her direct but absent stare focused on a mirror or into the distance as she tries to imagine a way she will feed her family for the day, the week? A tiny line of a mouth bespeaks her silence, even solitude. Though she has much to say, she will not. I feel a sad resignation but a clear sense of reality. Do I understand? Is that what Van Gogh intended? What should I try to remember?

"You have more questions than understandings, Mom." She's right, of course, but it crosses my mind that I prefer it that way.

The Metro streaks toward Virginia and we huddle over our notebooks. A thousand fragments of sound—train and people—reach my conscious thought but are easily put aside. I tell Elizabeth that I don't know if what I wrote has anything to do with what Van Gogh intended when he painted that portrait, but I was trying, like she was, to understand him and his subject, to feel what he felt, to give my concentrated attention to something worthy of remembering, worthy of understanding. In retrospect, I would call it a fervent need to understand.

"The best I can do is to write in my notebook until I figure it out."

She laughs. "Don't try to draw it, Mom."

"Nope," I say. "That's for you to do! But, you know what? Sometimes when I'm writing, words just come out of my mind and onto the paper and

I smile and think to myself, 'Yeah, that's what that painting is about.' I feel like all the writing was worth it because finally I understand better. I really want to remember what I wrote about the color in her cheeks doing open battle with her mortality because I think the conflict in that painting is about her impending death. Yet she still has energy and much left to say."

We pull out the exhibition catalogue to find the painting, but quickly have to stash it away. It would be just like us to miss our stop.

The conversation Elizabeth and I had in the fall of 1998 comes back to me as I write on this snowy morning. I left the National Gallery that day hungry to know more about Van Gogh. I devoured the exhibition catalogue and several other books with beautiful reproductions of his paintings and commentary on his work, but closed them dissatisfied. I wanted to understand the man. I wanted insight into his motives and ideas, his relationships and emotional life.

It wasn't until reading the letters between Van Gogh and his brother, Theo, that I began to live inside the artist's mind, to understand Van Gogh's psychopathology, his suffering, his bliss, and the mysterious forces that compelled him. I felt almost the voyeur as I read his letters filled with the details of his interactions with lovers and family, other artists, and doctors who tried to understand and treat the emotional demons that haunted him. I felt that I was listening in on internal conversations and, through those interactions, beginning, in the smallest way, to understand how Van Gogh understood his world.

Through the other books I collected, I was at least able to create images of the settings through which the artist and his contemporaries moved, and I realized that Van Gogh was driven to paint less to represent what he saw than to understand the world. His life was consumed by the need to understand. He was driven, literally through madness, to use color and composition to understand the world.

In 1888, Theo Van Gogh financed artist Paul Gauguin's trip to Arles, the sun-washed Provencal town in which Van Gogh was living and working, so that the two painters could work side by side. In letters to his brother, Van Gogh had fantasized about an artists' colony in Arles. He envisioned his contemporaries living and working communally, each driven with an intensity born of competition and inspiration. Van Gogh was at a fever pitch of excitement preparing his home for other artists when Gauguin arrived in October of 1888.

The much-anticipated artists' colony never materialized. Though Van Gogh revered Gauguin and was deeply influenced by him during this period, they clashed almost from the moment of the latter's arrival in Arles, and the tragic self-mutilation for which Van Gogh is remembered was the culmination of the short-lived cohabitation.

There are two paintings from this time, each depicting a single chair. In the painting entitled *Van Gogh's Chair*, we look down on a humble chair, abandoned but for his pipe and tobacco, positioned in odd geometry with half of a door and the red tile floor. The chair's stance is innocent and permeated with light from an unseen source; a simple box of belongings on which Van Gogh has chosen to sign the painting is tucked into the corner, reminding me of a child's box, labeled with his first name. The painter is nearby—we feel his movement in the room, anticipating the arrival, or perhaps the departure, of his friend Gauguin. We sense his almost childlike struggle to understand how his expectations about living and working with other artists have led to abandonment, bitter disappointment, and, once again, to solitude.

In *Gauguin's Chair*, the chair itself seems paternal. Arching arms and a curved seat soften the sharp angles and back. It is night and in this painting, the light comes from visible sources—candlelight on the chair, gaslight on the wall. The colors are deeper and more solemn—Gauguin, too, moves about just beyond the reach of the painting, we sense, but there is a terrible melancholy in the deep hues here. In place of the artists' conversation about color and light, form and shape, there is silence, punctuated by occasional violent quarrels. There is desperation—neither artist can afford to live alone, yet they cannot continue together. The chair may be Gauguin's late-night refuge—the books his temporary solace and retreat from the reality of his situation.

My amateur interpretations of Van Gogh's paintings would certainly never constitute a scholarly analysis, nor is that my wish, but I can, as a viewer of the paintings, pause until I sense the artist near. I can listen until I see him at work on these paintings, fervently striving to understand his world, and I can look to the lines and forms and shadows in his work for an explanation of that effort. I can take what I do know about his life in 1888 and impose my view on the product of his work. I can decide that there is a yearn-

VINCENT VAN GOGH
(1853–1890),
VAN GOGH'S CHAIR, 1888.
Oil on canvas, 91.8 × 73 cm.
© The National Gallery, London.
Reprinted with permission of
The National Gallery.

VINCENT VAN GOGH
(1853–1890), *GAUGUIN'S
CHAIR*, 1888. *(F 499).*
*Oil on canvas, 90.5 × 72.5 cm.
Reprinted by permission of the
Van Gogh Museum Amsterdam/
Vincent Van Gogh Foundation.*

ing in *Van Gogh's Chair*, a longing for acceptance that we all experience, and that Van Gogh must have sought from Gauguin, whom he longed to matter to—as an artist and a friend. I can begin to understand and even to describe how another person tries to comprehend his world.

As I study this painter and imagine certain qualities in his cognitive life, the commonalities in the human yearning to understand eclipse the time, language, and cultural differences between us. Though many regard Van Gogh as one of the world's greatest artists, the gulf between his processes of creating and understanding and our own isn't as wide as it might seem. Great thinkers, great artists, great writers, not unlike more ordinary learners—ourselves, our students—use their work to better understand their worlds. Imagining Van Gogh at his easel isn't unlike listening to children tell stories to understand the ideas they want to convey. They bubble over with detail, groping for the heart of their ideas as they speak, stumbling over the insight they want to share. Imagining Van Gogh in a field of sunflowers, painting with intensity and fervency, isn't altogether different from watching a group of first graders bent over their writing, working avidly to make their ideas understood.

For Van Gogh, painting provided the means by which he understood the people and places around him. Because he wrote so voluminously of the ways he struggled to understand the world, we have additional insight into how an artist with his prodigious gifts went about the work of comprehending—in his case, through painting and writing to his brother. For others, we can only imagine—but we should imagine.

DIMENSION: FERVENT LEARNING

- We are *fervent*—we concentrate intensively, we lose ourselves in the experience of thought, the world disappears, and we work hard to learn more. We choose to challenge ourselves.

Can we be so presumptuous as to imagine that we have insight into how *anyone* comes to understand? If our hope is for children to understand deeply and remember what they learn, we must. Undoubtedly there are dozens of important distinctions between an artist's life and our own, and much about Van Gogh's life and work we cannot and probably would not choose to replicate. But is there so great a difference between history's greatest artists and thinkers, such as Van Gogh, and the rest of us that there is *nothing* to learn from the ways in which they understood the world? When I read about Van Gogh, when I look at his paintings, I have to wonder, what can we learn, what can we extract from his approach to understanding the world and, from those insights, what can we teach that will enable our children to understand more deeply, regardless of their intellectual undertaking? What can we discuss with children that will enable them to immerse themselves in learning more enthusiastically, more fervently?

Van Gogh was, at every stage in his adult life, a fervent learner. He worked with great urgency, he challenged himself to tackle projects he believed beyond his skills, he lost track of the world around him, and, sadly, he let relationships languish and ignored health problems. In my research on Van Gogh's life, I read about an artist who was utterly lost in his work, who was so deeply immersed in painting that hours passed unnoticed and physical needs and challenges were forgotten. For example, Irving Stone (1934), in his novel about Van Gogh's life, describes his time painting in Arles:

> He became a blind painting machine, dashing off one sizzling canvas after another without even knowing what he did. The orchards of the country were in bloom. He developed a wild passion to paint them all. He no longer thought about his painting. He just painted. All his eight years of intense labour were at last expressing themselves in a great burst of triumphal energy. Sometimes, when he began working at the crack of dawn, the canvas would be completed by noon. . . . He did not know whether his painting was good or bad. He did not care. He was drunk with colour. (p. 375)

To learn with passionate intensity, to learn as if one's surroundings had blurred into an indistinct backdrop, temporarily irrelevant—this is to learn fervently. To be captivated, rapt, engrossed—this too is to learn, to *live*, fervently. Fervent learning needn't be just an occasional condition, an unintended consequence of finding oneself unexpectedly drawn to a new topic, text, idea, or interest. Neither is it something entirely beyond our control. Learners can *choose* to be fervent; we can choose to challenge ourselves, to tackle a difficult problem or an intriguing question with uncommon resolve, particularly when we are driven by a passionate need to understand.

But, we may wonder, can young children, children who struggle, or unengaged students of any age become passionate learners? Without question, they can *decide* to learn fervently—*if* they know what *captivated*, *rapt*, *engrossed*, *resolved*, and *avidly* mean; *if* they have models who can explicitly describe and show through their behavior what it looks and feels like to learn with persistence and passion.

Five-year-old Kevin, a kindergartner in a very low income school in rural Alabama, lay on his tummy in the corner of the room when I came into his classroom one morning in late February. His teacher, a brilliant woman named Johnnie Tankersley, nodded toward Kevin. "I don't know what's up with that kid, Ellin. He's been over there for three days."

I laughed with Johnnie. "Yikes, have you checked for a pulse?!"

She rolled her eyes at me and said, "Every time I ask him what he's working on over there, he says he can't talk about it now!"

"Okay, c'mon. He has to talk sometime, right? Can't we force it out of him? I mean, we're the teachers and he's not, right?"

"Sure, hotshot," Johnnie grinned. "Let me watch you try."

I approached Kevin, got down on the floor beside him, and asked, "Hey Kev, what's up, baby? What are you working on so hard over here?"

He didn't even look up and, in a solemn tone, said, "I can't talk about it now."

Johnnie and I stifled a giggle.

"Well, sweet Kevin," I said, "you're going to have to talk about it, because I'm only visiting the classroom today, okay?"

Exasperated, he turned to look at us over his shoulder, swiveled, and sat cross-legged, purposely blocking his work. "Okay," he said, and continued with great solemnity, "It all started with *The Stranger*."

I couldn't have been more baffled, but Johnnie knew immediately what he referred to. "Oh, Kevin, you mean a couple days ago when I read Chris Van Allsburg's book, *The Stranger*, to the class?"

"Yeah," he said, his voice thick with mystery. "I had to know how it really happened."

Eventually, we were able to sort out that Kevin had been fascinated with the book's theme, which has to do with the appearance of a stranger at a farmhouse each year at times that coincide with changing seasons. Kevin wanted to more fully understand how seasons change—as they were at the time. He had somehow gotten himself to the Sycamore School library and checked out a book entitled *The Universe*. The book outweighed Kevin by about thirty pounds, but somehow (ropes, pulleys, wagons?) he had gotten the book back to the classroom, found the section that addressed the vernal and autumnal equinox and the earth's angle on its axis, resulting in changing seasons. He had found four pieces of legal-size white construction paper and taped them together; by the time we arrived on the scene he had labeled them *FL* (fall), *WNR* (winter), *SRP* (okay, so he had syrup, not spring, but you see where he was going), and *SMR* (summer). He had labeled the Tropic of Cancer and Tropic of Capricorn and was in the process of labeling the equator. He then proceeded to describe the whole process of changing seasons to us.

What is it about the moment a kid does something brilliant that turns the adults around him into blithering idiots? I'm not sure, but Johnnie and I did not disappoint.

"OH MY GOSH, Kevin," I shrieked.

"You're amazing!" Johnnie yelled. "You did this all by yourself? You figured out all of this? I can't stand it, I'm so proud of you! This is incredible!"

Kevin became very agitated. *"Don't tell the kids!"* he hissed at us.

We were stunned. "Kevin, why not?" Johnnie asked. "This is such fabulous work—you've learned so much. Don't you want to share it with everybody?"

"No." Kevin was adamant. He waited a moment and whispered. "'Cuz they might think the axis is really there."

Now, for my money, that kid was understanding (and then some). Needless to say, *The Universe* was just slightly beyond his reading level, but he was driven, determined to find an answer to his pressing question, and somehow, with no assistance from adults (there is no librarian at the school, in case you're wondering), he had made very thorough sense of changing seasons.

What happens following moments like this with kids who are in the midst of understanding deeply? It seems to me we can follow one of two paths. We can choose to regale our spouses, friends, significant others, and (in my case because David doesn't really listen to my God Bless America stories anymore) basset hounds. We can tell them how great it was to hear a kid like Kevin describe his learning and how astounding it was that he was able to undertake something so complex by himself. We can tell them, as I told David, that *this* is why we teach! We can tell them that, though we make next to nothing, it is just this kind of reward for which we work every day! (I can already hear the strains of the music and see the eye rolling). We can burst into the teachers' lounge at lunch and tell the assemblage about Kevin and stand back as the first-grade team fights over him.

"I get him next year."

"No, wait just a second. I have a really tough group this year, *I* get him next year!"

"Ah, but you both forget, I had his sister, and I'm sure his parents are going to want him to have me—his sister loooooooooved me."

That's option one. It's based on "happy accident" thinking. We tell everyone within earshot because it's a great story, but that does little to ensure that Kevin and his classmates will continue to think and learn at high levels. Think back to the story I told in Chapter 2, when David asked me that provocative question following one of the "happy accidents" in my classroom: "Why don't they do that every day?" Why indeed?

We have a second option in responding to the moments of concentration and fervent thinking like Kevin demonstrated. We can sit in the quiet of our classrooms after school and try to analyze *exactly* what he was doing in his mind and in his life when he came to understand at a deep level. We can create language to define and describe, not the specific topic of changing seasons, but exactly what he did, in his *mind* and in his *life*, to understand.

Think back a moment to the Dimensions and Outcomes of Understanding model introduced in Chapter 2 (Figures 2.2a and b). Three of the dimensions were written, in part, because of Kevin and others I've observed who learned as he did. The three are:

- We are *fervent*—we concentrate intensively, we lose ourselves in the experience of thought, we work intensively, the world disappears and we work hard to learn more. We choose to challenge ourselves.

- We *dwell in ideas*—we need time to listen to our own thinking, to reflect purposefully on an idea. We rehearse and repeat to perfect our ideas; we need time to be silent and time to discuss our ideas with others.

- We *create models* to help us remember—we see patterns and discover new ways to consider our existing knowledge, to hold our thinking. We also generate new knowledge; we work to make a wholly original contribution to our world.

Think about what Kevin did. He concentrated intensively, lost himself in the experience of thought, took himself away from the rest of the class to work in relative silence, to listen to his own thinking. He was driven to understand. He created a simple model on paper to help him remember what he was learning and in so doing, he created new understanding. He made a contribution to his own and (it turns out) the other kids' understanding of changing seasons.

I say, "Let's tell the kids!" Let's get beyond "happy accident" thinking. If we give language to these processes, and if we discuss them with the children, I believe we can dramatically increase the frequency and quality of kids' thinking. I've seen it time and time again. We can use the dimensions and outcomes described in the model and/or we can engage colleagues and students in dialogues about what *they* find themselves doing when in the process of understanding. By giving language to those conversations, we can generate our own dimensions and outcomes.

I'm not suggesting a whole new curriculum or huge departures from what good teachers already do. I'm only arguing that teachers can not only talk about the value of learning, but also be specific about how fervent learning, or any one of the other dimensions or outcomes, can enhance understanding. Teachers can describe and model precisely what it feels like to be engrossed, rapt, engaged, passionate, and ardent and can reveal how exhilarating it is to live a life characterized by fervent learning. Teachers can help children realize that when they are fervent, when they *choose* to engage so deeply that the world around them disappears, the concepts they're struggling to understand become more clear, the texts they read become more multifaceted—in other words, they experience the outcomes of understanding, and the world, not just the classroom, becomes a more comprehensible place.

Are we up to that task? Can we really serve as models who describe the most intense of intellectual experiences? If not us, I would like to ask, then who will fulfill this vitally important role? In considering this responsibility, I realized I should reflect on experiences in my own life when I learned with passionate intensity, when I was fervent. I am loath to compare myself to Van Gogh, but I certainly recall experiences when I lost myself in a passionate endeavor; there are situations in which I have learned fervently (see the Dwelling in the Mind section later in this chapter). Learning a new piece on the piano during this, my encore attempt to learn, can so consume me that it is only in retrospect that I realize how deeply I've been concentrating and how long I've been at it. I recently completed Ha Jin's novel *Waiting*, during which I could think of little else, even when I wasn't reading it. I read it very quickly, if only to get back to the neglected aspects of my life, and still it lingered in my mind for days. I may not be a "blind painting machine," but are my experiences any less examples of fervent learning?

No doubt all of us can recall circumstances during which we experienced the dizzying and deeply gratifying feeling of losing ourselves completely in a book, a piece of writing, the creation of a garden, the weaving of a rug. Do those experiences qualify as fervent learning, as intellectual pursuits, or do we allow them to "count" only if they lead to the creation of a masterpiece? Why is it difficult for some of us to look upon our own fervent learning as fodder for classroom discussion right along-side conversation about the world's greatest thinkers and artists? If we dared describe our own experiences, might children see the quality of fervent learning as something within their reach? Might they then begin to grasp what the amorphous concept we call *understanding* means?

LITERACY ESSENTIALS: CREATING A CONTEXT FOR FERVENT LEARNING

When we consider what it might take to create or adapt classroom practices to accommodate and encourage fervent learners, it becomes clear that we need to begin with a classroom structure and climate that support in-depth learning. We need to take stock of what we *think* is most effective, but what for many of us has become habitual, and move toward a new conceptualization for the literacy block. We need to rethink the difficult-to-describe elements that come together to create a climate conducive to in-depth learning—every day.

In this section, we'll begin our exploration of the Literacy Studio model (Figure 2.4) and the What's Essential model (Figures 2.3a–d). Both models may provide useful structures to adapt for a variety of classrooms throughout the grade levels.

The Literacy Studio Model

The most fundamental of all the questions we must ask in order to create the conditions conducive to fervent learning concern the elements we may consider most mundane—schedules, routines, the daily processes that enhance (or inhibit) our students' propensity to think and learn with excitement and intensity.

In rethinking the reader's and writer's workshop models I have seen and used, I had to consider how teachers could create particular and distinct types of interactions with students for each of the components: crafting, composing, invitational, and reflection sessions. How does a crafting session or a reflection session differ from typical whole-class instruction or traditional sharing time? Equally important, how would the teacher's role and teaching tactics *differ* in a crafting session compared with a reflection session? I realized that we often move from one part of the workshop to another, but our teaching style, teaching tactics, and interactions with students are essentially the same. The very nature of our interactions with students during the different phases of the workshop needs to vary if we are to maximize children's learning and engagement. I want to illustrate these distinctions through three questions focused on each of the four components of the workshop:

1. What are crafting, composing, invitational, and reflection sessions, and what is the range of activity that occurs during each component?

2. What is characteristic of effective use of that component?

3. What would a visitor be likely to see (or hear) during that component?

You might skim the literacy studio components (described in Figures 3.1 through 3.4) and, assuming that your literacy block is already scheduled, decide the components are working pretty well for you (which they may be). Instead, however, read the descriptions more slowly, using a highlighter to flag specific aspects of your literacy block you'd like to rethink or refine. Mark the areas that may not work as smoothly or inspire as much deep thinking as you'd like. Ask some colleagues to do the same. When you're done, compare the results. Chances are, some colleagues will have strengths in areas you're concerned about, and elements of your workshop that are really humming may be troublesome for them. You've just created the perfect opportunity for professional learning. Get into your colleagues' classrooms and watch the literacy block in action; then offer the same opportunity in your classroom. Together, take a close look at subtle ways you might refine the structure, schedule, teaching tactics, and student involvement in your new literacy studios!

Of course, your school's schedule will determine how you lay out each component of the literacy studio and whether you have time to weave all of the elements into each day's workshop. For example, many middle school teachers with short class periods find that they must alternate crafting sessions that focus on reading and those that focus on writing, scheduling them on different days or even weeks—a week with deepest concentration or reading might be followed by a week with deepest concentration on writing. The reflection session provides a structure in which students and teachers can make connections between reading, writing, speaking, and listening. For more specific information on scheduling within the literacy studio, see Appendix C, "Conditions for Success in Reader's and Writer's Workshops."

I don't imagine for a moment that merely renaming the components or highlighting areas for improvement will automatically lead to a higher quality of instruction or more fervent learning for students. I do imagine,

Fig. 3.1. The Literacy Studio: Crafting Sessions

What is a crafting session?

- A time to study readers' and writers' craft so each child might practice the strategies and tools accomplished readers and writers use.

- A time when all class members gather as a group, typically on the floor (yes, even secondary students!), to experience the beauty of written language and the magnetism of story, but also to study the craft of other readers and writers.

- An opportunity to view oneself as an apprentice to the finest readers and writers, to gain insight into how they compose meaning, and to think about how we, too, can use those techniques.

- A time when all students see themselves as scholars, gathered to study the craft of other readers/writers.

- A time for students to observe the teacher model, think aloud, and demonstrate the strategies readers use to understand what they read, and the tools writers use to communicate meaningfully through writing.

- An opportunity for explicit teaching that extends well beyond a particular task or assignment. Teachers focus instruction not only on the day's text or assignment but on the qualities and characteristics of proficient readers and writers and how those qualities and characteristics manifest in *any* text or written piece.

- A time for precision and clarity in teaching. Teachers take care to use words precisely, to challenge students with new and more sophisticated sentence structures and vocabulary. They use silence judiciously and emphasize the need to take prolonged periods of time to think.

- A time for intimacy, rigor, and ritual. Crafting sessions are structured by rituals and may be serious or lighthearted in tone. Teachers encourage children to challenge each other's ideas and probe deeply.

- A time for teachers to invite students to apply what they've learned in composing. Crafting sessions end when readers and writers transfer their attention to independent reading and writing.

What is characteristic of effective crafting sessions?

- Crafting sessions are different from other types of lessons in that their content will be important to children in a wide variety of texts and in many different learning contexts, possibly throughout their lives.

- Teachers use superb fiction and nonfiction (usually short texts, picture books, or excerpts) to think aloud, model, and demonstrate the "craft" of reading and writing; teachers know the text very well and may have used it in earlier crafting sessions.

- Teachers focus on a few important topics in depth, modeled in a variety of texts and contexts over a long period of time.

- Teachers may use silent signals rather than verbal directions. They use silence frequently throughout the session, encouraging children to take a moment in silence to think.

Fig. 3.1 continues on next page

Fig. 3.1. The Literacy Studio: Crafting Sessions *(continued)*

- Teachers are primarily responsible for leading the crafting session, but involve students in sharing their observations, of the teacher's think-aloud or in sharing their thinking with a partner.

- Crafting sessions usually last between ten and twenty minutes and are usually held three to five times each week.

- A teacher may choose to hold one crafting session each day focused on a strategy that applies to both readers and writers or may hold two crafting sessions, one focused on reading and the other on writing.

What would you see during a crafting session?

- The whole class comes together in some ritualized way, perhaps when they hear a particular strain of music, the ringing of a bell, or some other inviting sound.

- Children gather in a predetermined spot where they can all see the teacher for modeling. This might be on a rug or in another place in the room comfortable enough for them to sit for up to twenty minutes.

- The teacher reads aloud from a short text, excerpt, or picture book, pausing occasionally to think aloud so that the children can learn ways in which a proficient reader uses a particular strategy (e.g., a comprehension strategy).

- The teacher writes on an overhead or a document projector, pausing to think aloud about the decisions she is making as a writer, perhaps with respect to using particular writer's tools (e.g., creating a compelling lead or writing persuasively about a character).

- The teacher and some students demonstrate new processes and routines in the classroom (e.g., participating in a "fish bowl" book club to show others how book clubs can work).

- The teacher introduces students to superb children's authors, beautifully written texts, extraordinary language, and the possibilities open to them as readers and writers.

- The teacher and students use precise, scholarly language when talking about the work of the reader or writer.

- Children share observations about the teacher's think-aloud or modeling; the teacher asks individuals to probe their thinking more deeply.

- Children try a skill or strategy by sharing with the whole group and/or turning and talking to a nearby student; they then quickly use the strategy before turning back to the crafting session.

- The teacher makes specific connections between the strategy or tool being taught and the students' independent work, both immediate and long term.

- The teacher builds excitement about the students' application of the strategy or tool in their own work and challenges them to experiment with their new skill during composing. The teacher tells the students that she will focus on that strategy or tool in conferences and invitational groups that day.

however, that if we want students to engage in the highest levels of thought related to their reading and writing, if we want them to share the quality of fervent learning with other great thinkers in the world, if we want to give more than lip service to the concept of highest expectations, we must consider ways to reshape, even subtly, our time and our interactions with students. We must propel our teaching forward, from good to great, from effective to artistic. We must do what may be hardest of all—*rethink what we believe is already working.*

Creating a Classroom Culture of Rigor, Inquiry, and Intimacy

The literacy studio is only one way to rethink what we believe is already working. Just as important, we need to rethink the ways in which we and our students engage in particular *roles* in the everyday life of the classroom—roles that contribute to a culture that supports fervent learning. Let's return to your hypothetical new colleague, Tracy, whom I introduced in Chapter 2. She has queried you about what matters most—what's essential to teach—and upon reflection, you have to admit that your school, in Nirvana Unified School District, has done a pretty good job of creating a school and classroom climate that is conducive to in-depth thinking. Your dilemma is that it's a bit tough to describe to a newcomer. What are those elusive elements that somehow come together to create an environment and a culture in which students thrive intellectually?

The best way you can describe these elements is to ask Tracy to imagine them as pieces of a puzzle—four interlocking pieces that collectively form an unseen culture of *rigor, inquiry, and intimacy* as well as a visible set of spaces for children to work. See Figure 3.5 (page 66).

If we use the What's Essential model, we can explore the concept of the balance or tension between rigor, inquiry, environment, and intimacy a bit further and perhaps get closer to defining the classroom community for Tracy. Look back to the What's Essential model in Chapter 2. There I outlined four sections that comprise the most essential elements of children's literacy learning, K–12, culled from research and experiences in classrooms throughout the country. The first section of that model, A Climate of Rigor, Inquiry, and Intimacy (Figure 2.3a), is relatively self-explanatory. The left-hand column outlines the teacher's role in creating this difficult-to-describe classroom environment.

As you try to explain your classroom culture to Tracy, you emphasize that there are dozens of ways to mix and match the guidelines in that

Fig. 3.2. The Literacy Studio: Composing Sessions

What is a composing session?

- An extended time each day for children to immerse themselves in reading engaging texts in a wide variety of genres, applying what they have been taught in crafting sessions.

- An extended time each day for children to write in their writer's notebooks, gathering and creating short pieces they may develop into more formal pieces later, or revising and editing their work into some form of "publication."

- An opportunity for children to select text they find interesting and appropriate, given their goals as readers. Students use this text to practice skills and strategies they've been taught in crafting sessions and invitational groups. Students have been taught to make wise text selections.

- An opportunity for children to select writing topics that have sparked intense interest and that permit them to apply what they have recently learned in crafting sessions and invitational groups in their writing. They may work on pieces in their writer's notebooks or in a more formal form. Students have been taught how to choose topics for writing.

- The time when individual children meet in conferences with their teacher to show their application of deep structure (meaning and comprehension) and surface structure (word learning and fluency) strategies recently taught and to set goals for their work as "apprentices" to fine readers and writers.

- The time when children read and write independently while their teacher hosts invitational groups.

- An opportunity for children to meet in pairs and small groups to discuss their application of recently taught deep and surface structure strategies in reading and writing.

- A time for children to meet in pairs and small groups to apply speaking and listening strategies taught during crafting sessions.

- A time for children to work on oral, written, artistic, or dramatic representations of their thinking about the books they have read.

- An opportunity for children to meet in book clubs to discuss books they have read in common and ways in which they have applied deep and surface structure strategies in those texts.

- A time to plan (with the teacher in a conference or with other students) what a student will share and teach others during the reflection time.

What is characteristic of effective composing sessions?

- Children are deeply engaged in independent work; they read and write with intensity for long periods of time.

- The classroom is filled with a sense of urgency—children are eager to apply what they have learned in crafting sessions. They work in texts that are challenging to them at the conceptual level and practice surface structure skills in texts appropriate for that purpose (leveled texts).

Fig. 3.2. The Literacy Studio: Composing Sessions *(continued)*

- There is an atmosphere that supports rehearsal. Children experiment with the deep and surface structure strategies they have learned, taking risks in their reading and writing, and spend a substantial amount of time rereading and rewriting.

- Children plan to demonstrate their new strategies for their teachers in conferences and with their classmates during reflection.

- Children feel independent and trusted to make the right choices—they know it is up to them to choose the right texts and writing topics. When they encounter problems, they know to attempt to solve the problems independently.

- There is a spirit of camaraderie. Children eagerly share their insights with others in small-group discussions and book clubs.

- Teachers move around the classroom engaged in a variety of tasks—observing the children at work, taking anecdotal notes and running records, conferring with individuals, encouraging experimentation, helping book clubs get started, and hosting invitational groups.

- Composing sessions occur every day and consume the longest period of time in the studio block—30–45 minutes for composing in reading and another 30–45 minutes for composing in writing. In middle schools with traditional schedules, reading and writing may be held on alternate days.

What would you see during a composing session?

- Children select books independently based on instruction on how to choose appropriate books.

- Children read independently chosen or assigned texts with a specific goal—to apply what has been most recently taught in a crafting session or invitational group.

- Children write on independently chosen or assigned topics with a specific goal—to apply what has been most recently taught in a crafting session or invitational group.

- Children confer at their desks with the teacher, who challenges them to demonstrate use of the skill or strategy and to take their application to a new level, perhaps in a new genre, with more difficult text, or by teaching what they have learned to others in a reflection session.

- Children meet with book clubs to discuss not only a book but their *thinking about the book*. For example, if children are being taught to use the comprehension strategy determining importance, they share ways in which they have used the strategy to better understand the text they are reading. They may have read different texts and and therefore might discuss the use of the same comprehension strategy in different material.

- Children occasionally turn to a partner for feedback on the books they are reading or pieces they are writing.

Fig. 3.2 continues on next page

Fig. 3.2. The Literacy Studio: Composing Sessions *(continued)*

- Children independently solve problems—the need for materials, the spelling of an unknown word, the unwelcome intrusion of another student, and so on—based on prior instruction on how to solve such problems without the teacher.

- The teacher asks students to pause in their independent work to "turn and talk" or reflect with another learner about their successes and challenges in applying the strategy or skill they're working on that day.

- The teacher moves about the room, alternately observing and conferring with the students.

- The teacher stops the whole group occasionally to remark on the progress a particular reader or writer has made in applying the strategy most recently taught.

- The teacher calls an invitational group together and meets with them while the rest of the children continue to read and write.

---

figure to create an environment that supports—and reflects—the students within it. The last thing you ever want to see, you tell her, is a bunch of cookie-cutter classrooms that all look alike and in which the teachers use the same types of activities and interactions with kids. The principles in Figure 2.3a allow for an enormous amount of creative variation; they're meant to provide general guidelines and direction, based on research and observations of successful classrooms. The ways in which Tracy might create a literacy studio and a learning environment will be entirely dependent on her students and her teaching style. The key point, you try to emphasize, is that each teacher, in his or her own way, has an opportunity to create a culture, a physical environment, a schedule, and a series of rituals that increase the likelihood that all children can think fervently and come to understand deeply every day.

In Chapter 4, I'll introduce readers to a classroom in which the literacy studio as well as the elements of rigor, inquiry, and intimacy come together in a stunningly effective learning environment for students in one of this country's lowest-income schools.

DWELLING IN THE MIND: FERVENT LEARNING

I graduated from college a quarter early and was so eager to begin my teaching life, I took a long-term substitute position at a rapidly growing school

Fig. 3.3. The Literacy Studio: Invitational Groups

What is an invitational group?

- A time embedded in composing when the teacher identifies small groups of children based on a shared need and pulls them together for intensive instruction and discussion. This may include acceleration into new areas of the curriculum or introduction or reinforcement of skills already taught. The group may meet one or more times, but is not a fixed, ability-based group.

- A time to read instructional-level texts in order to experiment with or reinforce deep and surface structure strategies or skills recently taught.

- A time for children to write short pieces in which they can experiment with or receive more intensive instruction in deep and surface structure writing strategies or skills recently taught.

- A time when a small group of children can explore ideas with an eye toward sharing them with others in reflection sessions.

- An opportunity to practice, with teacher support, surface and deep structure strategies recently taught in crafting sessions.

- An opportunity to observe the teacher think aloud in a more controlled, focused setting than in a large-group crafting session.

- An opportunity for the teacher to think aloud about a deep or surface structure strategy again and to observe children closely as they begin to apply it.

- An opportunity to introduce a surface structure strategy to a small group that the rest of the class already demonstrates independently.

- A time for students to read and write silently and immediately discuss with the teacher any problems they encounter.

What is characteristic of an effective invitational group?

- Invitational groups are short, focused, goal-driven, and active.

- Children are actively and enthusiastically involved because they have been effectively prepared; the teacher has created a learning environment conducive to eager participation.

- The group members have a spirit of support for each other.

- The teacher is free to focus exclusively on the invitational group, having taught the rest of the class to read and write independently for long periods of time. There are no interruptions.

- The teacher identifies students with a common need through careful observation and through conferences. However, other students may be allowed to join an invitational group if they believe they share the need the teacher will focus on that day.

Fig. 3.3 continues on next page

Fig. 3.3. The Literacy Studio: Invitational Groups *(continued)*

- Students and teachers plan to share what they've discussed with other children in the reflection time.

- The teacher creates a sense of anticipation and excitement for those invited to a group.

- Children who have participated in an invitational group are often invited to teach or demonstrate to others what they have learned during a reflection session.

- The teacher may or may not hold an invitational group every day; students' needs determine the frequency. Invitational groups generally last between ten and fifteen minutes so that students can return to their desks to apply what they've been taught and teachers can resume conferences with other students.

- Invitational groups are not static—the same group of children may meet one to three times to focus on an area of need, then disband.

- Invitational groups are not necessarily homogeneous (grouped because of similar scores on an assessment)—the children "invited" have demonstrated a similar need in their daily work.

- Invitational groups are designed to offer instruction in the group's zone of proximal development. In other words, instruction is directed to moving a child beyond his present performance level.

- Invitational groups are *not* simply a time for the teacher to listen to children read aloud in a round-robin style.

- When the teacher is working with an invitational group, the other children are reading and writing.

- When the teacher is working with an invitational group, he/she does not permit interruptions from other students nor does he/she initiate an interruption to manage other children.

What would you see during an invitational group?

- The teacher and a small group of students meet in a predetermined spot, possibly at a small table, set apart from the student work areas.

- The teacher sets a clear agenda for their work together and indicates how many times the group may meet.

- Students may be asked to bring their own books or writing in which they can practice the skill or strategy to be discussed by the group.

- Alternatively, the teacher may choose a text or excerpt in which all students will work. Each child has a copy, often just a page or two, in which they can gain further practice on a particular skill or strategy.

- The teacher may use think-alouds or modeling to teach or reteach a skill or strategy. Students apply the strategy immediately and discuss their successes and challenges.

Fig. 3.3. The Literacy Studio: Invitational Groups *(continued)*

- The teacher may introduce a new surface structure skill or deep structure strategy other class members have already demonstrated in their independent work or may introduce a new skill or strategy other class members are not yet ready to tackle.

- The teacher challenges the group members to continue to apply the strategy or skill in their independent work. She may announce the next group meeting or follow up with each student through individual conferences.

- A spirit of camaraderie and mutual support pervades the group.

south of Denver where new teachers were being hired in March for class size relief. I reveled in my new world, spending long hours at school and at home preparing for my fifth graders and reflecting on what was going well and on the obstacles we seemed to be facing. I had a great group of friends—the teachers with whom I worked (and played, on Friday afternoons after long weeks at work); I was seeing a fascinating man outside of work; and I had started on my graduate degree. I had a cozy little apartment and a loving family sixty miles away. I told a friend in late April that I had never been so happy.

It was midday on a Wednesday—May 3, a day when some years later I would celebrate the birth of my daughter—when my principal stood at the door of my classroom with the school secretary and asked to see me. The secretary was sent in to supervise my students and the principal pulled me out into the hall, his face somber. "Your father just called the school," he said, "and he wants you to head home now, just as quickly as you can. He will meet you in front of your apartment at one." I hardly had time to stammer, "Why?" before I was headed out the door and into traffic that was unusually heavy for that time of day due to a torrential thunderstorm. This, in an era before mobile phones, gave me time to wonder what on earth had gone wrong. Needless to say, I imagined the worst.

My father stood under the awning of my apartment building peering out through the driving rain. I wasn't even fully under the protection of the awning when he said, "Your mother was diagnosed this morning with acute lymphoblastic leukemia." She had been totally asymptomatic—she was just seeing the doctor for a routine physical. I'm going to take you home to see her in the hospital. Both my parents, madly in love since high school, were forty-nine, my age as I write these words.

As my father and I drove north to the town where I was raised, he spoke with a clarity and confidence I still remember. "We're going to beat this

Fig. 3.4. The Literacy Studio: Reflection Sessions

What is a reflection session?

- A reflection session is a time set aside three or four days each week for several readers or writers to teach others what they have applied in their own reading and writing. The focus of a reflection session is on a skill or strategy a child initially learned in a crafting session and successfully applied in composing.

- This is a time for readers and writers to reflect aloud about how a certain strategy or skill will help them on the immediate text or assignment and how what they have learned has changed them as a reader or writer.

- Early in the school year, teachers demonstrate how children can "teach" their peers in a reflection session. They emphasize that teaching requires a clear plan and a way to involve other students to ensure that they learn rather than just listen to the lesson.

- Before students conduct reflection sessions, teachers model various ways in which responsible learners learn from and respond to their classmates' work. For example, they may demonstrate whole-class reflection sessions, small-group sessions, and/or sessions conducted for children in other settings or classrooms.

- Teachers play a facilitator's role in reflection sessions—they may praise the successful use of a strategy; question the child's process, future plans, and ideas about how what he has taught will be useful to him or other students; suggest other ways the child can continue the work; and challenge (argue diplomatically about) what is being shared in order to push the child to expand his thinking.

- All class members need opportunities to conduct reflection sessions, but not as frequently as they may need time to share. Teachers make frequent use of "turn and talk" types of sharing to ensure that students have daily opportunities to express their thinking about what they are learning. Reflection sessions are a time for the group to benefit from hearing about something that a classmate did that will enhance their own work in the future.

- Reflection sessions may comprise the last ten to fifteen minutes of the literacy studio for the whole class or be more informal—the teacher might set up opportunities for small-group sharing in which one child leads the learning for three or four others during composing.

What is characteristic of effective reflection sessions?

- Reflection sessions are more than sharing; they provide a learner (or small group of learners) an opportunity to teach, making their own learning more permanent and allowing others to try the same strategies.

- The emphasis in a reflection session is on civil discourse, the use of scholarly language, and a focus on one student's thoughts rather than trying to make time for everyone.

- The teacher plays a facilitation role only.

Fig. 3.4. The Literacy Studio: Reflection Sessions *(continued)*

What would you see during a reflection session?

- Children are seated in a circle (usually on the floor) where they can all see each other.

- The children are in charge of the reflection session. If more than one child speaks, children have been taught to solve the problem through the use of silent signals—one child knows to withdraw from the conversation if she hears another speaking. They do not raise their hands to share, but interact as adults would in a group conversation (such responses have been the subject of demonstration and instruction from the beginning of the year).

- One child teaches the others what he or she has applied independently. The intent is not only to share the successes and challenges he or she faced, but also to ensure that other students can use what was learned in their own work.

- Children may create anchor charts to ensure that they all remember what was taught in the reflection session.

- The teacher may sit slightly apart from the group, guiding from the side and ensuring that the conversation is among students, not between him/her and the student who happens to be teaching.

- The teacher raises questions about how the strategy being taught is applicable to other learners and contexts.

- Students make specific plans to use what they have learned in their own reading and writing.

thing, Ellin," he stated emphatically. "We're going to get her the most advanced care in the best cancer centers in the country. We're going to study up on this thing and we're going to find every treatment option that is available. Our family is strong and we can figure this out together. I've already put calls out to Dr. Jennings, Dr. Osborne, and Dr. Mills [family friends]. They're going to help us in every way they can. They're going to tell us where to go, what kinds of experimental treatments are available. I know there is a great cancer hospital in Houston, and there's the Mayo Clinic, of course. We're going tomorrow to the medical library at the CU [Colorado University] Medical Center and we're going to get real smart real quick on this thing. It's a problem we can solve." The word *determined* doesn't come close to describing the intensity I heard in his voice, and though I was terrified by the situation, horrified at the thought of losing my mom, who also happened to be my best friend, I believed. I was twenty-one. I believed.

The next six months were, ironically, given the outcome, some of the most intense learning experiences of my life. We did study, we did travel,

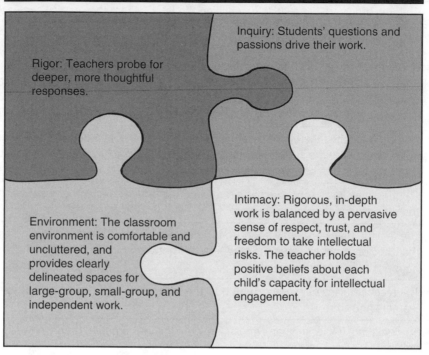

Fig. 3.5. Elements of a Classroom Culture That Fosters Fervent Learning

Rigor: Teachers probe for deeper, more thoughtful responses.

Inquiry: Students' questions and passions drive their work.

Environment: The classroom environment is comfortable and uncluttered, and provides clearly delineated spaces for large-group, small-group, and independent work.

Intimacy: Rigorous, in-depth work is balanced by a pervasive sense of respect, trust, and freedom to take intellectual risks. The teacher holds positive beliefs about each child's capacity for intellectual engagement.

we did get real smart, real quick; and in that pre-Internet era, that meant long hours with microfiche and medical textbooks that seemed impossible to penetrate. It meant reading everything from technical articles on hand-mirror cell-variant acute leukemia (only twelve recorded cases at the time of my mother's diagnosis) to Rabbi Harold Kushner's *When Bad Things Happen to Good People*. It meant schooling ourselves so that our questions of oncologists in four states would be so relevant and insightful that they would surely cause these learned men to think in new ways about the disease and to imagine new treatment options for her. It meant a divide-and-conquer strategy in which my father, my brother, and I each took on categories of study so that no stone was left unturned. It meant talking every day about what we were finding and how it might matter for Mom. Fervent learning? Without question, I had never learned so fervently.

Sadly, my mother died April 12, 1981, not even a full year after her diagnosis. I recall a beautiful spring morning not long after when I found my father with armloads of medical journals and articles, headed for the trash. His voice was thick with grief as he looked up and said, "All this did a lot of good, eh?" At the time, I shared not only his loss, but his sense of the futility of our study. All the hours we had spent trying to "solve this problem." No good had come of it.

With the perspective of over two decades, I can understand that time differently. It is true that all our study and all of our questions did not "solve this problem." The ache in my heart is as sharp and penetrating today as it was then, but I can view our search through different eyes. At the time of my mother's diagnosis, I did not see myself as an intellectual person, capable of great insight. I sometimes felt awkward in conversations with friends that took an intellectual turn—I wasn't altogether sure I had a lot to contribute. But there we were, reading, discussing, asking questions, reading some more, observing, asking more questions, trying to find well-reasoned strategies, searching fervently for answers. Though it was a heavily laden emotional experience, it was also an intellectually intense one. In the language I use today with children, we were questioning, determining importance, visualizing, relating new information to what we already had discovered, synthesizing it all, looking for common threads, inferring when there were no clear answers, and constantly monitoring to ensure that we were expending our intellectual energy wisely. We were, all four of us, fiercely determined to understand.

I believe we humans are always stronger in our broken places. Surely, that intense period of study and learning wasn't for naught. Is there some lesson I take away from that painful period that can inform my life and my work today? Without a doubt, during those difficult months I learned for the first time what extraordinary intellectual capacity my family possessed. In the face of a relentless disease that would, despite our effort, claim my mother's life, we vaulted forward with a life-and-death intensity, and nothing stood in the way of understanding the full complexity of the problem we faced. I had no idea I was capable of understanding that disease. I had no idea I was smart enough to learn what I learned. Therein lies a lesson I owe to myself and my family to apply today. We are, all of us, capable of intellectual fervency and, as teachers, that lesson has direct applicability to our classrooms.

I would like to suggest that we have all engaged in the kind of intensity of thought and action we read about when we study Van Gogh and other thinkers of his caliber, like Kevin in kindergarten. We have, whether in academic or family situations, experienced the feeling of losing ourselves completely in the study of something that mattered very much to us. When we revisit those experiences and sensations, we can bring something potently memorable to the children we teach and raise.

We can define and describe what it is to experience our own intellectual facility, and we can ask them to do the same.

Consider these questions:

- What intense intellectual experiences do you recall in your life?

- What characterized the learning you experienced during that time?

- What comprehension strategies did you use to understand your situation?

- What dimensions or outcomes of understanding did you experience that you can now discuss with students? In describing those dimensions and outcomes, focus on using language that makes the discussion relevant, not just for the experience you had, but to experiences children might have.

Many readers of this book will have studied comprehension instruction and worked hard to teach children to use comprehension strategies. One of the key instructional tactics we use in comprehension strategy instruction is the *think-aloud*. When we want children to understand how proficient readers use the seven comprehension strategies (described in Appendix A), we gather them around us and, using a provocative text, read aloud, pausing occasionally to think aloud—to show them exactly how we use the comprehension strategy we want them to use in their reading.

When we want children to grasp the dimensions and outcomes of understanding—what happens in our minds and in our lives—we can use another powerful instructional tactic: modeling. To think aloud is to show how readers, writers, and learners *think*, but to model is to show and describe how readers, writers, and learners *live*. To model is to show how we adults continue to explore our own intellect. We model when we talk with children about what characterizes the process of understanding, including dimensions like fervent learning. When we demonstrate what it is to learn fervently, we give our children the promise of living, sooner rather than later, a richly interesting intellectual life. (See Appendix G.)

I believe that our intellectual life is worthy of scrutiny because it holds lessons for our students, who may not yet have catalogued a vast set of intellectual experiences. They most certainly haven't had adequate opportunities to define and describe them. If we can share, not so much the experiences themselves, but the lessons we extract from them, we have an opportunity to introduce children to the intoxicating pleasure of understanding deeply—perhaps far sooner that we were privileged to do so.

It is an unusually cold morning in October as I write these words. My house is quiet, two dogs asleep at my feet, David and Elizabeth off to work and school. I think of the children in this country arriving in their classrooms this morning, a routine morning with announcements and calendar discussions and brief overviews of the day ahead. There is anticipation about Halloween, just around the corner, and they may sense their teachers feeling pressure as they near the end of the first quarter of work. Will those children have time to lose themselves in thought? Do they know what it is to be fervent in their approach to their learning? Have their teachers shown them how? Will they, as they read or write today, forget the world around them and think with an unprecedented urgency? Will they consider the subtleties and gradations of meaning; will they turn to others, as Van Gogh turned to his brother Theo, and ask questions like: Does this mean something? Do my words touch you; does my interpretation of this book influence you? Does my meaning matter? And when they do, will their teachers expect brilliant responses to these queries? Will they accept nothing less from every child, every day?

Childhood is certainly a joyful time when kids should throw back their heads with laughter every day. Teaching is also a joyful practice in which we should throw back our heads with laughter every day. But, our precious time with children also presents an opportunity we cannot afford to miss. It is the time when children meet their intellectual selves and learn that the greatest reward for learning is the opportunity to learn more. If we want them to beg for more intellectually challenging experiences, we must show them what it means to yearn for greater understanding. We must show them the urgency, the compelling need we feel to probe meaning more deeply, to learn fervently and live with intensity. We can tell them about people like Van Gogh and speculate with them what Van Gogh must have meant when he said, "Aren't we seeking intensity of thought rather than tranquility of touch?"

In this country's classrooms, we have a largely untapped opportunity—a chance to invite children to consistently learn with greater engagement and at much higher levels. Some children burst through our classroom doors each morning with "wild passion" and "triumphal bursts of energy" and others *appear* less intellectually interested and engaged. Too often we resign ourselves to these differences, assuming that they are the result of temperament or intelligence or the children's home environment—and thus are intractable. We have an entire lexicon devoted to describing children who struggle.

What if we *decided* that all children—*all* children—deserve an opportunity to be approached as great thinkers? What if we *chose* to teach children not just the content prescribed in our curricula, but *how to understand* as Van Gogh understood—fervently? What if we engaged in conversations with children about their own ability to think intensely? What would that look like in the classroom? How would children respond?

Perhaps those are unanswerable questions. I do know, however, that until and unless we speak with thoughtful authority about what it is to learn fervently, to understand at a level we may have thought impossible, the best we can expect is the occasional happy accident. To make fervent learning a way of life for all of our children will take some doing. It will take teachers who are themselves avid learners and who talk with their students every day about what it is to live that privileged life.

Chapter 4

Dwelling in Ideas

Early Sunday Morning
  — John Stone

Somewhere in the next block
someone may be practicing the flute
but not here

where the entrances
to four stores are dark
the awnings rolled in

nothing open for business
Across the second story
ten faceless windows

In the foreground
a barber pole, a fire hydrant
as if there could ever again

be hair to cut
fire to burn
And far off, still low

in the imagined East
the sun that is again
right on time

adding to the Chinese red
of the building
despite which color

I do not believe
the day
is going to be hot

It was I think
on just such a day
it is on just such a morning

that every Edward Hopper
finishes, puts down his brush
as if to say

As important
as what is
happening

is what is not.

MENTOR: EDWARD HOPPER

As important as what is happening is what is not. John Stone's final line in "Early Sunday Morning" (1995), a poem inspired by Edward Hopper's painting of the same name, stops me every time I read it. It forces me to lean in and *listen* to the painting, something I never thought to do with any work of art before reading this poem. To listen to a painting seems wildly counterintuitive, I concede, but it presents, for me, an extraordinary new way to look at paintings—in particular, those of Edward Hopper.

I discovered Edward Hopper while visiting the Art Institute of Chicago and later found a treasure trove of Hopper hanging at the Whitney Museum in New York. Edward Hopper was born in 1882 in Nyack, New York, and by the 1930s, had assumed a central role in American art as a leader in the movement known as American Realism. His interest, according to Wieland Schmied, author of *Edward Hopper, Portraits of America*, was in the closest, most precise observation possible of Americans in the most ordinary of settings.

EDWARD HOPPER (1882–1967),
EARLY SUNDAY MORNING, 1930.
Oil on canvas. Overall: 35³/₁₆ × 60¹/₄ in. (89.4 × 153 cm).
Whitney Museum of American Art, New York, Purchase,
with funds from Gertrude Vanderbilt Whitney, 31.426.

According to Schmied (2005), "The people who inhabit [the paintings] are certainly American—restlessly on the move and tired of being restless, lonely, and quietly despairing at their loneliness" (p. 11). He painted people in quiet desperation in run-down New York city flats and hotels, but he also painted landscapes depicting vast expanses of land and sky in rural America, broken only occasionally by a forlorn home or barn. His ubiquitous theme, to my untrained eye, is silence. And there is so much to hear in Hopper's silence.

I begin to think about how much *more* I can hear in Hopper's paintings because there are few visual details to build upon. The buildings in *Early Sunday Morning* are stark, no one visible. The scene could be in an evacuated city. When a writer or artist provides little detail to help us interpret a piece or painting, we are left in the silence of our minds to sort out what it means. As Schmied says, "Hopper provides only scant few details, but they are details charged with significance" (p. 40). I now understand—that is the draw Hopper's paintings have for me. I very much want to linger with them and invent the world they inhabit. I want to listen to the paintings, but also I want to extend my listening more broadly across the workings of my mind. I want to purposefully set aside time to listen to my own thinking; I reason that if I can teach myself to weave a deeper meaning by listening to my thinking, by listening to text and by listening to paintings, I can certainly invite children to do the same.

For example, if I take a moment in silence to listen to another Hopper painting, *The New York Restaurant*, the cacophony of sound I perceive is so vivid and immediate, so *real*, it changes the way I understand the painting. What at first glance appears to be an intimate conversation between the couple at the center of the painting is transformed by careful study, by listening in to what seems to be a gaping emotional distance between them, exaggerated by the noise of the restaurant. The sounds seem to prohibit them from speaking to each other for more

EDWARD HOPPER (1882–1967),
THE NEW YORK RESTAURANT, © 1922.
Oil on canvas. Collection of the Muskegon Museum of Art,
Hackley Picture Fund Purchase, Muskegon, Michigan, 1936.12.

than a fleeting moment. She can inquire about his satisfaction with his entrée, for example, but to engage in a protracted conversation here, in the bustle of this restaurant at the apex of the lunch rush, would be impossible. Patrons squeeze by this couple as they are shown to adjacent tables; the waiters speak in tones too loud for the setting; a couple argues at a nearby table. In my mind, the couple who is the central subject of the painting give up any attempt at conversation. They fall into the silence that has become their habit. She must wonder—when did that silence become so pervasive?

As important as what is happening is what is not.

When visiting museums and reading books with Edward Hopper paintings, I experiment with my newfound manner of looking at paintings and find that to listen is a potent tool. In *Hotel by a Railroad*, a balding man stares blankly out a window, bringing a cigarette to his mouth for the ten thousandth time. The sun is on his face, and a woman—his wife perhaps—sits nearby reading, indifferent to his presence. It appears to be summer—she is too warm, wearing only a slip, and he has said nothing for long minutes. It appears he will say nothing, that they are enveloped in a kind of all-encompassing silence that may have been nearly unbroken for decades. They are go-through-the-motions people, and few words of signi- ficance are necessary to complete their daily routines.

That is what I see when looking at the painting, but I have an altogether

EDWARD HOPPER (1882–1967),
HOTEL BY A RAILROAD, 1952.
Oil on canvas, 31¼ × 40⅛ in. Photograph by Lee Stalsworth.
Hirshhorn Museum and Sculpture Garden, Smithsonian Institution,
Gift of the Joseph H. Hirshhorn Foundation, 1966.

different interpretation when I *listen*. Her slippered foot, invisible to the viewer, pulls across a floor dustier than it should be in a hotel room and leaves the faintest of marks. The sound her slipper makes in that unconscious moment is deafening to me considered in the context of the overwhelming silence in the room. I hear him take a long pull on the cigarette and listen to the sound the resid- ual smoke makes issuing from his lips. The railroad track below, unseen from the painter's point of view, is cooling from the recent passage of a train, and as it settles back into the earth, my mind hears the ties adjust, no longer bearing the weight of the train. In that settling sound, I'm brought back to the couple in the room above the tracks who have also settled—their silence momentarily releasing them from the weight of whatever burdens they carry. As important as what is happening is what is not.

The well-known *Nighthawks* (1942) hangs in the Art Institute of Chicago, and I was initially taken in by its colossal size. At 84 × 152 centimeters, it dominates the room in which it is hung and draws us in to the all-night diner where a couple lean on a counter, the waiter bending behind it but still engaged with them; the back of a dark-suited man in the left center interrupts our gaze. The street beyond the diner is deserted, the windows in the nearby building dark, so dark the building may be abandoned. It is wartime and the brilliant red-orange of the woman's dress belies the shadow of that war hanging over their heads but may explain the unusual gathering so deep into the night. Perhaps they wait for word.

And there is the young waiter behind the counter. He is engaged with the couple though maintaining a proper "server's distance" from them. He is young, appears healthy—why has he not been called to war? It seems he has just responded, monosyllabically, to an inquiry from the man sitting with the woman. His attempt at courtesy hangs in the air. As I listen to his voice in my mind, I imagine that it carries a trace of guilt. Does he feel it's wrong to be here while his buddies are fighting on fronts he can't even envision? The guilt stoops his shoulders, dampens his voice, and has become a permanent facet of his being. His living is and, he imagines, always will be in the shadow of the technicality that finds him here rather than over there.

EDWARD HOPPER (1882–1967), *NIGHTHAWKS*, 1942.
Oil on canvas, 84.1 × 152.4 cm.
Friends of American Art Collection, 1942.51.
Photograph by Robert Hashimoto.
Reproduction, The Art Institute of Chicago.

And the man distant from the rest, whose presence becomes the apex of the triangle—not only is he apart from the conversations of the others, I imagine that he doesn't have the energy to listen to them. It is an effort to lift a coffee cup.

Perhaps he has had news, perhaps he sits here because it is the only place where he trusts himself not to weep. Hopper doesn't show his face, and only a small slice of his back is out of shadow. His leaning has a weight I can almost hear. He is silent and he fears that the rest of his life will be consumed by that silence. As important as what is happening is what is not.

Dimension: Using Silence, Listening Deeply

• We *dwell in ideas*—we take time to listen to own thhinking, time to reflect purposefully on an idea. We rehearse and repeat to perfect our ideas; we need time to be silent and time to discuss our ideas with others. We *create models* to help us remember.

Our lives are dense with noise. As I write these words, it is a quiet morning in my house, but still the tapping of my computer keys can become deafening if I concentrate on the sound they make. The basset hound sharing an ottoman with my feet breathes audibly, and occasionally I hear ice cubes drop from the ice maker in the nearby kitchen. A house is being built around the corner and the construction noise reaches my little office, though it is winter and the house is shut up tight against the cold. In these not-so-quiet moments, I have to work hard to shut out the distractions. I have to purposely *listen to my mind*, deciding what is important to include in these paragraphs and what may matter less, what I must exclude. I hear a critical voice telling me when the words I choose are tired or clichéd, and I begin to hear a version of my next points taking shape. I have a sort of conversation with myself; I hear the words I write or speak from the perspective of the reader or listener.

Similarly, when I think back to times when I've paused to dwell in a single idea, when I've pursued understanding beyond the literal, I realize that the process doesn't necessarily happen on its own. I may have to *choose* to dwell, I may have to be *purposeful* when I decide to reflect on an idea or concept—and that takes time. Reflecting on an idea is often spontaneous, but other times deliberate; there are times when we *decide* to examine an idea, turn it over in our minds, consider the many facets it presents—bewildered at some, acutely aware of others.

In the classroom, I want to take time to reflect, to consider and articulate far-reaching ideas and insights. I want to think aloud about issues that are provocative for the children—but that's going to take some time as well. When I teach, I try to model how it looks to take that time, silently, right in the middle of a lesson, in front of the children. What feels a bit awkward at first often leads to more thoughtful instruction and makes it more likely that children will retain and reapply what I've taught. It makes instruction more specific, far-reaching, and meaningful. I find that if I can not only think aloud about a comprehension strategy, for example, but also model a dimension like fervent learning or taking time to dwell on an idea, the children follow suit, generating inferences or questions that are far more profound and memorable than I ever expected. And in turn, those inferences are more likely to lead to the outcomes of understanding (shown in Figure 2.2a).

In our frantically paced classrooms, I worry that our children don't have the time they need to dwell in ideas in silence, to purposefully reflect on an aspect of text or a social studies or science concept they are learning. When I visit classrooms, the more common experience is one of rushing from lesson to activity to small group to learning center to music class or PE. By the time the kids are out the door, everyone is exhausted and would be hard pressed to remember what was important from the day. I observe teachers asking groups of children questions (often leading ones, getting the kids to say what the teacher already knows) and calling on the first child to raise his hand. Following a "that's great, Jennifer" kind of comment, they often move quickly to another child waving a hand, leaving little or no time to ask any one of them to push their thinking further.

We espouse thoughtful classrooms; we declare ourselves committed to the idea that all children can think at high levels—but I wonder who among us would be able to think deeply in many classrooms. If someone asked you a question that required a thoughtful response, would you be comfortable responding in the five to eight seconds we typically give kids to think before calling on someone? I worry that, without intending to do so, we are setting kids up to deliver convergent, vacuous responses or to give up, knowing another child will always be faster.

I wish we could take a collective deep breath and purposely slow the pace, allowing students to dwell in an idea. When a child responds, instead of saying, "Great, Jen, anybody else?" push for more: "Great, now what else can you tell me about that?" If the child says, "I don't know," say, "I know you don't know, honey, but if you did know, what would you say?" "I don't know" is merely a play for more time. When we assume that kids aren't doing high-level thinking, we may need to consider whether the conditions we create are conducive to high-level thinking. In other words, I wish we could give them time to think. I long for classrooms in which children don't try to respond quickly, where the norm is to take the time to develop a thoughtful response, even when other kids are waiting. I want to change our current emphasis from the number of kids participating to the quality of participation. Instead of getting as many kids as possible to speak, however briefly, give several kids time for longer, more thoughtful responses.

For adults, dwelling in ideas happens in the car during a commute, in the shower, even in the middle of a conversation with someone. We reflect while we're engaged in the routine tasks of daily life: stuffing too much white laundry into the machine, wiping a counter, waiting for the tires to be rotated. We reflect when we are speaking to others whose ideas and insights challenge us, when we are forced to defend a strongly held belief, when we're trying to clarify our thoughts in a letter. To take time in silence, to hold an idea in our mind, to reflect over time—this is how understanding happens in our lives.

Literacy Essentials: Creating a Climate of Rigor, Inquiry, and Intimacy

I have come to realize that my expectations for children's thinking have not always been what they should, and it is my teaching, *not kids' ability*, that determines the level of their responses. These lessons became clear in the dozens of classrooms I taught in or visited between June of 2000 and June of 2004 as part of the Cornerstone Initiative, where I served as deputy director. Cornerstone, the literacy and professional development project introduced in Chapter 1, is, at this writing, in its seventh year. The initiative focuses on serving teachers and children in some of America's most impoverished schools—thirty schools in ten districts that are considered among this country's neediest. In places like Jackson, Mississippi; Shannon County, South Dakota; Cleveland, Ohio; Horry County, South Carolina; Talladega, Alabama; Trenton, New Jersey; and Bridgeport, Connecticut, the Cornerstone Initiative seeks to build leadership capacity and professional knowledge in the theory and practice of research-based literacy instruction. Cornerstone's initial professional development is primarily undertaken with two coaches and the principal in each school, who in turn work with their colleagues to improve literacy teaching and learning throughout the school and district.

When Cornerstone was in the planning stages as well as in the early years of implementation, we were deluged with advice from "experts" around the country about how best to serve children and teachers working in high-poverty schools. We also heard a great deal from local educators experienced in working in low-income schools and were consistently cautioned that "these children" would come to us with few skills, little familiarity with the "building blocks" of literacy, and minimal background knowledge on which their teachers could build an instructional program. We were advised that the best approach would be to start with the most rudimentary skills and to work, in a slow, incremental manner, through a scope and sequence of literacy skills that would add up to proficiency if undertaken in the proper order. We were cautioned against using too much "critical thinking" and were told frequently that the kids in "these schools" wouldn't be able to handle instruction in comprehension strategies until much later in their school experience. We were told that the teachers serving these students would need to follow the same program for the sake of consistency, and that it was always going to be better to stick with "the basics." We were warned that it would be an almost insurmountable obstacle just to catch the kids up to where they should be at their grade level.

As I listened to this advice, I can't tell you how many times I wondered: If such approaches—ubiquitous in this country—are so effective, why haven't they provoked sweeping improvement in America's schools? If teaching a rigid scope and sequence of thousands of so-called essential literacy skills is the way to go with "these children," why don't we see far more of them at far higher levels of proficiency? The skill-and-drill approach has been around for decades, and, in my view, what we have in many schools is a whole lot of disengaged kids slogging through the essential skills in the right order, but who are starving intellectually.

We were also cautioned about working with teachers in high-poverty schools. They needed to follow the "protocols," we were told, because the kids needed to have instruction at their level and the programs, rather than the teachers, were to determine that level. When I met my colleagues at Cornerstone schools, I came face to face with hundreds of dedicated teachers who were using, in some cases, very prescriptive programs, and they were utterly stymied in their efforts to help children. They were discouraged beyond anything I had imagined, and they were sick to death of following formulas devised by the omnipresent "experts" as they watched children become progressively less engaged and no more skillful. Why, then, in too many schools and districts, do we continue—and even expand—approaches in which teachers are asked to present literacy lessons in a dogmatic, inflexible manner and kids become increasingly disengaged?

Worse, what I actually heard in all this advice was a systematic lowering of expectations for children *and* teachers in America's lowest-income schools and districts. What I witnessed, sadly, was a sort of thinly disguised racism, sexism, and classism I had hoped was forever dead in American public education. How is it that "experts" could propose continuing this approach when a mere visit to any one of the schools suggested that students weren't achieving because they weren't intellectually engaged? How could we continue down the same path with children who struggle, simply giving more of the same instruction—only louder? Isn't the definition of insanity repeating the same mistake and hoping for a different outcome?

My reaction was to try to think about the issues facing teachers and children in impoverished schools very differently.

In the Cornerstone Initiative, our goal was to engage children as thinkers from the very earliest stages of their schooling, introducing them to the internally rewarding world of learning at high levels *while* building a base of literacy skills and strategies they could apply in authentic literacy tasks, not on a series of skills sheets set up in some contrived order. I wanted to help children understand the *internal* gratification that accompanies in-depth learning about complex issues. I wanted them to realize that they absolutely had the intellectual capacity to learn at the highest levels and that, as they became more agile in using their intellect and articulating their insights to others, they were looking at a real opportunity to live beyond the expectations so many held for them. They were developing, should they choose to use it, a way out of the conditions of poverty into which they had, as random circumstance, been born. We meant to treat these children as scholars, and that is exactly what we did.

Our hope for teachers and principals was that we could identify a content framework and a variety of instructional approaches (as opposed to a program) that would simultaneously focus instruction on the development of the truly essential literacy skills and on the intellectual development students crave. Our hope was to help teachers understand the research fundamental to making *their own reasoned decisions* about the best instructional tactics for their students. We sought to reengage them in a professional and intellectual life in which they have ownership for decisions made in their schools. We wanted to create stimulating professional conversation in which teachers and principals could regularly discuss books and their own reading processes, then extrapolate to their students and classrooms. And, we knew that they could teach more authentically and focus their instructional attention on the essence of literacy learning if they had solid information about what matters most. We meant to treat the adults as scholars, and that is exactly what we did.

Many of the examples and stories I'll share in the remainder of *To Understand* come from Cornerstone schools. In these communities, we hoped to develop the sort of vibrant, sparkling intellect previously associated with "gifted" students. Beginning in this section, Literacy Essentials, I'll share stories of Cornerstone kids and others from my consulting work around the country whose thinking pushed my teaching further than at any time in my career; students for whom a deep connection with their own intellectual prowess opened pathways out of circumstances many of us would have thought beyond their control.

I have come to understand that saying we believe *all* children can learn at high levels is far more than rhetoric from some legislation or keynote speech. I want to describe some of the other Jamikas I've known (Jamika, you remember, inspired this quest) in order to help my colleagues around the country understand that following the programs, prescriptions, and formulas so common in America's schools is probably not the way to best serve children, particularly those in poverty. I want other educators to be continually surprised and heartened at the far-reaching thinking I heard from students who were thought too young and too limited in their use of English to be asked to think at such high levels. I hope that no one will read the stories of Cornerstone kids and decide that it's possible for children to think at high levels and grasp their own intellectual power in *those* schools, but not in his/her own. I want the readers of *To Understand* to know that my old notion of what it means to have high expectations for students was shattered in classrooms where kids taught me that if I could articulate it, they could understand it, and that they would move heaven and earth to engage intellectually. They showed me that if I started high and went higher, they would be right on my tail.

On the off-chance that you, like many educators, are feeling a bit beleaguered by negative media reports and ever-growing demands from communities and districts, I am delighted to confirm what you already know: There is much good news to report from schools, including those that serve this country's neediest children. As I observe in schools that are succeeding against all odds, I wonder—what is working when, even in overcrowded, underresourced classrooms filled with children who have been denied learning opportunities taken for granted in other communities, we discover that students are learning at unexpected levels? What is happening when children from the angriest neighborhoods imaginable, where they may witness two or three drug deals on their way to school each morning, but dive into their classrooms, books, and writing with fervor? What are educators doing to help children, even under the most challenging circumstances, reflect on abstract ideas, manipulate their thinking to understand more deeply, engage in spirited discourse about books and writing, read with fervency reminiscent of Van Gogh, and take time to dwell on an idea? How do these teachers manage to guide children to a place where they think at high levels despite the hardships they face outside of school? How is it possible that children in some schools already labeled as unsatisfactory go beyond what is expected and ponder important ideas in the manner of scholars and even artists like Hopper? And, conversely, what is happening in schools where children do not face the challenges of poverty, but are nonetheless disengaged?

Perhaps you have visited a classroom that was designed not so much around where the kids sit and where the teacher keeps his stuff, but as a purposeful attempt to enable children to beat the odds, to surpass our highest expectations. Maybe you have visited a classroom like that of Kathy Francescani and Jodi Snyder at Charles Lake School, in one of Cleveland, Ohio's, most impoverished neighborhoods. Their classroom is based on the principles of rigor, inquiry, environment, and intimacy outlined in the What's Essential model (refer back to Figure 2.3a) and is constructed around the Literacy Studio model (see Figure 2.4 for an overview and Figures 3.1–3.4 for detailed descriptions).

I approach Kathy and Jodi's classroom down an endless hallway, the kind I recall from my youth at Maplewood Elementary School. The green tile walls are anything but conducive to displaying children's work, but there hang third graders' drawings in the style of Matisse. The vivid colors and dancing figures really do bring to mind Matisse—perhaps the children have studied his work.

Strung from the ceiling tiles is a scale model of the solar system in bright papier-maché. There are photographs of each second and third grader and a sample of their writing, neatly laminated and hung at jaunty angles, but at eye level—the children's eye level. I can't help myself and

I pause to read some of their writing—an adult has translated the Spanish into English on some of the pieces. I'm delighted to find several rows of small bookshelves in the hall, each perched on a garage sale rug with a sign inviting the visitor to the second- and third-grade "mini library." Several children move among the shelves selecting books. They are focused, their faces serious, and by the time I approach, two of the three have selected a book and moved back into various classrooms.

A small lamp on a tiny table glows at the entrance to Kathy and Jodi's classroom. There is a placemat under the lamp—red polka dots set off the bright red base of the lamp. The lampshade has been decorated with bright markers by eager second- and third-grade hands. The scene on the shade seems to depict the first day of school. There is a sweetness to this scene, no doubt, but it is far more than cute. It feels inviting not only for children, but for adults. I realize that this hallway and this room actually beckon *me* as much as the children. This is intimacy.

I enter the classroom to the fragrance of vanilla from a glowing candle tucked safely away on a far corner of the teacher's desk. My eyes scan the empty room and my first impression surprises me. Where is the clutter generally found in primary classrooms, the piles of, well, primary kids' stuff? The tables seat two children each and are clustered together so that three pairs face each other. In the center of each group of tables are baskets with pencils, sticky notes, small notebooks, and markers. There are two meeting areas; one that accommodates the whole class seated on a rug bordered by bookcases, the other space smaller with a cozy, upholstered rocking chair and four or five beanbag chairs, also defined by low bookcases and cubbies. The teachers' desks are tucked away in a corner but facing each other. These are not standard-issue teacher's desks—they're much smaller, permitting far less clutter. I notice an extensive professional library on a nearby shelf. There is a sense of order to this haven—not rigidity, but simplicity and warmth and, above all, predictability—the comfort of routine serves as a counterpoint to the intellectual rigor I am about to observe. This is an environment conducive to in-depth learning, responsive to kids' need to dwell in ideas over time.

The children return from music, and as they come in chatting, I notice that they go immediately to their cubbies, remove stacks of books—some novels, some picture books, some nonfiction—and find places around the classroom where they settle in to read. This is an eager, joyful place, and I have to remind myself that the joy is coming from the kids—neither teacher has yet said a word. Some of the children curl up on beanbag chairs, others at their tables; two others share the rocking chair and read quietly to each other. Their joy is filtered through a sense of urgency in their work—they seem driven by goals. The teachers stand back, observe, record a few notes, and pull up next to individual readers to begin the morning's reading conferences. Strains of Bach form an auditory backdrop to the peaceful atmosphere. The children are pursuing great questions in their reading and writing. This is inquiry embedded in intimacy.

I greet the teachers (who share a classroom because they are also freed half time to coach colleagues) and begin to listen in on a reading conference. Kathy is conferring with a tiny, Spanish-speaking girl who is holding a wordless picture book. Kathy gently urges her to select a book from the pile that has words. She reminds her that she has worked with wordless books for two days, and now it is time to challenge herself with English words!

"Rita, do you remember when I read this book to the whole class?" Rita almost nods and says, barely audibly, "Four times."

Kathy laughs, "You're right, Rita, we've read it together, as a class, four times—that's a lot, and you'll remember that we focused on what we thought was important each time we read it. That's one of the reasons I just know this is a book you will be able to read. Shall we give it a go together?" Another nod, this time noticeable.

Kathy asks Rita to recall aloud everything she remembers that was important from the book. The book is not, as we might imagine given that Rita is an English learner, a book with a painfully simple plot, and I'm eager to see how Rita approaches Alan Say's *Grandfather's Journey*. It is a sophisticated tale of emigration from and return to Japan that spans several decades.

"I remember this book," Rita begins slowly. "It's about when the author's grandfather couldn't pick where to live."

"What else?" Kathy presses her.

"I don't remember."

Kathy smiles almost to herself and pauses.

"Rita, take time in silence to listen to the voice inside your mind that speaks to you as you read. As I turn these pages, Rita, think about what might be most important, what might matter most. Just listen to your mind as it speaks to you. What might matter more than the grandfather and the places he has lived, what *ideas* do you want to think more about?" This is rigor.

Rita looked uncomfortable as Kathy thumbed through the pages of the book. I even wondered if she might cry. Several times, Kathy spoke in an almost inaudible voice, "What matters most? What do you want to spend time thinking about? What ideas seem true for all people, no matter where they're from? Don't say something quickly, Rita, reflect and listen to your mind at work."

Long moments later, Rita gasps, "Oh! That the grandfather loves partly Japan and partly living here."

I exchange a glance with Kathy, because the ambivalence of the central character is indeed a very key theme in the story. I expect Kathy to turn triple back flips, but her response is far more productive. "Rita, I remember that too. I remember that the grandfather in this book was happy in some ways here in the United States and happy in other ways when he was in his native Japan." Rita nods gravely.

"Do you also remember, Rita, how we talked about some parts of books mattering more than others? We said that there are some ideas in a book that you may want to remember for a long time. We've been talking in our crafting sessions about how each reader decides which ideas are most important for them to remember."

"Oh yeah, and I say I just know how he might want to live here, he might want to live in Japan, but he lucky he have both to remember." This is what happens in classrooms when intimacy and rigor coexist.

"I do remember you saying that, Rita. You were saying that you have Mexico to remember and sometimes you want to live there and sometimes you're glad to live here, but no matter what happens, you'll always have memories from both that are an important part of you, and that this book reminds you of those memories."

Rita nods again, presumably slipping back into the memories she carries.

"So, Rita, I guess you'll be reading this book."

Rita looks at Kathy with wide eyes. "Isn't it too English for me?"

Kathy and I exchange another glance, "Well, let's see, you have heard it four times, you remember what is important about the book; let's see if you can read any of the words." Rita opens the book to the first page and runs her tiny fingers over the print. "Yeah, I know a lot! I know *when*, *it*, *the*, *grandfather*, *boat*, *wide*, ..." The list went on. "There are words I don't know."

I wait for Kathy to tell her the unknown words but, again, she does something far more productive. She encourages Rita to try to read as much as she can, recalling the key themes and using the words she knows to decide what the unknown words might be.

"Now, Rita, remind me what you can do when you don't know a word."

"Sound it out," are the first words out of Rita's mouth.

"And what else?"

Rita peeks up at a large chart on the wall. Under the title "What We Do When We Come to an Unknown Word," the children had brainstormed and Kathy had listed a host of strategies including, but not limited to, sounding out words. This, too, is rigor.

As Rita tells Kathy all the strategies she could use to identify an unknown word, I become distracted by the room around me. Numerous charts hang neatly on the walls, but none was commercially produced. As I study the charts I become aware that all are records of the children's thinking. The charts include What Great Readers Do to Make Sure They Understand; Topics We Want to Write About; Surprising Language We Found in Books; Poetic Language We Discovered in Books; Quotes We Love (this one has two columns, one for quotes from books, one for quotes from each other); Book Recommendations (this chart includes children's recommendations to other children); and Ways We Use Schema to Better Understand What We Read.

My eyes are drawn back to the children. Most are still reading intently, but a group of four has seated themselves at a little table in a far corner of the room. It is lit softly by a floor lamp and covered with a tablecloth. As Kathy launches Rita into *Grandfather's Journey*, I wander toward the book club to eavesdrop; they are engrossed in a discussion about the book *Gleam and Glow* by Eve Bunting. They are helping themselves to a bowl of pretzels from the center of the table and, as I watch, one child leaves and returns bearing four water bottles collected from the cubbies of those gathered at the table. As he seats himself, the others thank him and continue in their conversation. One of the other students, Jose, asks if he would like to share his thoughts, given that he didn't have an opportunity while getting the water. Ray Paul, the water gatherer, says, "Yes, thank you, Jose," and begins to speak.

"See, I think these kids aren't just worried about their dad being off fighting a war. That is a lot to worry about, but"—he pauses for a very long moment—"it's really more about losing everything they got used to seeing every day—their house, that pond, their rooms, the places they ran around outside. It's not just the dad, it's that everything is changed and if everything changed for us, we'd be sad too."

I begin to wonder if I'm dreaming. This is rigor driven by inquiry balanced by intimacy embedded in an environment conducive to in-depth learning.

Charles Lake is a school where the odds are stacked against the children, but in this classroom, there is an oasis for the mind and spirit. Children enter the room to the sounds of running water from a gurgling fountain or to the strains of classical music from a small CD player—

clearly a dorm room castoff. There is a pervasive feeling of calm; silence is not imposed, but treasured. Kathy and Jodi purposefully keep their voices very low, which causes the children to lower their voices. The children have been taught to interact with one another in a civil and courteous manner, and they rise to the occasion. They know the routines and schedules and they expect to be engaged. Kathy and Jodi are less angry than sad when someone isn't engaged, and these kids would rather eat spinach followed by broccoli than disappoint Mrs. Francescani or Mrs. Snyder.

To explore how we might transform all classrooms into environments conducive to in-depth learning, look back at Figure 2.3a, the first part of the What's Essential model—A Climate of Rigor, Intimacy, and Inquiry—which was introduced in Chapter 2 and explored further in Chapter 3. Kathy and Jodi's classroom is a great example of a literacy studio, noted in the first item in both columns of the figure.

Teachers	Students
Create a predictable daily workshop that ensures abundant time for independent reading and writing—a literacy studio	Read and write independently for extended and growing periods of time each day; actively engage in all four components of the literacy studio

Their classroom clearly represents other attributes listed in the model. It is evident that children are treated with the deepest respect and expected to say and do brilliant things every day. They are trusted to solve their own problems whenever possible, and the reward is a greater sense of freedom, more authentic interactions with each other, less need for the teachers to set up ways to "control behavior." The environment is carefully crafted to be inviting and cozy for children as well as adults. Children's work is proudly displayed along with photos of them engaged in various elements of the literacy studio. Some children read at their desks, others in beanbag chairs or on the rug; there are gingham curtains at the windows and scented candles and tablecloths on the tables; the lighting comes from lamps decorated by the children, not harsh overhead fluorescents. The room is uncluttered, the books organized sensibly, every square inch of space used thoughtfully. The spaces set aside for learning accommodate the whole class, small groups, and individual work. There is easy access to materials and to other learners.

This classroom reminds me that a healthy climate and environment isn't about having cute things on the wall or spending countless hours preparing bulletin boards. Classroom community means having a classroom that, visibly and invisibly, provokes intellectual development in an intimate setting. Listening in on the conference with Rita made me understand that creating rigor means pushing the children to attempt new things in their reading and writing with the full understanding that those challenges may be just outside their grasp. Most teachers would have considered *Grandfather's Journey* too difficult for Rita. Yet, as I checked back in, I watched her read it, start to finish. She had the time and the determination; she had heard it before (four times!); she had the strategies she needed (for word identification and comprehension). Many of us would have told her to try something easier, and what an extraordinary loss that would have been. Kathy showed absolute faith in Rita's ability to read *Grandfather's Journey*, and that belief went a long way toward convincing Rita she could. There was a velvet-hammer quality to Kathy's leadership in the conference. Her voice was sweet, supportive, very quiet, and tinged with humor, but she was emphatic that Rita could take on the significant challenge. Kathy didn't just send her off to read a difficult book without the tools—word identification as well as comprehension strategies. But she didn't let Rita's status as an English learner prejudge what Rita could and could not handle. There is no question that this classroom represents the tension between *rigor* and *intimacy*.

Eavesdropping on the boys' book club led me to see that, if children are taught explicitly how to interact with one another, they will use those skills in authentic conversations about books. If they are taught to defer to each other, they will. If someone has modeled how to bring another child into the conversation, they will do that. And if they have been taught how to push each other's thinking by saying things like, "What else? I think you have more to say" or, "Tell me more about that until I can understand it as well as you do," they will do that as well. Moreover, if someone has modeled the dimensions and outcomes of understanding (Figures 2-2a and b), including using silence as a tool to deepen understanding and dwell in important ideas, their lives will gradually begin to reflect those as well as the other dimensions.

The question is—are we teaching them? Jodi and Kathy certainly are. The reason that both rigor and intimacy are in such evidence here is that Kathy and Jodi model those qualities every day in every move they make in the classroom, and the children follow their lead. As I retreat down the hallway, past the mini library, the solar system, and eventually the Matisse-like drawings, I begin to grasp that the elusive, yet vital, quality that lies at the heart of creating classroom community is the teacher—the person who fully expects brilliant thinking from every child every day and creates a world specifically to support that expectation.

If I tried for a hundred years, I could never do justice to the appearance and climate of Kathy and Jodi's classroom and dozens of others like theirs that I've visited. There are hundreds of subtle, thoughtful details they have worked years to refine that nearly defy description. They, as well as many of the Cornerstone teachers, learned a great deal from Debbie Miller's extraordinary book, *Reading with Meaning* (2002), and her videotape, *Happy Reading* (2002), as well as from briefly working with Debbie directly when she helped Cornerstone teachers in their classrooms. Her influence is irrevocably woven into my own and Cornerstone teachers' sensibilities about the conditions necessary for in-depth learning at consistently high levels.

So much of what Debbie taught us, and what Kathy and Jodi realized so beautifully in their classroom, is difficult to describe. But part of creating a literacy studio is to be clear about the conditions necessary (see Appendix C, "Conditions for Success in Reader's and Writer's Workshops") for children to think deeply, and then to retain and reapply the concepts they learn. I think about the myriad of classrooms Cornerstone teachers have created and can identify some fundamental elements—seen and unseen—in each of these extraordinary places where language and thought have a life of their own. I have come to believe that classrooms like these dramatically enhance the development of intellectual character and quality. In such environments, students are more likely to be intellectually engaged and to manifest the dimensions and outcomes of understanding—what happens when we begin to truly comprehend our world. Whether designed for kindergartners or middle schoolers, these classrooms resemble a cozy den or a reading area in a lovely public library or independent bookstore, but with one significant added element—the expectation of intellectual engagement from every inhabitant, every day.

DWELLING IN THE MIND

After that fall morning in Jackson, Mississippi, when Jamika asked, "What does 'make sense' mean?" I forced myself to focus on what happens when we understand. When teaching comprehension strategies, I pushed children to talk, not just about how they used a strategy, but where that strategy led them. What did they come to understand that they might have missed had they not inferred, created images, determined importance, synthesized, and so on? I sought to describe not just the process of comprehending, but its outcomes. As I mentioned in Chapter 2, I wanted to describe what it means to understand in a new way—one that extends our traditional ideas about comprehension, which are often limited to retelling and correctly answering questions.

Eventually, the evolving definition of understanding branched in two directions: what I now call the dimensions and outcomes of understanding (see the full descriptions in Figures 2.2a and b). The dimensions describe the *experience* of understanding and what that process means *in our lives*. The outcomes describe the *cognitive* effects of understanding—what happens *in our minds*. You will notice, inevitably, a great deal of overlap between these two categories—one set of traits rarely exists without the other. You will also notice that the outcomes relate primarily to reading comprehension, whereas the dimensions relate to any type of comprehension experience.

The dimensions and outcomes emerged following hundreds of workshops with teachers and demonstration lessons with children. When asked what happens when we understand, children and teachers described particular traits and processes, some behavioral, some cognitive; I merely labeled those traits and processes when I saw patterns.

In one such workshop, I had an opportunity to record two teachers discussing the poem and Edward Hopper painting at the beginning of this chapter. Their conversation is illustrative of several outcomes and dimensions of understanding and is typical of discourse when adults are asked to describe what they do and how they think when they are working to understand.

"*Nothing's happening,*" Sarah was emphatic. "I can't stand paintings like that. I'd rather look at a Remington where horses and cowboys are kicking up dust, kicking up a fuss!" Having just read "Early Sunday Morning," Sarah paused and looked back up at the image of the Edward Hopper painting projected on the screen at the front of the high school auditorium where 150 teachers had gathered for a workshop. "I just don't know what a painting like this is supposed to do for you. In a Remington, there's something happening. And the poem"—she glanced down to the copy of the poem in her lap—"'as important as what is happening is what is not.' What is that supposed to mean? How can something that isn't happening be important?"

Her colleague, Audrey, paused as if she were deciding whether to respond and said hesitantly, "Well, I don't see it exactly like that. I think

it's intriguing to imagine who is behind those shades on the second floor.
I sense someone there and, I know you're going to say I'm crazy, but I feel
her loneliness." She indulged a long moment of silence before a tumble of
thoughts spilled out. "I find it amazing that the painting and the poem,
really, can be so simple, so pure, in a way, and still say so much. Doesn't
it just make you wonder if it's during the Depression or if the town is
struggling economically? And doesn't it look like the door on the right side
of the painting is open halfway? Has someone just come in? Is there something wrong or is it just the shopkeeper stopping by to check on things
before church? What does it feel like, sound like, smell like in those quiet
shops? I can almost see the merchandise on the shelves in those places.
Dust settling into the spaces on the glass shelves. So quiet."

"I guess you could do that—I mean what you're doing—you could
make up all the action rather than having it presented on the canvas like
Remington did. You're just bolder than I am, I guess," Sarah laughed.
"You're not afraid to invent what isn't there. I don't know if I can do
that."

"You know, I don't think you have to worry that you might be inventing it wrong," Audrey responded. "Artists and authors, when they put
their work out in the world, they are really agreeing, I believe, to let the
readers or viewers interpret it, and if I see things or wonder things that
Hopper doesn't want me to see or Stone doesn't want me to wonder about,
well, I guess I don't care!"

"Yeah. I guess I just need to think about it some more." Sarah and
Audrey looked back up at the painting and the poem in silence. Following
a long pause, Sarah said, "I'm still not sure I can say I like this painting,
or the poem for that matter. Where's the action?"

Audrey reflected, almost talking to herself, "This reminds me of the
town I was raised in. It was in central Missouri and you could walk downtown on a Sunday morning, and it was just so silent and so dead it was
almost scary. Everyone, and I mean everyone, would have been home getting ready for church. And then everyone would go off to church and then
home for Sunday dinner, which was the big meal of the day—at noon. The
shops in this painting are so much like my town . . ." She paused, rereading a section from the poem, "I love this line, 'as if there could ever again
be hair to cut, fire to burn'; it's almost like he's saying that this could be a
town deserted, just left behind by all its inhabitants. Maybe that's what
Hopper was trying to paint, you know? A kind of desertion, an imagining
of 'middle America,' whatever that is, as sort of desolate—empty. That
rings true for the town I grew up in. Never a surprise—ever! I see this

painting and this poem sort of calling us to question—is that kind of predictability healthy? Don't people need to be shaken up a little, to know they're alive? Shouldn't there be a little, I don't know, *texture* in daily life? Doesn't conflict actually play an important role in our lives? If there are no problems to solve and life is this quiet, is that right, healthy?"

"You were thinking all of that?" Sarah asked, incredulously.

"Well, no, not exactly, not at the time I first read it, but as I talk to you about it and as I stop to think about it, I guess I become more aware of what I was thinking about. Now we should add that to the list we're supposed to be making," Audrey said, getting back to the task at hand. She wrote *talk to another reader* in her spiral notebook.

"That makes sense and I think, even though I didn't really like the painting that well, you taught me that a reader, or a viewer, can 'make up' what they don't know, or don't understand from the painting," Sarah acknowledged. "I learned from the way you just invented a meaning, even without knowing what the author or painter really meant. You just gave it your own meaning and, now that I'm thinking about it, it reminds me of all the books on teaching reading that I've read where they talk about 'constructing your own meaning.' I never really understood that before, but I think that's what you were doing."

Sarah and Audrey paused again. The tape recorder shows that they were silent for nearly a minute before Sarah said, "Now that I look back at the painting and the poem, I can see more of what you see but . . ." There was another long pause during which Audrey did not try to finish Sarah's thought or ask any questions. Sarah finally added, "I think there is something about the way this poem and painting go together that is very lonely and empty to me, maybe even frightening, and I didn't realize it until I was thinking just then."

Sarah and Audrey were seated toward the back of an auditorium filled with teachers. I had asked the teachers in a workshop outside Chicago to reflect on their own thinking as they viewed the painting and read the poem. I asked them to consider the question, How do you come to understand? When your mind first encounters something like a painting or a poem, how do you begin to make sense of it? I asked the teachers to listen as I read the poem, then to reread it silently and to consider the painting about which the poem was written until they could take some notes about how they go about the business of understanding. Then I asked them to talk to a neighbor, not so much about the poem and painting, but about their experience and cognitive work in coming to understand them. I asked that they make a list to capture the various *ways* in which they found themselves beginning to figure out what the poem and painting were all about.

I moved around the room eavesdropping, listening to conversations like Sarah and Audrey's, trying to prompt the teachers to consider not just their interpretations and feelings about this particular poem and painting, but to think about the work that goes on in their minds and their lives when they're trying to understand something. I emphasized that it might take several readings and many viewings before anyone felt they truly understood these pieces, but that I was interested in how they reached their initial understandings.

Sarah and Audrey were getting to the heart of their discussion when I interrupted the group. They started by talking about whether they liked the poem and the painting and how they interpreted them. Not surprising, since most of us went to school at a time when, if we were asked to comment at all, we had to limit our reactions to fairly strict interpretations of the piece, feeling we had little latitude to invent meaning, much less talk about how we construct meaning.

But when Audrey politely disagreed and provided a different interpretation, she was beginning to explore the question they had been assigned. *How*, exactly, do we go about comprehending? The connections, visual images, and inferences Audrey made were certainly tools (comprehension strategies) she was using to comprehend both pieces, but she didn't describe *how* those inferences, images, and connections helped her understand more about the painting or the poem. Audrey was also correct in suggesting that paintings and poems are subject to the readers' and viewers' interpretations once they're in the public eye, and she had plenty of connections to her own life, but didn't say how those connections supported her understanding. But when Audrey realized that she came to some of her conclusions *because* of their conversation, she was beginning to articulate *how* she engaged in the process of comprehending. There is a subtle and very important difference.

When I asked for insights from the large group to help explain how they went about understanding, I recorded the list in the left column in Figure 4.1 on a blank transparency. The teachers' first observations are in the left column; as I pushed them to say what they came to understand, to describe the outcomes of their work, I recorded those comments in the right column.

They were able to articulate with real clarity what it was that they came to understand—when I *pushed them to say more*. This, I told the

Fig. 4.1. Strategies and Outcomes for Understanding

The Process of Understanding	The Outcomes of Understanding (parentheses refer to outcomes as described in the model, Figure 2.3a)
Used visual images from my background knowledge.	I began to feel the presence of the unnamed people who inhabit the painting and began to imagine what their lives were like. *(character empathy)*
Decided what was most important in both the poem and the painting—the common elements.	I was able to focus on one concept/one section of the piece, then extrapolate from that section to understand the whole piece. *(recognizing patterns)*
Reread multiple times.	Picked up on details and subtle facets I wouldn't have noticed with only one reading—like thinking about the role towns like this played in American history. *(setting empathy)*
Suspended disbelief—decided I'd "give the poem a chance" when my first impressions were negative.	It became more believable and credible. By going back and forth between the poem and the painting, I started to think about the people who did live in these quiet little mid-twentieth-century towns and what their lives were like. I found I actually liked the poem and painting more! *(believability)*
Used long pauses in the conversation just to think about the piece.	I lingered with the portions I found most emotionally touching or aesthetically pleasing *(a sense of the aesthetic)*
Filled in the parts I didn't understand (inferred or made them up).	Once I got comfortable with the fact that I was just going to "make up" the parts I didn't get directly from the poem or painting, I started to see a real beauty in both pieces—I wasn't so fixated on "getting it" and I could actually enjoy it. *(a sense of the aesthetic)*
Used the text structure to infer separation of ideas.	I could actually get on a roll with the piece—I got a sense of the rhythm of the language and a sense of the bigger meaning, once I had that rhythm in my mind. *(a sense of what's next, the general order of things)*
Posed questions, discussed them with a partner.	Once I realized that my partner had some of the same questions and once we started to fool around with some of the possibilities, I felt a lot more able to discuss the poem and painting intelligently. *(confidence)*

teachers, is the level we want our students to reach. We want them not only to state which comprehension strategy they're using—an inference or connection, a question or image, but to go *three steps beyond*. We want students to:

1. Say *how using that strategy deepened their comprehension* of a particular piece and how that same strategy might be used in future readings.

2. Say what they came to understand in the piece *because* they used the strategy.

3. Say *what conditions contributed to their understanding* of the piece (e.g., discussing it with a partner or having time to consider it in silence) and how recreating those conditions might help them in future readings.

I gave the teachers an opportunity to return to their conversations and explore ways in which the exercise had relevance in the classroom. In what ways did scrutiny of their own process of understanding apply to their work with children? They went back to work, and the tape recorder started turning on Sarah and Audrey.

"Well, I know one thing for sure that I will take back to my classroom," Audrey began. "I didn't realize how much I thought until I articulated it to you. I don't think I encourage my kids to talk through their understandings nearly enough. This is really bothering me. I just read aloud, tell them what I want them to think about the strategy I'm demonstrating, and then I tell them to try it in their own reading. I think that's good for teaching them to use a strategy like making connections, but I don't think it helps them to really see *how* they are understanding. Sarah, you showed me that, in order to think more than just what flies through my mind while I'm reading, it helps to talk to someone and sort of 'make up' the meaning as I talk."

"It's interesting because I don't think I give my kids enough time to talk either," Sarah replied, "at least not about something so abstract as how they come to understand something. I'm just so concerned with getting them to be on task and get the work done; I honestly don't think I ever considered whether they could have that kind of conversation in fourth grade, much less if it would benefit them. But I took something else away from this for them," Sarah said. "I just realized that what helped me understand this poem and painting was the time you and I took to just think about them. You know, and I think this is because we know each other so well, we were comfortable being quiet and just thinking about the poem and the painting. That says something to me about my kids. How do I get them to feel comfortable in silence like we were—not always feeling like they have to answer quickly or fill in where someone leaves off? See, I think you just let me think about these [the poem and the painting] and it wasn't until I did, that I began to think about something other than a kind of knee-jerk reaction—I don't like them because there's no action."

Audrey was curious. "Do you mean that it was *because* of the silence that you started to understand, because isn't that the opposite of what I was saying?" She didn't wait for Sarah's response before asking, "How can both be true—how can I need to talk to someone, you in this case, in order to understand and then find that you need to think in silence in order to understand?"

They laughed together as they realized what they had concluded. "Different kids are going to do it differently," Audrey said.

"And they have to have an opportunity to do both," Sarah added.

"I think, by far, the hardest thing for me when I think about how I am when I'm with my kids is going to be the silence part," Audrey continued. "I think you're really onto something—kids could use more time just to listen to themselves think. But when I think about how I sort of *fill* every quiet moment with talking to them, it's going to be really hard to encourage silence. I think I only really demand silence when I've just had it with them. I can just hear myself saying, 'Okay, everyone just needs to be quiet for a minute so we can refocus and get going again' or something like that. I impose silence punitively, and you're saying it's a different kind of silence—it's like the silence in this poem and in this painting. It's the kind of silence where you become acutely aware of what's around you and what you're thinking."

"Right," agreed Sarah. "It's interesting to look again at the Hopper painting now, and don't laugh because I know I'm the one that said I didn't like it that much, but now I look at those storefronts and I think about the silence and it isn't silent at all—I can almost sense the hubbub on a weekday, the commerce, the activity, and now it's almost like I prefer the stillness in this painting to a painting that shows all of that going on. I know, you're laughing at me, the big Frederic Remington fan, but I really learned to appreciate that stillness and to listen to what might be happening—what isn't happening now, but will be again."

"Oh! Did you hear what you just said?" asked Audrey. "It's just like the end of the poem—'as important as what is happening, is what is not.'"

When I reviewed the transcript and listened to Sarah and Audrey discussing how both discourse *and* silence contributed to their emerging understandings of the poem and painting, I realized I had neglected, in my teaching, a potent tool children can manipulate to deepen comprehension. Though I had often encouraged children to engage in discussion as a way to understand more about a text, I hadn't given thought to the role silence plays in children's learning lives. To understand the power of talk I have only to think of my own book club. We pool our ideas, argue, laugh, interpret, and take all kinds of liberties in peeling back the layers of the books we read. I understand how vital their interpretations are to the decisions I ultimately make about the books; without the conversation, I would have only a unidimensional view. But following the conversation, I know far more about what we read than I would have left to my own devices. Their perspectives enrich my interpretations. And, I've gone the next step to consider what all of this means in the classroom. If our understanding is intensified by discourse, surely the same thing is true for children. (See Chapter 8.)

However, I hadn't considered what Sarah and Audrey concluded—that it wasn't just the conversation, it was the comfort they felt in being *silent together, taking their time to think* that allowed them to strengthen their interpretation of the text. They concluded that, in those moments where, side-by-side, they regarded the painting, reread the poem, and listened to their minds at work, much of the hidden fullness of the painting and poem came to light. Their insights made me think about how much fuller life would be if we gave ourselves the gift of silence to consider more subtle meanings in what we read. I also realized, in that silence, we may be more prone to regard the world through auditory rather than just visual channels. I began to wonder what impact we could have if we taught children how to create silence around them, to listen to the voice in their minds, and if we coached them to hear the meanings in texts and concepts they seek to understand deeply.

Through work in Cornerstone classrooms and in other schools around the country, I no longer have to wonder about the effect on children when we teach them how to create silence around them or take the time to dwell in important ideas. More times than I can count or recall, I have observed the potency of thought and expression children generate when a teacher models and then asks them to give themselves the gift of silence—time to hear the workings of their minds.

I worry about the external rewards we think we must offer to "motivate" children to read and learn. I have found they are altogether delighted with the rewards born inside. I see it in the expression of wonder and disbelief on children's faces after they have shared an insight about a book or concept they're working to understand. They don't realize how brilliantly capable they are, and it is one very pleasant surprise when it dawns on them. That's what brings them back for more.

And, by the way, that's why I teach. I unapologetically admit that I teach so children can discover the brilliance inside and so I can watch! Observing as children of any age make that discovery keeps me coming back for more, and I know the same is true for the thousands of teachers with whom I've worked around the country. Discovering one's own intellect is its own greatest reward for teachers as it is for children. No pizza parties necessary, no contests to see if one class can read more books than another, no need for principals to promise to shave their heads if the kids read ten thousand books. Just the simple, silent moment when a child dwells in an idea and explores his intellect, just the astonished revelation of a found insight—that's enough for me, that's enough for them.

Chapter 5

To Savor the Struggle

MENTOR: REYNOLDS PRICE

"Why would you intentionally put kids in the position of having to struggle to understand something? Honestly, in the school where I teach, their lives outside school are hard enough. I just can't imagine intentionally trying to make it harder for them. School needs to be a nurturing place where they know they're safe, where they're willing to take a risk, where they don't have to struggle for a few hours every day."

The teacher speaks with sincerity, conviction, a trace of anger. It's the kind of interaction I've come to expect from teachers when I conduct seminars at Teacher's College, Columbia University, in New York. I know that the spirit of challenging so-called experts isn't the norm in many graduate schools and professional learning settings around the country, so I'm always relieved to find it at TC when I work with teachers there. This teacher was taking me on after I'd suggested that one of the greatest gifts we can give students is the experience of having to struggle to understand an idea. Though her comments didn't alter my belief, I fully understood her point. In the schools where I most frequently work, kids' lives often are unimaginably difficult. To throw challenges their way runs counter to many of our instincts, but I've come to believe that when we do and provide the instruction they need to surmount the challenge, we introduce them to a world of possibility, not defeat—to the unlimited potential of their minds.

I responded to the teacher that way and then asked the whole group to call to mind someone they know who has faced what seemed an insurmountable challenge and to consider, in writing, what cognitive energies have gone toward conquering it. Curiously, when I sat down at the table in the front of Milbank Chapel to write alongside the workshop participants, I found myself recalling a commentary I had heard on National Public Radio (NPR) by the author Reynolds Price, whose books and poetry I had read and admired for years. Price had spoken, in one of his three-minute NPR monologues, about his tenth-anniversary MRI scan—the tenth of the magnetic resonance imaging tests he has endured to confirm he remains cancer free. A ten-inch-long tumor invaded Price's spinal cord in his early fifties and could not be removed by a surgeon. MRI scans, which would have made such a surgery possible, had not yet reached major American hospitals at the time of his diagnosis in the early 1980s. The only available therapy for Price was massive doses of radiation, administered every day for five weeks. The radiation held the tumor at bay, but was administered in such enormous quantities that the treatment paralyzed him from the waist down. His subsequent writings and commentaries frequently touch on his struggle and the insights that have come from it. (See the bibliography.)

Personifying the saying "we are always stronger in the broken places," Price's writing meanders from religious insights to moments of blinding clarity about his place in the world to poignantly funny anecdotes about the predicaments a paraplegic faces in our fast-paced culture. In the commentary I remember, he speaks of the interminable experience of being prone in the MRI tube with the incessant and deafening banging of the magnets immediately above his head while being told he must not move, even to swallow. I can relate, having endured four such scans, and recall how ludicrous it was to try to calm myself by listening to music in the earphones testing centers provide. You can't begin to hear the music over that banging. In *Feasting the Heart* (2000), Price writes of finding, in this most vexing of situations, a "few techniques for tolerating those close quarters without beginning to rave." He speaks of reciting "the contents of my long-term memory—poems I learned in childhood, one-word mantras that have helped me through hard times, the famous Jesus prayer, and more adult poems (some of Shakespeare's sonnets and Milton's 'Lycidas')" (p. 86). He wonders why he

> always felt a curious peace in that coffin . . . a special calm seems to protect me in the tube, a trust that has always risen like a clean breeze in those stifling quarters—not that I'll never die or never again know agony—but that for now I roll ahead through life on a benignly thick sheet of ice till I've done all the honest work my mind contains.
>
> One week after this year's scan, for instance, I completed my eleventh novel. And this year's scan was again clear of cancer. (p. 87)

Price writes of a life turned upside down, but throughout, reveals his surprise at not only surviving, but thriving intellectually, and not in spite of, but *because of* his struggle. In *A Whole New Life*, he describes his outlook in the months just preceding his diagnosis—his tenth novel was about to be published; he had enduring and fulfilling relationships with friends and family, work he loved, and a home that was also a sanctuary for writing and cherished solitude. Following the initial treatment, though, he was utterly broken, experiencing unendurable pain and completely dependent for the first time in his adult life. Yet, in the twelve years following his diagnosis, he completed as many books as he had in the twenty-six previous years—prolific beyond anything he imagined as an able-bodied person. This new pinnacle of productivity, he comes to believe, would never have been realized without the adversity.

I wonder, what is it that enables some individuals to leverage intellectual productivity out of adversity? Is it some dynamic amalgamation of grit, anger, determination, and too much time on one's hands? Is it a process of thumbing one's nose at the forces that conspired to place a man like Price in such a situation? Or is it a peaceful turning inward, a conscious commitment to explore the emotional landscape that accompanies an ordeal like serious illness?

I lose myself in writing about Price, alone in the company of others at Teacher's College, beginning to understand through my own words that his struggle opened countless dimensions in an already rich and accomplished life. He may never have known those dimensions without the terrifying diagnosis and the accompanying irony of a treatment that simultaneously saved him and paralyzed him.

Price's story is, of course, not unique. Thousands of writers, artists, musicians, and scientists—think Virginia Woolf, Van Gogh, Beethoven, and Steven Hawking—have used their art and their minds to understand adversity in their lives. In the first edition of *Mosaic of Thought*, we wrote about a piece lifted from Viktor Frankel's *Man's Search for Meaning* in which Frankel survives his time in a Nazi concentration camp by living, inventively, in his mind.

There are far less visible examples in those around us, including children who not only coax insight and intellectual productivity from hardship, but who actually *seek* intellectual struggle. I remember Chrystal, a fifth grader from a low-income, rural school in Alabama, who was tenacious in her efforts to write memoir. She had read *The House on Mango Street* (Cisneros 1984) and was only interested in writing something her readers could visualize as clearly as she was able to imagine the scenes in Cisneros' memoir.

Her first efforts were fairly standard fare—a chronology of her life, holidays, friends, teachers, and birthdays, but she went back to *The House on Mango Street* dozens of times, and started her writing from scratch, over and over, doggedly determined to try something hard. "I don't want it to sound like fifth grade," she told us. "I want people to read it and think, 'Sandra Cisneros could have written that.'" Chrystal was well aware that she was reaching for something just beyond her grasp and was willing—almost eager—to experience the hardships writers endure. Part of the pleasure for her was in living to tell the tale—she wanted to be part of the confederacy of writers whose experience is characterized by exertion and trial.

How do children, like Chrystal, *decide* to undertake intellectual challenges they know may be beyond them? How do we create the conditions in our classrooms that encourage all kids to decide to challenge themselves far more consistently?

I snapped out of my reverie and written ponderings about Reynolds Price, realizing that I was leading a workshop, and it was probably best not to spend the rest of the time writing while the participants dozed off or balanced their checkbooks. I asked the teachers to share the written descriptions of people they had known who struggled. I was moved, but not surprised, by the stories they shared. It seems we reach new levels of understanding when we persevere through difficulty. The respect that permeated each teacher's story of a person who had fought adversity revealed the silver lining we all suspect lies within struggle, but seldom articulate.

Of course, none of us would wish certain kinds of trials—illness, loss, failure—on others, but a truth does emerge. We are not only stronger emotionally, perhaps spiritually, at our broken places, but our understanding of the world and our place in it—our cognitive life—is often enriched by struggle. We see more clearly, we understand more incisively, we focus more intently, we remember more permanently. In what small way can we extrapolate lessons from a life like Price's that apply to our work with children? What lessons lie here for teaching and learning?

DIMENSION: TO SAVOR THE STRUGGLE

- We *struggle for insight*; we savor and learn from the struggle itself; we venture into new learning territory and fight the debilitating influence of judgment.

It was Irish Literature 208. I was a sophomore at the University of Denver discovering the joy of learning for the first time in my life (with the brief exception of my high school death penalty project). It was Professor Bernhardt. It was a paper on William Butler Yeats. He gave me a B. I was very offended. I looked up his office hours on the syllabus and marched in, B paper in hand. Okay, to tell the truth, I think it was a B+.

"What's the problem with this paper," I demanded, unaccustomed to getting B's. "Aren't the bibliographic citations correct, isn't it the right length, wasn't I supposed to write about William Butler Yeats, and didn't I, in fact, write about William Butler Yeats?" Dr. Bernhardt had a faint smile as I completed my diatribe. He probably wanted to laugh out loud (or slap me—I definitely deserved it). I waited for his response, thinking I'd caught him giving me the wrong grade and that he would humbly apologize and let me watch while he changed the grade in the book.

"Miss Oliver, there were no problems with the bibliographic citations, your paper was the right length, you stayed on topic." He paused. "But, you should know that I don't give A's in this class when the papers include no original thinking. This paper reflects nothing original. There are no fresh insights or thoughts that give pause. Should you wish to rewrite it with the inclusion of original thought, I would be happy to reconsider it. You don't need to focus on the length and the bibliographic citations—Miss Oliver, you need to learn to think."

It was a long, lonely walk back to the dorm. I couldn't be indignant because I knew he was right. I knew I didn't know how to think, knew I'd never really been asked to think, but the most terrifying realization was that I knew I didn't know how to *learn* to think. How does one go about *getting* an original thought? I knew I wanted one, but to start again, with a blank sheet of paper in my IBM Selectric typewriter, seemed daunting, to say the least.

Many teachers with whom I speak have had similar experiences. It wasn't until college or graduate school that we were challenged to extend our thinking beyond recall, retelling, restating, and regurgitating. We "did school" well enough to earn a decent GPA and go on to college, but we were not taught *how* to think, to understand. When finally we faced significant intellectual challenges, many of us weren't sure we had the capacity, much less the tools, to address them successfully. Many, like me, weren't prepared for the struggle and, for a significant time in our learning lives, didn't realize any value in such rigorous effort.

In our K–12 schooling, we only rarely experienced the unforgettable gratification of working doggedly to understand something, wondering if it would ever make sense, nearly giving up, making a decision to persevere, and finally, *finally*, gaining insight and understanding. And, if we were lucky enough to experience that process, we were forced to see ourselves, our own capacity for intellectual rigor, in a very different way. For most of us, these kinds of experiences were either accidental or forced by a professor like Dr. Bernhardt.

What if all students routinely experienced intellectually engaging and challenging learning lives? What if they were *taught* that ideas worth understanding are worth the struggle? What if teachers modeled the power of struggle so that students wouldn't fear, but embrace difficulty and challenge? Might children develop more positive regard for their intellectual capacity earlier and more permanently? Might they come to respect the nearly limitless power of their own minds, thus leading more of them to pursue higher levels of learning in high school and college? Might our students expect to be asked to produce original thought? What would Dr. Bernhardt say to that?

Many teachers to whom I speak not only worry, as did my colleague at Teacher's College, about asking kids to struggle, but also wonder whether teaching kids how to work hard to understand, how to think, is even possible. Isn't this the era in which our kids spend a huge percentage of their time outside of school in front of screens (movie, computer, video game, television)? Isn't theirs the generation of immediate gratification? Don't too many of them experience too much difficulty in their lives without our adding to it? Isn't it tough enough to motivate kids to read and learn as it is? Should we really be thinking about making it tougher?

I clearly recall conversations with professors during my teacher-preparation years in which we teachers-in-training pressed them to tell us more about how to motivate kids to read. How can we get kids to become "lifelong readers and learners"? How can we make learning fun? How can we get kids excited about books? How can we ensure quick success for students? I wonder now if we were asking the wrong questions. The question isn't how *we* motivate them to read; it isn't how *we* work harder to get them excited about learning. Instead, we should think about helping kids build their *own* internal drive to learn. Our work is not about making things easier or more fun, or more entertaining, but about helping kids discover the powerful capacity of their own minds, which is, in and of itself, intoxicating (and by the way, fun!). No contests, no prizes, but the biggest reward of all—the certainty that they have the facility to understand deeply, to create original ideas.

I can remember saying to my own students things like, "Hey you guys, we're going to do this really fun, exciting project and it's going to be really easy and we're going to be done by lunch!" I thought I was getting them psyched. My message, inadvertently, may have been: "You need this to be fun and easy and short. You may not have the intellectual wherewithal to undertake something that requires stamina and will be, at times, bewildering." I didn't realize it, but I was really saying, "It's my job to pump you up to do an activity that may not be worthy of your intellectual attention in the first place." Of course, that is the last message I ever wanted to send. Where did I ever get the idea that easy, quick, and fun was the way to engage students? Why didn't it occur to me that my most important job was to teach students how to overcome intellectual challenges and discover the far more lasting pleasure that brings? Could it have been that, at some unconscious level, I didn't trust that my students were capable of serious intellectual struggle?

To overcome obstacles is to know our own strength. Anyone who has confronted a complex problem—whether chosen or thrust upon them— knows what it means to realize just how much we are capable of understanding. Often, though, this awareness must overcome an incessant internal voice arguing to the contrary. The demon of negative judgment, of self-doubt, is for many of us alive and well. As I write later in this chapter, many of the words in this book fought their way to the screen through a chorus of voices in my head screaming, "Nobody CARES, Ellin!" To return to writing after *Mosaic of Thought*, this time on my own, was an act that required me to repress the voice that tells me I'm a lousy writer and that my ideas won't matter to anyone. It was, for me, a full-out battle with the fiendish influence of self-doubt. That self-doubt is part of the struggle. I desperately wish someone had taught me, explicitly, how to do battle with it when I was young.

To struggle, especially while fighting the debilitating influence of judgment, whether from oneself or from others—is an all-important dimension of understanding. Are our classrooms set up to capitalize on that dimension, while providing children the needed support? What does intellectual struggle look like when productively woven into literacy work? What can we do to reverse negative associations of struggle and instead work toward a school and classroom culture that savors such challenge?

We must model ways in which our own insights and understandings have grown because we struggled, and lay out learning opportunities that do not lead to immediate gratification. I believe our classrooms should include actual experiences and explicit discussion of what it means to struggle toward understanding. We need to talk about the *internal* gratification—not just a tangible product—that results from working hard and eventually coming to understand. We can ask kids to articulate their own dimensions of understanding, use those I've proposed, or merge the two, but we should be explicit about the pleasures and struggles of the thinking life.

In Figure 5.1, I propose a smattering of ideas meant to entice kids to explore new facets of their intellectual selves through confronting complex challenges.

There are, of course, numerous ways to build an ethic that values intellectual struggle. I have observed teachers who create and then celebrate circumstances in which they ask children to take their time to think deeply, and to use oral and written language as well as artistic and dramatic options to develop their thinking. I have watched children share their insights and ideas to inform others and teach their peers to use their minds in new ways—in other words, to work hard in order to understand at an unprecedented level.

How do you create a classroom culture that celebrates rigor? I've visited classrooms in which a banner over the door announces "Scholars work here." I've observed children who clearly differentiate and move flexibly between the scholarly language used in crafting sessions and invitational groups and the neighborhood or playground language that characterizes their more informal oral interactions. I've seen classrooms in which teachers talk to students about their own repeated attempts to read Tolstoy or write a eulogy, emphasizing qualities such as perseverance and patience. These teachers are clear in telling their students that, though they are young, they have the same qualities inside, just waiting to be practiced.

Any one of these tactics used in isolation may prove empty, like just another poster hanging unnoticed on a wall imploring kids to "try your hardest every day." However, integrated into a classroom culture that takes thinking seriously, that invites children to look inward for gratification, these tactics can raise the standard of thinking for every child, every day. Who wouldn't want that?

LITERACY ESSENTIALS: MAKING TIME FOR WHAT'S IMPORTANT

I acknowledge that it takes a significant amount of time to model for children what it looks like to concentrate intensively, dwell in ideas, and rel-

Fig. 5.1. Teaching Students to Value Struggle

In a classroom where intellectual struggle is valued, students and teachers demonstrate the following behaviors:

- Students know they are working toward reading progressively more difficult text—not only because the words are more difficult or the text longer, but because the complexity of ideas is greater, the genre new, or the text structure less predictable.

- Teachers give students time to consider their responses to text in silence. For example, in crafting sessions and invitational groups, teachers encourage children to value thoughtful responses over hasty answers. A child who says, "I don't know" or "I forget" is given more time to think. Students are taught to wait in silence while peers consider their responses and understand that the best thinking often takes the longest.

- Teachers challenge students to describe and defend their opinions in crafting sessions and invitational groups as well as book clubs—students *expect* to be asked to elaborate on their ideas or defend their conclusions.

- Students purposely, as well as spontaneously, apply comprehension strategies in demanding text. For example, if a text is heavily loaded with new concepts, students need to determine importance—to decide what matters most and what is worthy of remembering.

- Students explore the progressively more subtle insights and understandings that come from rereading texts. Teachers can ask children to describe what they understand on a second or third reading of a text that they didn't understand the first time around.

- Teachers show students how to challenge another reader in a civil, but provocative manner—for example, asking a student who has shared to probe the idea further or tell how using a comprehension strategy helped him understand the text more deeply.

- Students experience the gratification of spending progressively longer periods of time reading and writing (composing) independently every day, celebrating as the time spent in independent reading or writing increases.

- Students are exposed to the most sophisticated oral language possible. For example, from the earliest grades, teachers might explain what metacognition is and how students can use it to reach deeper understandings. However, students should also confront sophisticated vocabulary based on content they're studying.

- Students are trusted to solve intellectual problems, particularly when the teacher has demonstrated the means for doing so—for example, asking students to reread from the point of view of several characters before determining what is important in a chapter.

- Students go beyond reporting or retelling after reading; they are asked to share their thinking about a text (what they inferred, images they created while reading, questions they pursued, etc.) rather than just report what happened.

Fig. 5.1 continues on next page

Fig. 5.1. Teaching Students to Value Struggle *(continued)*

- Students are challenged to share their thinking about a text in a variety of forms—written, oral, artistic, and dramatic—and to invent new ways to report, not on the book, but on their *thinking about* the book.

- Teachers ask students not just to share their new learnings as readers, but to actually craft lessons (reflection sessions) to *teach* others to do what they have done. For example, if a child learns to apply a comprehension strategy, such as inferring, in a new genre, say poetry, the child should be invited not only to share what he has learned but to actually teach other children to infer in poetry.

---

ish ever-greater challenges. At first glance, it seems that focusing on the dimensions and outcomes of understanding will take time from instruction on the skills your district directs you to teach. I want to take a closer look, however, at which of those skills are truly essential. I propose that there is far less essential content than we perceive (and that some states include in their literacy standards documents) and that, if we focus instruction on what matters most, we have more than enough time to teach children to comprehend deeply, to experience the gratification that comes as struggle leads to understanding. But the question remains: Do we know what matters most in K–12 literacy?

The difficulty of this question is amplified when we read professional books and attend conferences in which colleagues promote instructional practices associated with *one* aspect of literacy, such as phonics or comprehension, without fully acknowledging that teachers are asked to teach *all* literacy content. Earlier in this chapter, for example, I encouraged you to model the internal gratification that comes from struggling with, then finally grasping, a difficult idea. In the last chapter, I suggested that the best thinking sometimes takes the longest, and therefore we should encourage kids to take their time to think. What I haven't addressed yet (and what too many literacy educators fail to explain) is how you're supposed to take on these worthy goals when you have 10,006 other things to teach—in literacy, by Thursday! The truth is that all of those objectives exist and, if you're like most teachers, you've seen the list of goals grow longer each year, with absolutely nothing removed from it.

It's time to recognize this dilemma and propose some solutions. If we want kids to *live* the dimensions of understanding and *think* about the outcomes of understanding, something in the current curriculum has to go. I'd like to explore ways in which we can find time to model the dimensions and outcomes by focusing on the concepts that matter most, K–12.

Let's return to the conversation you've been having with your hypothetical new colleague, Tracy, who expresses some of this frustration.

Tracy stops by your classroom one afternoon several weeks before students return to school and confesses that she is uncertain about the literacy *content* she is to teach. She wonders if Nirvana Unified School District is clear about what content matters most for literacy learners. Just a little question, you think.

"There are just so many lists of skills, so many sources that tell us what to teach," she begins. "Do we rely on the state standards, district curricula, test preparation materials, units that have been developed by colleagues, our own ideas about what's important to teach? Really, I feel like there is so much content, so many skills, I'm not sure what matters most. In the state I just moved from, there was this huge standards document—pages and pages of scope and sequence and all these student activities we were supposed to teach, and now I get here and it's a whole new document, much of which is different from the standards in my old state. I just wonder—who got it right? If my former state's content standards are, in fact, a list of the most essential skills and strategies, then why is this state's document so different? How do you decide what's most important to teach in this district?" She mentions that she asked the question in her interview with your district and it seemed to cause some confusion among the interviewers. There's a surprise, you think.

I believe all of us must be able to answer this fundamental question if we ever hope to have time to teach children what it means to understand deeply and give them opportunities to do so. I believe that the reason we feel so pressed for time is that we are trying to teach far too much literacy content—more than may be necessary. It is no surprise to anyone reading this book that some educators—especially policy makers—can't bear to delete content from curriculum documents and literacy materials, but they are all too happy to add it. We're trying to teach every skill that anyone ever thought important, and the result is teaching that lacks focus and depth. We use multiple sources for the content we teach—standards documents, district curricula, literacy program scope-and-sequence lists, lists of skills that *may* be tested, and our recollection of what we were taught when we were in school. The result is that we veer ever further from what I described in Chapter 2 as the important conditions for human learning. I argued that people learn best when a *few important concepts* are taught *in great depth over a long period of time* and when they have opportunities to apply those concepts in a *wide variety of texts and contexts*.

I've also observed that we teach activities as if they were curriculum. When we teach learning strategies such as graphic organizers, semantic maps, KWL (what I know, what I want to know, and what I learned), and think-pair-share, we must be very clear that while these activities may be useful to organize and share thinking, they are not essential literacy content. These should be taught only if they will facilitate children's thinking about the real literacy content, but many state and district standards and curriculum documents don't distinguish between the content itself and activities that facilitate learning. Obviously, the emphasis must be placed on the true content—what research tells us is essential for all literacy learners.

Do state and district curricula and standards detail what is essential? Some well may, but I find that these documents differ dramatically from state to state and, frankly, I'm not surprised. The processes many states and districts use may be far from the ideal way to define and describe essential elements in a literacy curriculum. Many documents do reflect much of what is essential, but may include much more. How can teachers make informed decisions about what content to emphasize more, what less?

In fact, though state and local standards and curriculum documents differ dramatically, there is real consensus—bordering on unanimity— among researchers who have examined what content matters most for children, K–12. There are legitimate differences of opinion among researchers about *how* that content should be taught and what *emphasis* should be given to particular skills at particular stages in children's schooling, but there is widespread agreement about the most essential literacy content. We could speculate forever about why states, school districts, and individual schools have created such widely disparate (and lengthy) curriculum and standards documents in light of this consensus, but that is a quagmire into which I'm not able (the publisher says this book cannot exceed 10,000 pages) or willing to wade.

If we return to the conclusion that we learn most effectively when we learn a *few important concepts* at a time, taught *in depth over a long period*, and apply them in a *variety of texts and contexts*, then it becomes clear that we must be very clear about those few concepts. I find the fact that researchers agree on the essential content liberating, particularly because the list of essential skills and strategies is quite brief when compared to many state standards and basal scope-and-sequence documents. We really do have time to teach comprehension in much greater depth, including time to teach students to think deeply, *if* (and it's a big *if*) we choose to focus on the most essential skills and strategies all along the grade continuum. I believe it makes sense to have these essential skills and strategies in mind when reviewing district and state standards. Knowing what matters most will help us set priorities for our precious instructional time with children. All of this leads me to ask, wouldn't it be possible—given a much more manageable set of standards—to weave into our daily conversations with children instruction on how to understand, how to think critically? Wouldn't we, under those circumstances, dramatically increase the probability that students would actually *remember* the essential content they have learned? Or is this making too much sense?

So, what are the most essential skills and strategies for learners in grades K–12? How would you respond to Tracy's query? Perhaps you would begin by looking again at the What's Essential model introduced in Chapter 2 (Figure 2.3a–d) and further elaborated in Appendix B. The model is not designed to provide an exhaustive review of the research or suggest specific teaching tactics. Rather, it can provide teachers like you and Tracy with a viable set of content outcomes for their literacy instruction. My hope, of course, is that this outline will enable you to focus on the literacy content that matters most, leaving ample time to explore the nature of understanding with your students.

You sit down with Tracy and remind her that you've already discussed the first category of the model, A Climate of Rigor, Inquiry, and Intimacy (Chapters 2 and 3). Your instruction should rest upon that foundation, which encompasses classroom environment and lots of time for focused, independent reading and writing. Look now at the second category (Cognitive Strategies). Because you work in Nirvana Unified School District, your faculty has cheerfully agreed (you're always cheery in Nirvana) that this outline comprises what matters most in terms of the *content* in your literacy classrooms.

Figure 5.2 recaps the six cognitive processes people use to read, write, speak, and listen effectively: graphophonic, lexical, syntactic, semantic, schematic, and pragmatic strategies. In the model, I've configured the cognitive strategies (known by some theorists as cueing systems) into two groups: three *surface structure* systems and three *deep structure* systems.

Surface structure systems are the cognitive processes and skills language users must employ to identify words and read fluently—the graphophonic, lexical, and syntactic systems. Researchers (such as Rumelhart 1985) have referred to them as surface structure systems because they have to do with the surface, or visible and audible, aspects of language use. Proficient language users employ these three systems collectively and independently for three key purposes:

1. To identify unknown words (in or out of context)
2. To read fluently (orally or silently)
3. To understand how words, sentences, and longer pieces of texts are configured and structured

Deep structure systems are the three cognitive processes that enable language users to understand words, interpret meaning, and communicate— the semantic, schematic, and pragmatic systems. Researchers refer to them as deep structure systems because they have to do with comprehending and enhancing understanding. They are largely invisible and inaudible cognitive processes. Proficient language users may use these systems consciously or subconsciously, collectively and independently for four key purposes:

1. To understand word meanings (from literal to inferential) in text
2. To understand an author's intended meaning and glean information from text
3. To interpret meaning and consider ideas and themes at the whole-text level
4. To enhance comprehension by considering a range of interpretations and perspectives and by speaking and writing about ideas and text, thereby discovering more subtle meanings

We understand that these six systems (three surface and three deep) are used *simultaneously* by proficient readers. Researchers, including Rumelhart (1985), argue that the six systems develop simultaneously, are used simultaneously, and therefore are best taught simultaneously. To understand what that means, let's take a closer look at the description of each system in Figure 5.2.

You and Tracy discuss and actually highlight those areas in the figure that you attend to most frequently in your classroom. Tracy highlights the graphophonic and semantic systems because her former district encouraged teachers to focus most on ensuring that kids could decode (graphophonic) and were building strong vocabulary (semantic). You highlight the syntactic and pragmatic systems because you find yourself working a great deal with grammar, text structures, and conventions (syntactic) and pride yourself on creating lots of ways for students to share and discuss books (pragmatic).

Tracy asks about faculty discussions. Do your colleagues actually sit down to discuss all six systems, she wonders? And what about in classrooms? When you are conferring with a child, do you focus on one or two systems simply because you understand them better, or do you try to keep

Fig. 5.2. What's Essential for Literacy Learning
Cognitive Strategies

Surface Structure Systems	Deep Structure Systems
Sets of skills that help readers/writers identify words and read fluently	Sets of skills and strategies that help readers/ writers comprehend literally to grasp plot, comprehend deeply to probe ideas, and extend and apply their understanding
Graphophonic System: Letter/sound knowledge, alphabetic principle, phonemic awareness, decoding	**Semantic System:** Understanding word meanings from literal to subtle; discussing or writing about associations related to words; precision and word choice in writing
Lexical System: Visual word recognition based on frequent visual exposure to words; visual memory for *all* words	**Schematic System:** Constructing meaning at the whole-text level (can be literal or inferential understanding of themes, ideas, and concepts); storing and retrieving relevant knowledge; connecting the new to the known
Syntactic System: Understanding (usually auditory) and use of language structures at the word, sentence, paragraph, and whole-text levels (see Figure 2.3d, Text Structures)	**Pragmatic System:** Multiple experiences with ideas we've read or learned; sharing and applying meaning; constructing meaning through oral, written, artistic, and dramatic means; writing for specific purposes and audiences; revising thinking based on interactions with others; adopting the habits and mores of readers and writers

all six in mind as you're assessing the child's progress? You reply that your faculty is working to discuss and thoroughly understand all six because they work in concert and that you have developed a form that helps you focus conferences with children on all six systems (see Appendix D, "Conference Record").

My conclusion from visiting classrooms around the country is that we teachers understand certain systems (usually the graphophonic, syntactic, and/or semantic) better than others and therefore direct much more of our instructional attention to those areas. Given that it is the simultaneous use of all six systems that permits readers to be proficient, I am arguing that, without solid knowledge of all six, we may well be selling children short. Let's take a moment to explore each of the six in more detail so that no matter what grade you teach, you can rely on a fuller knowledge base when setting instructional priorities for your whole class as well as for individuals with specific needs.

Cognitive Strategies: Surface Structure Systems

The three surface structure systems—graphophonic, lexical, and syntactic—have to do with the visible and audible aspects of language and permit readers to identify unknown words and to read fluently.

Graphophonic System

Teachers have been bombarded with information about the graphophonic system and the need for systematic phonics instruction for over a decade. We have programs and procedures and activities and games and centers representing every conceivable approach to phonics instruction; I'd like to pare this system down to its essential elements. We need to ensure that children know four key components of the graphophonic system:

1. Letters and the specific sounds associated with each letter (46 distinct sounds associated with the 26 letters)

2. The principle that letters have specific sounds associated with them (the alphabetic principle)

3. How to produce the sounds of words in isolation (phonemic awareness)

4. How to blend the sounds to accurately pronounce an unknown word

The content is really very straightforward, and I cannot recall ever hearing or reading that the graphophonic system is unimportant. The graphophonic system *is* important (to readers of languages with alphabets), but I worry that much of the recent emphasis on phonics instruction represents overkill in teaching one system to the exclusion of the other five. Remember that all six systems are learned simultaneously and used simultaneously, leading to the conclusion that they should be *taught* simultaneously. I appreciate Isabel Beck's clear, straightforward explanation of the graphophonic system in her book *Making Sense of Phonics* (2006). Anyone reading this short book will learn how to design a clear and systematic approach to phonics instruction—without the need for outrageously expensive and inauthentic programs. (See Appendix B, "What's Essential," for a more comprehensive list of essential phonics content and effective ways in which children need to practice phonics in order to become rapid, accurate word decoders.)

Children who are successful in using the graphophonic system have had explicit phonics instruction (naming the relationship between letters and sounds), and that instruction tends to follow a particular sequence (systematic). For example, we know it makes far more sense to begin with consonants and short vowels and build to more complex consonant clusters, digraphs, and dipthongs (Beck 2006). Playing with words, word building, creating new constructions within word families, and manipulating letters to form a variety of words are all important opportunities for children to practice, but the most effective form of phonics practice is to read texts (at an appropriate level) and to write every day. Children in our primary-grade classrooms require widely varying amounts of instruction and support as they learn phonics. I worry that in too many classrooms, we have forgone thoughtful assessment to determine student's specific needs in phonics and replaced it with a one-size-fits-all approach to phonics instruction. Though there's no question it's more challenging for teachers, the most effective way to approach phonics instruction is to identify individual and small-group needs and provide instruction tailored to those needs in small groups and individual conferences. If a child understands the alphabetic principle, can pronounce sounds individually, and can use that knowledge to decode unknown words, continued phonics instruction is probably not necessary. Once she knows the process, she needs opportunities to apply it in independent reading and, especially important, in writing!

We have long debated what has been called "invented spelling"—inviting children to make their best guess at the spelling of a word in their writing. I wish whoever coined that phrase had called it what it really is—invented phonics. Using approximated representations of words while writing is one of the single most effective ways to practice, not spelling, but phonics. When a child takes care to represent each sound she hears in a word she writes, she is getting invaluable phonics practice. I worry when schools declare that there will be no invented spelling. Will we substitute that important phonics practice with dozens of worksheets filled with nonsense words presented out of context, which are therefore unlikely to be remembered, much less reapplied in new contexts? I hope not. Learning to use the graphophonic system takes more than just systematic phonics instruction—it is critical to practice by reading and writing for extended periods of time every day.

Lexical System

With all the hoo-ha about phonics, I wonder how much professional discussion you have heard about the lexical system. The lexical system has to do not only with the recognition of basic sight words (remember that dude named Dolch who came up with five hundred of them?), but of *all* words we are able to recognize and pronounce instantly, without having to pause to sound them out. Frequently, theorists describe this visual word-recognition process as part of the graphophonic system (they may call it fluency or automaticity), but I find that integrating it into the graphophonic system leads to too much emphasis on the letters and sounds within words, and too little on holding words in visual memory so that they can be pronounced (and spelled) instantly, without further decoding, the next time they are encountered.

When we recognize a word, we can say it. We may or may not know the meaning of particular words (that aspect falls on the deep structure side, the semantic system), but using the lexical system, we need not sound them out in order to pronounce them—we recall the words from visual memory, in rapid succession, and we can say them (whether reading silently or out loud). We are reading fluently. The lexical system may well be the most used system of the six—our eyes move over and perceive every (or nearly every) word we read. I've seen many children successfully decode and pronounce a word, but fail to hold a visual memory of that word so they can pronounce it without first decoding when they encounter it again. This overuse of phonics makes them *disfluent,* but many teachers who haven't heard of the lexical system believe that the answer is to do more phonics work. What these children need is more practice in the lexical system. They need frequent visual exposure to many, many words in their classroom environment and in books.

The lexical system has everything to do with reading fluency, yet many teachers know very little about it and therefore do less to help students build a large "lexicon"—a mental library of instantly recognized words. Our goal is for every child to sound out a word when necessary, but never do so twice for the same word. The word is stored in visual memory and the child understands that no matter what form it takes (capital or lowercase letters, large or small print, cursive writing, etc.), the word will always be read the same way. Appendix B contains an extensive list of ways we can ask students to practice using the lexical system, particularly if they have difficulty with visual memory for words.

The lexical system also relates to children's spelling ability. Children who spell well are able to create an instant picture of the word in their minds as they write it.

Children who use the lexical system well are typically those who are surrounded with books and print in their classroom and home environments. They are children whose teachers and parents point out words in the environment, have fun playing with words, find words remarkably interesting, and talk to kids about the words they see. In many primary classrooms the walls are filled with wonderful environmental print—there are words everywhere, labeling everything in the room, capturing kids' thinking on anchor charts, and adding to their lexicons with rapidly growing and changing word walls. Primary teachers tend to focus more on the celebration and wonder of words, but intermediate, middle, and high school classrooms can be too sterile—in some cases nearly devoid of words. I'm baffled by this, because content areas provide rich fodder for a constantly changing array of words. If kids are to be able to read *photosynthesis* and *anthropomorphism*, they need constant visual exposure to the words (as well as great discussion and investigation related to their meanings). Learners of all ages build a lexicon of instantly recognized words through continual exposure to them.

Syntactic System

While the lexical system is wholly visual, the syntactic system rests on human auditory processing—our mind's ear. We "hear" when language is structured correctly at the word, sentence, and whole-text levels. For example, if a child tells you he "runned and fell at recess," you gently correct his past tense—ran. If order begin out write I to of (If I begin to write out of order), you "hear" the improper grammatical structure (even if you are reading silently). Our mind's ear even reacts when we hear more subtle grammatical inconsistencies. As a child I would run wildly into my house and tell my mother that "me and my friends are going to ride bikes." She shuddered and said that language like that "made her teeth itch"—a rather unusual way of saying it sounds incorrect. It's a phrase I find myself using with my students and my daughter to this day! We *hear* (even if we're reading silently) when language doesn't sound like language.

When reading a novel or longer piece of text, we react to syntactic or structural irregularities such as flashbacks, fast forwards. or parallel plots. Sometimes we find the liberties authors take with the plot irritating, and other times we marvel at the author's skill in manipulating time and plot so adeptly. These are all, essentially, auditory reactions to our knowledge of the correct structure—the syntax—of language.

Children who have a well-developed syntactic system are typically those who have heard and used increasingly complex forms of oral language throughout their lives. They have been given time to express their ideas and encouraged to use ever more sophisticated ways to construct sentences and tell stories. They have read a lot, and read increasingly complex forms of language as they mature.

But the single most important way children become strong in their use of the syntactic system is by speaking and writing frequently, formally and informally, for different audiences and purposes, and across content areas and genres. The syntactic system is a developed "sense" of what sounds right, what elements in text fit together, and how words can be manipulated to work well in written forms. We can develop the syntactic system in children by encouraging them to listen for subtle differences in what we read aloud or say to them. We can say, for example, "Which sounds more like language—the children ran on the playground or the children runned on the playground?" We can adjust these exercises to be more obvious or more subtle depending on the needs of the child. Children who are learning to speak English benefit not only from these types of exercises, but from hearing increasingly sophisticated and complex sentence structures through read-alouds and conversations with their teachers and peers.

The surface structure systems are essential if children are to read, write, speak, and listen independently. They form the visible and audible components that make language users proficient. The surface structures facilitate our use of the deep structures, but we have all seen what happens when a child has had too much instruction in the surface structure systems, to the exclusion of the deep structure—meaning making—systems. These children tend to read robotically, make nonsense substitutions as they read, and frequently don't monitor to ensure that what they're reading makes sense. They are also the children who become disengaged from the whole literacy process—they tell us they're bored, they say they hate to read, they complain that it takes too long, they act out, they struggle, and too often, they are channeled into special education (whether or not they're part of the very small percentage of children with an identifiable learning disability)—where they may get more surface structure instruction, and the cycle repeats itself endlessly. Teachers need to ensure that they provide an appropriate balance between surface and deep structure systems. While children are still learning the graphophonic system, at least 50 percent of instructional time should be devoted to deep structure instruction; thereafter, the percentage of instructional time devoted to deep structures should increase dramatically.

Cognitive Strategies: Deep Structure Systems

The three deep structure systems—semantic, schematic, and pragmatic—have to do with the literal and inferential meanings of texts and enhancing understanding of ideas we read and learn.

Semantic System

I have observed teachers with a passionate interest in words and watched how they share this love with children, and I find it very hard to describe how they do what they do. No book on vocabulary instruction or set of activities can accomplish what these teachers do, spontaneously, in the classroom. They pause during a read-aloud to marvel at an author's word choice; they reread lines just to let children appreciate the cadence of the language; they interrupt everyone during composing to share the word one writer has chosen because it perfectly captures the meaning he strives for. There are words and quotes posted throughout their classrooms, pulled from children's writing and well-loved books. They share their pleasure when the words an author uses surprise them. They wisely select a few very relevant words to study at a given time, helping children to build a conceptual (rather than definitional) understanding of each word by associating other terms with it. They create situations in which kids discover and teach each other words, and they ensure that children are hearing—and using—an ever more sophisticated vocabulary as they speak and write.

The semantic system encompasses all we know and are able to do with respect to understanding word meanings, from the most basic knowledge of a word's definition to the subtle ways writers precisely choose the best word for a particular context to all the associations, feelings, and memories we have surrounding a word or phrase. We have long understood the need for vocabulary instruction that creates a conceptual base for new words, helps children build a personal set of associations for the words they know, and encourages students to use increasingly subtle and complex words in their spoken and written language. Sadly, there is still too much focus in American classrooms on handing out long weekly word lists, then asking children to look up their meanings and write sentences that use the words in an appropriate context.

Effective semantic system instruction focuses on building an extensive vocabulary that is enriched by the user's experiences, emotions, and memories related to the word. We remember word meanings when they are associated with other words and background knowledge in long-term memory.

Great semantic instruction encompasses words used in daily conversation, words essential to content area themes and topics, and words students are curious about. Teachers emphasize the oral and written use of increasingly sophisticated vocabulary and find numerous ways to reinforce students' attempts at more complex vocabulary. The most effective vocabulary teachers not only select, introduce, and discuss words, but they also have children speculate on and confirm the myriad meanings many words hold.

We have to remember that the most effective way to help children build a broad and deep vocabulary is for them to spend extended periods of time every day reading independently, particularly if the books they're reading contain vocabulary slightly more sophisticated than their own. It is also crucial that children are exposed to increasingly sophisticated vocabulary in their daily oral interactions with the teacher and other children.

We also know that focusing on words from content area study—discussing all possible meanings for the word and, equally important, what the word *doesn't* mean—can be very effective. We can use semantic maps and other advanced organizers to help children link newly learned words to existing memories, knowledge, and emotions. We want children to work with words, to spend time considering multiple meanings, and to hear interesting, multifaceted words during read-alouds as well as oral interactions in the classroom.

Our goal is for children to use a wide variety of words in written and spoken contexts for a particular purpose or effect. We want them to get excited when they hear or read new words and be eager to work them into their own vocabulary. We need to teach them, by modeling, to pause when reading to marvel at an author's use of words, perhaps recording them in reading journals or sharing them with other readers. We must encourage them to experiment with new words in their spoken interactions and, in writing, seek to use words to greatest effect; they know that readers' reactions are often the best barometer of their success.

Have we given up hope that, like their teachers, like great writers, children can be in love with words? I don't think we can expect kids to come to us with this love of language, though some will. But we need to build the love of words and language from the time they come to us in kindergarten until they stand at the podium on graduation day. The most powerful arbiter of a child's evolving sophistication as a language user is his teacher—someone who loves words and shares insights about words fluidly every day, throughout the year.

Schematic System

In many schools and districts, comprehension is described as a discrete set of skills that include being able to recognize main ideas and details, retell, and answer comprehension questions. While it may be useful for students to use these skills, curriculum and standards documents tend to miss the bigger picture. Those skills are all part of the schematic system—a set of cognitive processes that govern how information is understood at the whole-text level. When we read, we draw conclusions, make judgments, and create general frameworks to help us understand the text as a whole—our comprehension moves well beyond understanding individual word meanings, though it is certainly dependent on them. The schematic system involves the storage and retrieval of ideas and information by connecting new ideas to our background knowledge. But the schematic system encompasses far more.

The schematic system is the set of cognitive processes that are at work when our heart quickens while reading a compellingly written passage. It is the system that leaves us with indelible memories of books from our childhood and allows us to remember when we first went beyond the literal meanings of words to speculate about the unwritten messages—those ideas the author *may* have considered when writing a particular text. The schematic system is responsible when we become frustrated with an author's style, put the book down, and grab something else because we find it unsatisfying or hard to relate to. It is the system that was at work when I looked up from a book to find I had missed my stop on a train running from Philadelphia to Trenton one morning. The schematic system is at the heart of our personal interpretations and our drive to read more. It also reshapes our existing knowledge, belief systems, feelings, and opinions by accommodating newly learned or discovered ideas. It includes understanding at the most profound level as well as our ability to answer literal comprehension questions and retell. It is what makes us seek answers to the pressing questions in our lives through reading, writing, speaking, and listening.

Teachers who focus effectively on the schematic system are teachers who think aloud frequently, telling students how they think and how they adapt their use of comprehension strategies to meet the demands of the text. They speak to students often about connections they make from the text to their own lives, other texts, and their knowledge of the world. They speculate about a range of different meanings possible in a single piece of text; they have scrutinized their own learning enough to be able to articulate it to children. When teachers think aloud, they are literally showing children how and where they store newly learned information in their brains and how they retrieve it when needed.

The schematic system, in particular, is enhanced by the comprehension strategies we discussed in *Mosaic of Thought* (see Appendix A, "Cognitive Strategies Defined"). We use the comprehension strategies as tools to understand larger themes and ideas in text, to create personal interpretations, to be critical and skeptical, to question, and to act in our lives on what we learn through reading. We want kids to use comprehension strategies if these tools serve to deepen their understanding. When it is appropriate to use them, we must ensure that children can be:

1. Independent: They learn to use strategies without teacher support.

2. Flexible: They can use any, all, or none of the comprehension strategies, depending on the demands of the text.

3. Adaptive: They can purposefully use one or more comprehension strategies—"turn up the volume" on those strategies—to meet the demands of a given text.

Our goal with the schematic system is to teach children to fully use all seven strategies and to describe and appreciate the advances they make in comprehension when they do. We want them to pause in their reading to consider interpretations and implications from the text, seek a wide range of possible meanings, and focus on relevant details or zoom out to consider the bigger ideas. We want kids to experience a sense of urgency to seek more information about a topic of passionate interest, or to reread a section of fiction or a stanza of poetry simply because they are in awe that an author crammed so much meaning into such a small package. Of course, I want children to develop the lifelong habit of reading, but that phrase has become so banal as to be almost devoid of meaning. That's why in this book I propose a new way of thinking about what it means to understand—the dimensions and outcomes of understanding—a new set of standards that define in far more specificity what it looks like, what it feels like, what it means to understand.

Pragmatic System

When I join my book club for one of our monthly discussions, I often leave my neighbors' homes wondering if I read the same book as the rest of my group! These women of diverse ages, backgrounds, and life experiences project a thousand shades of color on the pages of the books we read together, bringing perspectives, ideas, and interpretations I had never imagined. They cause me to turn back to sections of text I thought I understood, reread them through a surprising new lens, and in so doing, discover meaning I didn't know was there. But just about the time I become intimidated by the quality and depth of their insights and the surprising spin they apply to the books we read, they tell me I do the very same thing for them. Though I've never named it for them, it is the pragmatic system that permits each of us to understand a book and the ideas that emanate from it more deeply, more completely, *because* of the others. We each bring our own understanding of the books we read, but when we talk, we broaden what we know with the perspectives of others. This is part of the pragmatic system, and it permits us to retain and reapply what we understand far more effectively.

The pragmatic system involves enhancing our understanding through multiple experiences with ideas from text. It can be as simple as rereading portions of the text or as involved as writing about text. We know that to understand deeply, to probe meaning beyond the superficial, often involves reliving the ideas in some way, having more than one opportunity to explore them. In classrooms as in the real world, this often involves several children working together, exploring each other's interpretations and perspectives. Children are using the pragmatic system when they interact in book clubs, use reader's theater or a skit to interpret a book, write responses to or interpretations of what they have read, and sketch or draw to show their thinking about a book.

Most teachers realize that we never understand something so well as when we teach it. We know that if we want students to learn, we have to find several ways to define and describe the concept and that, in turn, forces us to focus on the core principles and to express them clearly and precisely. In other words, we have to know something very well to teach it well. The process of studying and rethinking an idea so extensively that we can teach it is an example of the pragmatic system in action.

To *do* something with ideas we understand, to *act* on our insights, to *reorganize* our understanding in order to share it cogently with others—all this is to use the pragmatic system. The pragmatic system has everything to do with whether children (or adults, for that matter) will retain and reapply what they have learned. If they don't manipulate, restate, and apply the ideas, children are far more likely to shrug and say, "I don't remember" than not.

When I ask children to explore their thinking using written, oral, artistic, or dramatic means, I'm asking them to use the pragmatic system, and I know that they will understand more deeply, retain more, and be far more likely to reapply what they understand in new contexts. Using the tools listed in Appendix E ("Beyond Reporting on the Book"), for example, I'm asking them to linger with and rethink the ideas in their books.

I'm asking them to reread and to supplement their understanding with the insights of others as they write or interact or create artistic and dramatic representations of their thinking.

I have to be careful, though. If, for example, I ask children to keep double-entry journals or to use the think-pair-share strategy to talk about a book, I don't want them to use that format to *report what happens in the book*. Rather, I want them to use their journals and group discussion to *record their thinking about the book*. The comprehension strategies provide a useful language for recording thinking about a book. For example, if I'm teaching the comprehension strategy determining importance as students read various works of historical fiction, I'll model how children might use one column to record what they think is important and the second column to reflect on how they decided an idea was important and what they understand about the text because they paused to consider what was most important. This is most certainly not a typical book report! Children who are proficient in their use of the pragmatic system frequently choose to capture their thinking in some written form—not to retell the events from the book, but to hold on to their ideas so they can remember and reapply them later. Sticky notes can be useful, as can sketches, anchor charts, and different kinds of reader's notebooks, but for most children, the most potent use of the pragmatic system is discussion about their thinking related to a particular text.

I want to offer another caution about using the pragmatic system: We are too prone to ask children to use oral and written means to capture their thinking in inauthentic ways. In other words, we ask children to complete projects and use advanced organizers when we wouldn't consider doing so in a real-world context. I use my book club as a barometer when considering ways for children to share their thinking. Would I, for example, walk into my book club and suggest that everyone rewrite the last chapter of the novel we've just read and write themselves into the plot? I'd never suggest something so preposterous, but that is just one example of the hundreds of "activities" I see proposed in materials that purport to "teach" comprehension. The members of my book club would accuse me of actually drinking wine *before* I got to the meeting, a cardinal sin in our unwritten bylaws! I would never suggest that we all sit around and rewrite a chapter, but I *might* propose that we discuss alternative endings the author may have considered. We could talk for an hour on that one and have a wonderful time arguing and debating what the author would or wouldn't have considered as a conclusion to the novel. When we're debating and discussing, we're using the pragmatic system as proficient readers do—naturally and authentically—to enhance and deepen each person's understanding through the perspectives of the others.

Let's add one more layer to our understanding of the six systems. In the last portion of Figure 2.3b, the Cognitive Strategies section of the What's Essential model, I list some of the skills and strategies students use to show us they are using the six systems effectively. Repeated below, this is by no means a comprehensive list, but a sampling of what may be a "body of evidence" to demonstrate proficiency in each set of systems.

These types of strategies comprise forms of evidence that children are using all of the six systems. If children are decoding, reading fluently, holding words in visual memory, and self-correcting when they pronounce a word incorrectly, they are showing evidence of successful use of the surface structure systems. When they use strategies such as monitoring, schema, inference, and images, they are demonstrating their use of deep structure systems as well.

Our job is to ensure that children continue to apply these skills—use all types of cognitive strategies—in progressively more difficult text and

What children know and are able to do when using surface structure systems	What children know and are able to do when using deep structure systems
Use decoding strategies such as identifying word families, chunking, point and slide, cross-check across systems (does the word make sense, sound like language, do the letters match the sounds), etc.	Monitor for meaning
	Activate and/or create relevant background knowledge (schema)
	Infer
Recognize sight words and other words in environment visually; repeated use of recognized words	Create sensory and emotional images
	Determine importance
	Question
Use word analysis strategies such as identifying affixes, compound words, and derivations	Synthesize
Use text-management strategies such as rereading/reading ahead, deep reading, skimming/scanning, using text features such as boldface and italics	

in a wider variety of genres (which I'll address in Chapter 6). The graphophonic system should be taught in the first three grades of elementary school, but the remaining five systems continue to develop and should be taught throughout grades K–12.

It isn't within this book's purview to explore all six systems in depth, but interested readers will find much more complete descriptions of each of the six systems in Appendix B, "What's Essential." For each system, I have included a complete list of the skills and strategies we need to teach in order to help children fully develop that system and a matching set of outcomes that comprise a "body of evidence" that children know and are able to use it. Appendix B is meant to provide more comprehensive information about what content matters most in K–12 classrooms.

When working with teachers, I find that many have had opportunities to learn and teach two or three of the six systems (usually the graphophonic, syntactic, and semantic), but haven't had professional opportunities to explore the other three or four. This is analogous to suggesting that we can ride a bicycle without the handlebars or chain. We can probably make the contraption move, but it isn't working at the optimal level of performance. It is very legitimate to suggest that your faculty pursue deeper understanding of all six systems in order to ensure that you're focused on what matters most for kids and not wasting time teaching nonessential skills.

I'm aware that many district and state policies require teachers to teach literacy content that isn't really essential, while omitting skills and strategies that are. That is why, in this chapter, I posed Tracy's hypothetical question: What really matters most in literacy teaching? While I would never encourage teachers to omit critical elements of curriculum, I find it just as vexing to suggest that we need to teach *everything*! The bottom line is that teachers need to be well informed about what matters most and raise critical questions of policy makers when they become aware of requirements that fall outside those boundaries.

This chapter focuses on the dimension of understanding related to struggle. In many ways, I think this decision—what *not* to teach—is the ultimate struggle for teachers. It comes down to questions each teacher asks in her classroom every day: Is what I'm about to teach worthy of children's attention? What will I emphasize? What will I put on the back burner—or remove from the stove altogether? What will I teach in great depth over a long period of time and ask students to apply in a variety of texts and contexts? Will what I teach bring intellectual richness to their lives? Is it essential?

I am fully cognizant of the range of restrictions and requirements teachers face, but I am also aware that there are opportunities to exercise professional judgment, perhaps far more than most teachers realize. I see "wiggle room" to do the right thing for kids within the system and, when necessary, to exercise just a bit of civil disobedience. I have found that when very well-informed teachers approach policy makers with questions and *alternatives* as well as evidence from their classrooms to show that those alternatives lead to student learning, policy makers are quite receptive to change. I worry when teachers feel certain that things will never change, because they may decide not to ask.

Let's return to Tracy. You really do have something of an answer to her important question—what content matters most. By describing the three surface and three deep structure systems, you are describing a model based on decades of research and practice that suggests there is far less content than many of us are struggling to teach. We don't have to worry about teaching three thousand skills and strategies—we're really talking about six cognitive processes and the skills and strategies kids use that show us whether they are successful with all six or struggling to use some of them. Whether or not you decide to provide explicit instruction (that is, tell the students what the systems are and how they work) is up to you. I have seen children become more independent when they learn what the six processes actually are, but it is imperative that *we* understand each of the six systems and provide well-balanced instruction, based on observed needs, for each one, and that we minimize or eliminate content that doesn't support the development of the systems.

I'm saying that we *must* understand the essential content, if only to be able to respond when our curricula become obese! We need to argue that to teach deeply and well, the curricula have to slim down, and that we have a very clear idea about what is essential. Focusing our limited instructional time on that essential content allows us to explore with children the nature of understanding and permits us to do what we've always known to be most effective—to teach a few important concepts in depth over a long period of time, and have students apply them in a variety of texts and contexts.

It's ironic that, in a chapter extolling the virtues of struggle, I argue for a very simple approach to understanding essential content! But, I side with Oliver Wendell Holmes, who said, "I wouldn't give a fig for the simplicity this side of complexity, but I would give my life for the simplicity the other side of complexity." To me, he is reveling in the clarity of thought that surfaces after we've dealt with complexity. We teachers have had to find our way through voluminous, confusing, and complex claims about what content matters most for children's literacy learning before we could reach a more commonsense and certainly clearer view—six systems, taught in great depth over a long period of time and in a variety of texts and contexts, will get us where we need to be. That simplicity couldn't be seen without the struggle through complexity, and I am grateful to generations of researchers who have led the fight and to classroom teachers who have the courage to focus on what's most essential.

DWELLING IN THE MIND

I have struggled to write this book. I mentioned in the prelude that I could find a million and six things to do to ensure that I never quite had the time to sit down and write. And, unlike *Mosaic of Thought*, where Susan and I had to plan our schedules around getting together to write, I had no pressure from a colleague to crank up the rpm's. I had a lot of time to think and a lot of time to decide I wasn't up to the task. Wonderful friends and colleagues offered support and finally threw up their hands in frustration (one or two suggested that I should "ice it" for a while). The structure— four sections for each chapter that can be read "vertically" (as we usually read chapters, from beginning to end) or "horizontally" (reading the same section in each chapter—say, all the Dimensions sections—before going back to read another section all the way through)—was particularly difficult to envisage. I knew what I *didn't* want to write—a "how-to" manual for teachers with specific, scripted lessons—but I was several years into it before I knew what I *did* want to write. Once I had decided what the book wasn't and what it was, I merely had to sit down and write, right? Not so much!

Trying to generate new thinking has been one of the most daunting intellectual experiences of my life. Bruce Morgan, my dear friend and author of *Writing Through the Tween Years*, in one of our ten thousand discussions about my, shall we say, slow start in writing this book, finally said, "I don't know who ever told you it was going to be easy. You seem to think that you should just be able to sit down and hammer this thing out, but it doesn't work that way. You're trying to reshape our thinking about what it means to understand, and you think that should be easy? Get real, honey." Bruce was only partially right. I certainly didn't expect that writing a second book would be easy, but I did imagine that once I had the structure in mind, I could sit down and crank it out fairly quickly. I imagined that it would be hard work in terms of long hours and multiple revisions, but ultimately a matter of sitting down and just writing what I know. Not so much!

When *Mosaic of Thought* was first published, colleagues often asked how long it took to write. My flip answer was "thirty-nine years" (my age at its publication), but I now realize how true that was. To know what I believe, to experiment with children, to launch ideas with teachers, to eliminate illogical ideas, to restart, rethink, reflect, and reorganize is, for me, the work of years. I have come to understand that all of that mind work (and field work), all the false starts, and the need to wrestle with the this-doesn't-matter-to-anyone-but-me demon are the texture, the struggle, that makes my thinking stronger, but my thinking certainly isn't formulated only when I sit at the keyboard. I find myself writing to discover what I know, think, believe, feel, and do.

I write to figure out what I think and what I have learned from working with children and their teachers. I reflect on times when children surprised me with the clarity and complexity of their thinking, trying to figure out *what they were doing, exactly, in their minds and lives, in order to think at that level*. And then I have to find the language to define and describe it so that other teachers can create the conditions for their students to do the same.

When I say that this book has been a struggle, I must emphasize that it has been, in no way, painful to write. I still feel great pleasure, bordering on joy, when I see new insights appear on the screen as my fingers move across the keyboard, and I've discovered that the joy is born directly of the struggle. If it wasn't difficult, would it be so gratifying? If I didn't have to battle self-doubt, would I be as careful with my words and ideas? I have come to realize that the challenging circumstances we humans are all too ready to avoid are their own greatest reward. I have learned that I savor the struggle and, though the timing may not match my own (or my poor, ever-patient publisher's) timeline, it is the way I learn.

Reading Reynolds Price convinces me I'm not alone. Price's epic struggle to survive and draw meaning potent enough to move forward each day is captured in his lengthy letter to a young medical student waging his own war with cancer. In *Letter to a Man in the Fire*, Price writes:

> The most nearly honest and hopeful guess I can make is that, if you survive this ordeal in working condition, you're almost certain to be a far more valuable medical doctor and person than you'd otherwise

have been. Poets more ancient than Aeschylus have hymned the awful paradox that humankind can apparently only advance through suffering but no one has cut that paradox in deeper letters than Aeschylus—

It is God's law that he who learns must suffer. And even in our sleep, pain that cannot forget falls drop by drop upon the heart, and in our own despite, against our will, comes wisdom to us by the awful grace of God. (p. 64)

I hope it goes without saying that I wish no one the suffering that Price and his correspondent endured; rather, in this chapter I wish to illuminate that from suffering or struggle come our most memorable insights, our enduring strength, and an increased capacity to empathize—surely all traits we wish for ourselves, our loved ones, and our students. From complexity can come simplicity, the courage to focus on what matters most.

In thinking about the children we serve and raise, our instinct is to free the path from obstacles, make their way clearer and easier. However, yielding to those instincts may not be in their best interests. We can manage, guide, define, and describe the intellectual challenges and the resultant learning we desire for them, but to limit their opportunities to learn through struggle is to tame one of the most dynamic forces in their intellectual development. We do so at our peril.

Chapter 6

A Renaissance of Understanding

MICHELANGELO (1475–1564), *SLAVE AWAKENING*, 1519–1536?
Reprinted with permission of Polo Museale Fiorentino.

MENTORS: THE THINKERS AND ARTISTS OF THE RENAISSANCE

Our heads were heavy with a jet-lag hangover when we arrived in Tuscany. On that day in 2003, we had flown from Denver to Chicago, Chicago to London, and London to Milan, then driven four hours from Milan to Greve, a village outside Florence. The day in which we began traveling had long since faded to black in the western United States; we weren't even sure what day it was in Italy, but there in the square, waiting for us at the prearranged time, sipping an Orangina and looking rested and refreshed, were my father, his wife, and her daughter. I couldn't help thinking how extraordinary it was that we could come halfway around the world on three planes and one automobile and end up in a tiny town square in an off-the-beaten-path area of Tuscany at the exact hour we were expected. I can't figure out a way to show up on time for dinner at a friend's house five blocks away.

My dad leapt from his spot in the shade and helped us unload the paraphernalia we'd dragged along for a ten-day trip to Italy. Elizabeth and I do not travel lightly. We have a family rule that you don't take what you cannot carry for the duration of the trip, but she has a build-big-biceps-and-endure-the-pain philosophy—one *does* need all those shoes, of course. And I had come with books—always a smart thing to pack for overseas travel—lots of books on Italy, the Renaissance, the great artists, the city of Florence, all in an effort to compensate for my underdeveloped knowledge of places distant in time and place from my own world. The overweight charge Alitalia airlines felt compelled to charge us on the return flight was the cause for a scene in the Milan airport that my family still refers to as "Mom goes postal," but that's another story.

The next day was my birthday, and I indulged myself in a little sermon to Elizabeth about how I was visiting Italy for the first time at forty-five and she was doing the same at fourteen. I wondered first if she understood how lucky, how unusual, how rare this experience was and, second, if she would be able to truly grasp the beauty, complexity, and profundity we were about to experience. I should have been far more concerned about my own ability to absorb it all.

We began our time in nearby Florence by visiting the Galleria dell' Accademia because my dad wanted us to see Michelangelo's *David*. As we approached the *David* by walking through a long gallery, my eye was drawn to my right where a series of Michelangelo's "unfinished" sculptures (reproduced here) lined the gallery wall. They were intended for the tomb of Pope Julius II, but were unfinished as other projects impinged on his monumental plans for the tomb. The original conception was to have three levels of sculpture in a freestanding structure, the lowest level of which was to include statues of military victory alternating with statues of slaves. Ultimately, only three (of the planned forty) of Michelangelo's sculptures came to grace the tomb, and it was the "unfinished" slave sculptures that caught my eye.

Elizabeth still tells the story of the day her mom stopped and "cried in front of the whole museum" as we paused to look at the sculptures. She can recall in painful detail how "off-the-charts embarrassing" it was. She is absolutely right. I was riveted to the sculptures and found futile each attempt to regain my composure. The family glanced at one another, shook their heads, moved away in tandem, and pretended to speak only Swedish when they saw me, but I could not stop the tears. I circled around the exquisite *David*, but went right back to the *Slave Awakening* and cried some more.

It took me hours to recover and years to understand my reaction that day—initially I wrote it off to jet lag—and any words I use to describe the sculptures would be inadequate at best, but I experienced a moment of insight that I will never forget. I won't pretend that I understood the sculptures the way Michelangelo intended, nor would I lay claim to an emotional or intellectual experience that millions before me haven't had; but for me, on that day, in those circumstances, I glimpsed a rare (for me!) insight about art, the aesthetic life, and my own passionate interests.

The image of the torment and strength in those sculptures is seared into my memory. Because they're "unfinished," the viewer sees the human figure literally tearing itself from its moorings in stone. The faces in each reveal, to me, the agony of indefinite confinement coupled with the unquenchable desire to be free. The viewer glimpses, simultaneously, the anguish of enslavement in stone, the irony that stone is so brutally unforgiving but yields such exquisite beauty, and the clarity of purpose oppressed peoples throughout the ages have exhibited. They also divulge Michelangelo's method as a sculptor. His wasn't a process of envisioning the end from the beginning—rather, he sensed what the stone held and worked to free it. That process seems universal for people engaged in creative work—art, writing, sculpting, dancing, learning—we sense what the (metaphorical) stone holds and work to release the meaning.

The sculptures and paintings I saw that day and in the days we spent in the Uffizi and the other Florentine museums told me more than all the books I schlepped to Italy. They spoke of humankind's yearning to be released, to be reborn, from the darker, more repressive time that was medieval European life—the stone.

I began to wonder what the Italian Renaissance had to say to me and to relate the Renaissance to my understanding of teaching and learning. I was fascinated by the notion of intellectual liberation, and I began to wonder what it means to be a Renaissance learner in the twenty-first century. I thought about those who taught the Renaissance thinkers. In what ways were Michelangelo and Leonardo da Vinci influenced by their teachers? But to understand the idea of the Renaissance, one has to understand the world that came before it. I went back to all those books and discovered how little I knew about the medieval and Renaissance periods.

Imagine living in a world dominated by suspicion, fear, xenophobia, and terror—where invention and discovery are severely limited by authorities more concerned with maintaining their power than bettering the lives of citizens. Medieval life in Europe was characterized by "a mélange of incessant warfare, corruption, lawlessness, obsession with strange myths, and an almost impenetrable mindlessness" according to William Manchester (1992), author of *A World Lit Only by Fire: The Medieval Mind and the Renaissance.*

Manchester describes a Western civilization in which the best minds were devoted to superfluous debate about doctrinal minutiae. Ordinary people were tortured and killed for disagreeing with church dogma, and discourse about ideas outside religious teaching was forbidden. The idea of introspection, of reflection on the state of one's society, or any thought of criticism of the state or the church was unthinkable for centuries. Historians largely agree that there was systematic repression of independent thought and individual autonomy that lasted the better part of a thousand years, from the sack of Rome (AD 410) to the fall of Constantinople (1453). I started to wonder if there isn't a little of the medieval in every era and couldn't help but feel the weight of that dogma and the centuries-long repression of ideas as a tragic waste of human potential.

Then, a curious confluence of world events—changes in Europe's economy and the emergence of a few people whose political power coincided with the flowering of ideas about returning to and perfecting ideas from ancient Greece and Rome—led to what we now think of as the Renaissance. I began to study, in my brief visit to Florence, the conditions necessary for sculpture and architecture to flower again.

We think of the Renaissance as a time when great thinkers revisited the progressive ideas of the Greeks and Romans but also as a more general rebirth of European culture, a rebirth into the light of ideas—among them, the intellectual movement known as humanism. Humanists believed (and believe) that humans hold nearly unlimited potential to invent, create, and solve problems. They believed that beauty is a divine gift, and they invested extraordinary resources in the creation of an aesthetically pleasing world of visual arts and ideas. They sought a more egalitarian society in which individuals from all social classes have access to ideas and autonomy in their beliefs and actions. The more I read about the humanists, the more I thought about teaching and learning today—*an egalitarian society in which individuals from all social classes have access to ideas and autonomy in their beliefs and actions.* Wasn't that the original ideal in American public education?

I was driven to read more about Renaissance thinkers after I returned home, and I learned that the ideals of humanism and the rebirth of the arts and invention didn't necessarily lead to a contented existence for the central players in the Renaissance. Michelangelo's lifelong personal torment may be reflected in the churning, agonized images we see in the slave sculptures. He was unceasingly and bitterly self-critical, torn between his devotion to the church and his perception that his own life fell far short of his religious ideals, ambivalent about his sexuality in light of church doctrine, and divided between a desire to complete projects and a chronically restless mind that longed to move on.

I am stunned by how strongly the twisting images of his fifteenth- and sixteenth-century sculptures echo our own ambivalence and conflicts. In these pieces we see the straining against oppression, the nearly impossible task of breaking free from the bonds of poverty, prejudice, and war. If these pieces have that kind of staying power, might the lessons learned from the Renaissance, and the repressive times that preceded it, shed light on today's schools?

DIMENSION: RENAISSANCE THINKING

- We become *Renaissance learners*—we're driven to explore a wide range of topics and interests, texts and genres. We work to understand how ideas are related, to see patterns. We become *passionately interested* in particular topics and ideas and are willing to expend considerable time and energy in seeking to understand them; we dig deeply to discover previously unknown facets of an idea.

We explored Florence in record heat and humidity, and as I took refuge from the heat in cool sanctuaries—museums, churches, and piazzas—I struggled to connect the idea of the Renaissance to contemporary schooling and children. I tried to understand what my emotional reactions to the sculpture and art might mean for teachers and children, in the context of American schools.

Slowly, images took shape—the face of a young child coming to school for the first time, consumed with curiosity. She bursts through the door of kindergarten each morning with another discovery, a story to tell, a treasure discovered on the way to school. She has endless questions and seems constantly distracted because every new object she encounters holds more interest than the last one. She sometimes feels frustrated because she can't yet grasp all her mind wants to know. She is a learning machine because nearly everything is new in her young life and no one has yet told her she should sit down and focus on only one task at a time.

Another image came into focus—an older child discovering a passion and becoming aware of how much of himself he is willing to devote to his growing obsession for science, a sport, the arts, or history. He experiences for the first time the delicious feeling that the more he knows, the more he knows how little he knows—surely the most intoxicating realization for someone who desperately wants to learn more. He shifts priorities to make it possible to pursue his passion. He becomes aware of how much more he is capable of than he ever believed—harder work, deeper insight, greater achievement. He is driven to get better.

Then, sadly, a third image came to mind—this time of a conversation among teachers of older students who lament the loss of children's curiosity and drive to learn. They describe kids who will work hard only for external incentives and wonder why they misbehave or have become sullen and disengaged. I have heard so many of these conversations, I've lost track. I even hear myself worrying, alongside colleagues, about the loss of intellectual fervor and curiosity as if there were nothing we could do to prevent that loss once it occurs. We blame it on the testing culture; we argue that we have so much content to cover we haven't time to let kids explore their interests or follow their questions into interesting research projects. We shrug our shoulders and give in to the inevitability of kids being more interested in social rather than academic engagements as they grow older. How different that image is from the one of the young child early in her school career.

As I wandered around Florence, considering these ideas for the first time, I began to wonder if the decline in that initial curiosity and energy for learning *must* be inevitable. I know that some students seem more likely to lose their interests and passions, but I also know that some never do. Why do those few retain the freshness of desire to learn? And, if a few do retain that intellectual fervor, might we study it to better understand how to help others do the same?

I know that children's development must include the processes of enculturation and socialization and that adolescents adapt their behavior to align with peer's norms and expectations. But I wonder how so many of us came to accept the conventional wisdom that children don't engage in social development *alongside* compelling academic interests. Might intellectual passions provide a focal point for kids who are otherwise floundering? Why don't we consider that option as our first defense against the uncertainty of adolescence? I wonder how we have come to feel so helpless in the face of children's changing bodies and social lives. I wonder why, too often, we decide we can't more actively intervene to prevent or reverse this phenomenon.

Can we model what it looks, sounds, feels, and tastes like to retain the spirit of curiosity and the passionate interest in a wide variety of topics with which children come to us? Would it be easier if we had the language to define and describe this kind of learning for kids? Is it beyond them? My experiences tell me it is not, and that kids are fascinated and deeply affected when they are introduced, not only to the players of the Renaissance, but, more important, to the kinds of thinking in which they engaged.

I find it ironic that, as a society, we claim to admire the qualities of Renaissance thinkers. Five hundred years after the Italian Renaissance, we refer to people with a wide range of interests as Renaissance people. We respect our friends and colleagues who can converse with a wide range of people on a variety of subjects and ideas. We regret that we don't possess more of those qualities.

But in schools, are we set up to create Renaissance kids? I worry that with schedules driven by different subject areas, curriculum created around tests, and a society that demands perfect completion of everything kids attempt, we are unwittingly contributing to the demise of the Renaissance person— creating our own medieval age. Renaissance thinking has to do with finding connections among disciplines, seeking the highest form of aesthetic expression, inventing new thinking, pursuing a wide range of interests, creating models to capture our thinking, speculating about the possible, and seeing almost unlimited potential in each person.

If we live in a society that values Renaissance thinking, but in schools that work against it, is it possible to help young children sustain and older kids rediscover the Renaissance person in themselves? Do all young children come to us with those qualities? Is it possible to devote time to the pursuit of pressing questions on a wide range of topics? Can we encourage kids to wonder, to pursue new ideas through their own discovery and research? And, if we decide that it is important to promote the notion of Renaissance learners, where do we begin, given the constraints of our professional and personal lives?

Michelangelo, Leonardo da Vinci, and their Renaissance contemporaries seem, from my brief study of this period, to have retained a very childlike curiosity throughout their lives. The questions they generated led them deeper into painting, sculpture, architecture, agriculture, poetry, engineering, politics, religion, medicine, music, rhetoric, and science. They read widely (given what was available) and kept copious notes related to their questions and speculations. They surrounded themselves with others who could enlighten and extend their thinking. They tested, experimented, drafted, sketched, and otherwise tried out ideas. They didn't finish everything—as a matter of fact, they finished far less than half of what they began, but they *worked* their ideas; they followed the big questions and tried to bring the answers to light.

In the context of recent education theory, researchers interested in inquiry-based learning (often science educators) and library media specialists have broken a trail in this area. They have long understood that when children have choice, when they are encouraged to pursue through research and inquiry a wide variety of topics interesting to them, they are more likely to be engaged and more likely to learn—to retain and reapply concepts. Theorists from Jerome Bruner and Howard Gardner to David Perkins, Ron Ritchhart, and Dennie Palmer Wolf have explored the role of questions (both teacher- and student-generated) and teachers' encouragement to pursue topics of great interest in providing multidisciplinary opportunities for students to learn at unprecedented levels.

Librarians work with teachers and students to facilitate the exploration of those questions and help learners grasp the relevance of their findings for the world. Kids pursuing their own questions often discover many other intriguing lines of thought to explore and realize that their interests are more far-reaching than they knew. These are not new ideas—I just don't hear about them much anymore. I wonder—should we rethink our priorities so we can reintroduce children to their own curiosity, passionate interests, and the means to pursue them?

I am not advocating an approach to teaching and learning that lacks standards and accountability; rather, I'm suggesting that we more appropriately balance our agenda with the students' in order to prevent the disengagement we so often see as kids grow older. I'm arguing that we may be perilously close to robbing children of the initiative and intellectual curiosity we hope will define their adult lives. My conclusion is that we aren't doing enough to create Renaissance thinkers—kids with the same qualities we value in adults—yet this goal is well within our control.

We may be constrained by the age-old notion that intellect is fixed at birth, and it's the one-in-ten-million child who has the genius of Michelangelo or da Vinci. That may be true of raw genius—some people are born into the world needing little encouragement to simply release their brilliance. But the children with whom I've worked have convinced me that the rest of us have an almost unlimited capacity to develop the curiosity, focus, productivity, insight, and originality we have long believed are characteristic of only a few. In my view, it is we teachers who can create the conditions and engage in the modeling necessary for children to experience and become intoxicated by the scope and power of their own minds.

What would it actually look like in today's classrooms, given their myriad demands, if we capitalized on what we know about the Renaissance? What can we do, whether on a large or small scale, to promote Renaissance thinking in the early years of the twenty-first century? I propose just a few ideas in Figure 6.1, with a promise to develop them more completely in the next section.

Fig. 6.1. Classrooms That Promote Renaissance Thinking

In a classroom for Renaissance learners, I suggest that children and adolescents would have an opportunity to

- generate, record, and reflect upon hundreds of their own questions—questions about the natural world, art, science, history, geography, animals, people, religion, society, and dozens of other topics

- propose direction for independent and group study, deciding which questions they want to follow

- refine and revise their questions through speculation, prediction, hypothesis, and frequent discussion with others

- abandon some (if not most) of their questions in order to pursue others in greater depth through research (formal and informal, text-based, Internet-based, interview-based)

- pursue topics that encompass several disciplines

- test ideas, revise their thinking, and work on projects that are relevant to them and applicable in the world

- share their understandings by teaching others using a variety of methods and media

- exercise choice in a wide variety of classroom situations—choosing which books to read, topics to write about, and questions to pursue; ways to share their thinking; and the timing and pacing for some assignments, especially research projects

- read and write about a wide variety of topics at varying levels of difficulty

- use art, music, and drama as well as written and oral means to articulate their thinking and emotions

- track changes and revisions in their thinking over time; discuss what led to those revisions

What if, in your classroom and the classrooms of, say, half a dozen colleagues, you experimented with some of these principles and generated your own ways to promote Renaissance learners? Suppose a group of children experienced "Renaissance" classrooms for even two or three years during their elementary, middle, or high school experience—what would become of those children?

Take a moment to imagine that small group of children as adults. I envision them as people who treasure the freedom to disagree, to challenge authority in a respectful way; who are unafraid to take risks that may lead to failures. I can foresee that they will be people willing to experiment and to constantly revise their thinking. Because they are still consumed by questions, they would continue to contribute to society and to the knowledge of their age. They would be the people who work in communities around the world to create conditions more conducive to the development of human potential. I have to wonder if they might, finally, become the generation that strives to ensure that all families have access to basic housing, health care, food, and education, and that the learning opportunities accessible to the advantaged are increasingly available to all. I see them as they become the people who apply original solutions and political tactics to broaden access to freedom of thought in this country and around the world.

What if your students, simply because you promoted the generation of questions and pursuit of ideas, grew up to apply their understandings to the most complex social and scientific problems of their age? Might these kids be the generation whose knowledge and insight lead to the inventions, entrepreneurial ventures, and aesthetic production that makes theirs the next Renaissance age?

Are you thinking that all of this is not our job? If not us, who? Do you want to be the one who says, "No, I don't have time for my kids to pursue their questions and interests because my agenda, the district's agenda, the state's agenda, is too important"? Are you thinking, "Well they have to have the skills down before they can tackle higher-level thinking"? Really? In twenty-five years of teaching, observing teachers, and reading literacy research, it is clear to me that the acquisition of basic skills occurs *simultaneously* with the development of intellectual interests when children are given an opportunity to control part of their learning—to generate questions, pursue topics of relevance, and engage in vigorous discussion.

I won't suggest that kids spend all day, every day posing and answering questions. I acknowledge, as I pointed out in Chapter 5, that there is essential content that must be taught. But I believe that, if we focus on the essential curriculum and carve out time for the preceding principles, our students may startle the world with their contributions. Those opportunities to question and study may be woven into the fabric of the existing curriculum or set aside as a time each week for students to explore, debate, and study—or, ideally, a combination of the two. I don't propose that there is a "right" way for teachers to create Renaissance learners—that would be oxymoronic—but I shudder to think that mine may be the generation of teachers who did not seize the opportunity to value and replicate what Renaissance thinkers once brought to the world.

I think back to the moment when I first saw, in Michelangelo's sculpture, the outline of a person straining to break free of the stone, and I can't help but relate that to our lives in teaching. Can we commit to liberating our children from the rote and routine, the drill and kill, the mind-numbing repetition that characterizes too many classrooms? Can we agree at least in part with the humanists of the Renaissance and proclaim that all of us have nearly unlimited capacity to produce original thought?

Literacy Essentials: Text and Genre Variety

To answer those questions in a practical way, let's return to your conversation with Tracy, who is still trying to pin down what your school and district consider essential content in literacy instruction. You tell her that your faculty has made a collective decision (I told you this was hypothetical!) that teachers should:

• focus instruction on a few important concepts

• teach them in depth over a long period of time

• permit students to apply these concepts in a variety of texts and contexts

You remind Tracy that you and your colleagues want to create a school-wide culture based on the principles of rigor, inquiry, and intimacy (discussed in Chapters 3 and 4) and focused on the six cognitive systems (described in Chapter 5). You are committed to providing the time necessary for students to learn and apply the skills and strategies known to promote development of those systems (see Appendix B, "What's Essential").

Tracy has another question. "That's an extraordinary commitment," she says, "and I really appreciate the clarity that provides. I need to ensure that I really understand all six of those systems and the skills and strategies kids need to use to demonstrate that they are using all six. I am beginning to understand my content focus in literacy, but now I have questions about the last element of your faculty's commitment—using a variety of text and contexts. I'm not at all sure what you mean by that. In my old district, we did extensive preassessment to find a kid's reading level and then tried to move each child progressively through the levels. We had a book room from which teachers could choose books for kids at their level, and that's what they read every week. How do you get the variety in?"

You (hypothetically) realize that you're not going to get your desk organized on this particular morning, and instead grab another cup of coffee and motion for her to join you at one of the students' tables.

"Well," you say, "we look at things a bit differently here. While we think it's important to assess each student's present performance level and to know where he or she can read comfortably for surface structure practice, a couple of basic premises do guide our own and our children's selection of materials and texts. We are big believers in variety—we want kids to be Renaissance learners, to have broad *and* deep experiences in a wide variety of text levels and genres."

You pull out your model, What's Essential for Literacy Learning (look back at Figure 2.3). You ask her to look at the third category, Text and Genre (shown again here as Figure 6.2). These two columns summarize what we know about the use of materials for particular purposes as well as the variety of genres needed to pique children's interests. And, of course, to promote Renaissance thinking!

Genre Variety and Genre Study

You explain to Tracy that the left column of the model includes many genres with which we hope students will become familiar at some point in their K–12 years. I have listed them in this particular order because of a survey I once saw (but have long since lost) in which ninth-grade English teachers from around the country were asked, "With what genres should your *incoming* ninth graders be adept, as readers and writers?" This list reflects their responses in descending order of priority. It surprised me that the ninth-grade English teachers have quite an extensive list of genres with which *incoming* students should be not only familiar, but adept as writers. I am certain that, as a classroom teacher and as a staff developer, I never came close to incorporating that kind of variety. It does rather beg the question, what do the ninth-grade English teachers plan to teach, but we'll leave that for another author and another time.

Their priorities also surprised me. They placed at the highest level of priority biographies, textbooks, and persuasion, and look at what is dead

Fig. 6.2. What's Essential for Literacy Learning

Text and Genre

Distinguish Among Genres	Use Different Level Texts for Different Purposes
Study genre characteristics; read and write in that genre	Vary the text difficulty depending on the task

Biography Historical fiction Textbooks Reference texts Web sites Persuasion Realistic fiction Poetry Memoir/autobiography Science fiction Mystery Journalism Opinion/editorial Tests Expository texts—narrative Picture books Photo essay Promotional materials/advertising Fantasy/science fiction	Work in instructional level text for: • practice in decoding • practice in word recognition • practice in oral reading fluency • practice in word analysis Work in more challenging texts (including read-alouds, wordless picture books, and texts that have been read aloud multiple times) for: • application of comprehension strategies • study of writer's tools • analysis of text structures • book club discussions • reading with a partner • learning new content (especially when there are text features such as graphs, charts, bold print, and/or familiar text structures)

last—the stuff lots of adolescents most like to read. Sorry, Harry Potter, J. R. R. Tolkien, et al.! And whatever led to the elevation of the biography? I like a good biography as much as the next person, but . . . top of the list?

Whatever the validity of this list and its particular order, it calls our attention to the fact that those who teach older children expect (I believe with some justification) their students to have experience with a wide range of genres before they get to high school—a much wider variety than has been common in our K–8 classrooms. I say that there is justification for their point of view for all the reasons I've discussed in this chapter. Human beings with a variety of questions and passionate interests won't be satisfied with a few types of text. When I consider my own reading habits—and I'm certainly not a Renaissance woman—it's very clear that without being fully conscious of the variety, I read a broad range of material.

For example, I always have a novel in progress, usually to share with my book club; I love travel writing, so I read travel essays, especially in the summer; in recent years, I have read widely about the artists and authors in the Mentors and Dimension sections of this book; I read several auto-biographies or biographies every year; I read professional journals, reports, reviews, and books; I subscribe to four magazines: *Newsweek*, the *New Republic*, *Real Simple*, and the *New Yorker*; I read the *Denver Post* when I'm home and the *New York Times* online every day; I read the poetry my daughter recommends as well as a lot of her writing; I've been known to buy *Vanity Fair* in an airport and chew through it as I criss-cross the country; I refer to Web sites for information almost daily; and I'm a rabid consumer of any gardening book. If you took time to list what you read every week, your own list would be similarly diverse. Our own daily reading fare is much broader than what we provide for children. That leaves me wondering—if we limit their exposure, how do we expect them to develop wide-ranging interests in many genres?

Sierra, a fifth grader in one of Trenton, New Jersey's, lowest-income schools, taught me a lesson I'll never forget about the inner Renaissance person we all have. I was conferring with the children in her class one morning and noticed that, as I moved closer to her, Sierra performed the old "switcheroo," a move with which, after twenty-five years of working in classrooms, I'm very familiar. The "switcheroo" occurred when Sierra swiftly slid the book she was reading into her desk and removed the book she was supposed to be reading. I smiled to myself and approached her, saying that I was curious what book just went into her desk. Sierra, looking a bit defensive, said, "I'm a Beverly Cleary reader." What?! I indicated that I didn't know what that was and she said, "Mrs. Johnston found out I can read Beverly Cleary and so she gave me seventeen." I must admit I was still a bit unclear until I realized that, in her zeal to match kids with books, Sierra's teacher had discovered that Sierra had read and enjoyed several Beverly Cleary titles and steered her toward the entire classroom selection of Beverly Cleary books—seventeen in all. "Mrs. Johnston wants me to read them all because she says I like them and they're a good level for me."

I began to understand exactly what happened, because I've done it myself. Upon discovering a "good match" between book and reader, Mrs. Johnston had suggested that Sierra dig into the rest of Cleary's books. I can almost see her thinking, "Whew—Sierra's taken care of for a while; now, let's see, who still needs new books to read?"

Still curious, I asked Sierra what book she had been reading when I approached. I couldn't believe what book had gone into her desk in the "switcheroo": *Little Women* by Louisa May Alcott. *Little Women.* I am not proud of the admission I'm about to make, but I was stunned that a fifth-grade African American child in a twenty-first century inner-city classroom had chosen to read a rather tattered and physically uninviting copy of the classic. It had probably been on the school's shelves for fifty years. I wish I could say that I showed great joy and enthusiasm, but giving in to my lowest reactions, I asked Sierra if she had seen the movie.

"What movie?" she asked.

Okay, I thought to myself. I wonder if she's really reading this book—if her teacher thinks that Beverly Cleary books are her speed, could she really be reading *Little Women*? I asked her to read aloud, which she did with fluency and virtually no word identification problems. You'd think I would have repressed my biases and doubts, but, shamefully, I went on. "Sierra, wow, you're a great reader in that book. Can you tell me now—what would someone who has never read that book really need to know to understand it? I know that, in your classroom, you've been studying the comprehension strategy determining importance. Are there ideas you think are important for a person to get a sense of what it's about?" I was assuming that she was reading the words (using surface structures well) but not comprehending (using the deep structures). Wrong again.

"Well, you should know that if Jo—she's one of the girls in the book; I know that sounds like a boy, but she's a girl—if Jo went to this school, she'd be in Dr. P's [the principal's] office about as much as I am. And"— here she took a deep breath and studied me—"I don't know you very well and I'm not sure if you get sad, but I think Beth—that's another sister—is about to die." Comprehending? I think so.

Sometimes I think my presuppositions about children should be grounds for malpractice. Maybe I should be forced into a career in retail sales. What business did I have to assume that this child wouldn't be interested in or capable of reading and understanding *Little Women*? It was disgraceful on my part. Sierra was embarrassed to have been "caught" reading a book that revealed her interest in times and places distant from her own. But the truth is that she "caught" us—her teacher and me—in assuming that her assessed level indicated that she should be reading only Beverly Cleary and that she wouldn't have an interest in the adventures of a group of sisters in mid-nineteenth-century New England. Shame on us. Sierra was a Renaissance kid. What were we doing to provide a variety of reading materials for her and the other Renaissance kids in her classroom? You can bet I have rethought my presuppositions and biases.

If we were to create a palette of reading options for the Renaissance children in that Trenton classroom, what would it look like? Such a library would certainly include selections from most, if not all, of the genres listed in Figure 6.1 and would encompass a range of levels, reaching both below and above the current performance levels of the children in our classrooms. It would be arranged in an inviting, accessible manner with many book covers face out, with abundant labels to quickly guide readers to the books they seek while making the range of options evident. There would be conspicuous places for readers to record their reactions and recommendations and a book of collected reviews written by children and teachers for other readers.

Our obligation to expose children to a variety of texts and reading materials goes beyond availability and accessibility. We need to *teach* as well as help children discover for themselves the qualities that characterize each genre, and we need to provide abundant opportunities for children to write in each genre.

In many of the schools in which I have worked, teachers create at least one genre study each quarter. During this time children can still choose what to read, but their choices are limited to the genre under study. Teachers design their own genre studies, but do so within a set of broad guidelines (see Figure 6.3).

I have found that, by adhering to these guidelines and ensuring variety in the genres studied each year, students became much more enthusiastic and engaged in reading a wider variety of books than they ever had.

Teachers with whom I've worked also found that they could "divide and conquer" genre study across the grade ranges K–2, 3–5, 6–8, and 9–12. Certainly children will read within the fiction, nonfiction, and poetic genres throughout each year, and there is nothing wrong with repeating any genre study in more difficult text—for example, studying biography several times across the elementary years in progressively more complex examples. But teams of teachers often decide to designate certain grades for the study of each genre in greater depth, ensuring that students would have instruction in all genres some time during their tenure at the school.

For example, some kindergarten through second-grade teachers decided to provide specific genre instruction in picture books; poetry; realistic and historical fiction; expository (narrative and didactic) writing; nurs-

Fig. 6.3. Genre Study Guidelines

Genre study focuses on the qualities and characteristics of a particular genre and includes abundant opportunities for children to read, study, and write in the genre.

1. *Qualities and characteristics:* Children should review several dozen examples of the genre, studying the physical and other characteristics sufficiently to generate a class list or rubric that reflects the qualities of the genre. This list should be revised throughout the genre study and, when completed, should include all the major physical and stylistic characteristics of the genre. Children should be invited to bring examples of the genre from home or the library. They may wish to create a genre "museum" containing examples and artifacts reflecting their study of the genre. The "museum" can be reworked throughout the study.

2. *Variety within the genre:* Children should read (not necessarily in their entirety) a range of examples of the genre, representing different periods and authors, and discuss (in small or large groups) the variety present within the genre.

3. *Focus on the purpose and audience:* Children should have an opportunity to discuss the range of purposes served by the genre. They may survey (rather than read in their entirety) several examples from the genre to discover the range of purpose and audience common within that genre.

4. *Focus on the author:* Children should discuss authors within the genre under study and, learning a bit about several, speculate on why that author became a writer within that genre and whether he/she wrote widely in any other genre.

5. *Exposure and discussion—reading:* Children should have many opportunities to read independently within the genre as well as to hear examples read aloud. They should read (and reread) in greater depth at least one (depending on the genre) example of the genre that is considered excellent—an award winner, a highly reviewed sample, etc. Rereading is the hallmark of effective genre study. Students should discuss their responses, opinions, and evidence of propaganda or bias, and create their own recommendations regularly throughout the genre study.

6. *Experimentation and revision—writing:* Children should create several (depending on the genre) written pieces that reflect the major qualities and characteristics of the genre. Each child should undertake revision and publication (for the classroom or beyond) of at least one piece. Revision is the hallmark of effective genre study. They may review peers' submissions using the list or rubric they've created (as described in the first guideline).

ery rhymes, fables, fairy tales, and folk tales; and fantasy. Similarly, intermediate-grade teachers decided to conduct in-depth genre studies in a wide range of nonfiction, historical and realistic fiction, autobiography/memoir, biography, photo essay, opinion/editorial, tests, mystery, myths, and fantasy during those three years. Middle and high school teachers can make similar choices to ensure that the variety of reading and writing expected of students extends to their secondary school experiences.

Genre study should be designed not only to expose students to a variety of texts and to prepare them to read effectively across genres and disciplines, but to help children find new passions as readers. I often see interest surveys and reading interviews in which students are asked to list their favorite book, genre, author, or topic (all singular). I applaud our efforts to get to know our students' preferences, but I think we're asking the wrong question. Instead, I'd like to ask children to list *all* the books, genres, authors, and topics (all plural) that have moved them or caused them to rethink their feelings, beliefs, values, and opinions. Authors write books to *change* us, not to help us become more like ourselves, and it takes more than one book, genre, author, or topic to help us rethink our most fundamental ideas and become Renaissance thinkers.

Let's return, for a moment, to your hypothetical colleague, Tracy. Her next question, after you have spoken so eloquently about your school's philosophy related to genre variety and study is, inevitably, "but what about reading programs or a basal?" You consider suggesting that a few glasses of a good Cabernet Sauvignon may be necessary for you to get into that one, but instead you tell her that teachers in your district often use selections from their school's basal readers. You tell her that, increasingly, reading programs include wonderful stories and nonfiction pieces, and that those selections are used routinely in the way that any literature or nonfiction selection might be used. You tell Tracy that the related materials (worksheets, teacher scripts, student activities, and centers) are rarely used because they take time away from students' independent reading and writing—the single most important component in any literacy "program."

The bottom line, you tell her, is that your district understands (we can dream, can't we?) that a well-informed teacher is worth all the programs ever invented to "standardize" reading instruction. A well-informed teacher, your district believes, understands the essential content, knows how to address that content with the most effective instructional strategies and models, and, most important, views children as individuals with unique learning needs and preferences. To that end, the district is making the necessary investments in professional learning to ensure that is true for all teachers. No program, with all its related materials, can ever replace that knowledgeable and compassionate teacher. No program, you tell her, has ever been written in accordance with your district's (Nirvana Unified) understanding about human learning: namely, that people learn (retain and reapply) most effectively when a *few important concepts* are taught in *in depth over a long period of time* and when students have an opportunity to *apply those concepts in a variety of texts and contexts.*

Level Variety

Tracy indicates that she is beginning to feel as if she has died and gone to heaven, but still has another question: "Okay, if you're not using a program, how do teachers figure out their students' reading levels?" Now here is the moment when I'm glad it's you and not me answering this hypothetical teacher's queries, because my somewhat irreverent sense of humor and disdain for authority has gotten me into trouble over the years. You think as I stare down fifty I'd learn to censor my thoughts a bit more effectively. I'll let you know if I ever learn to do that.

I was recently in a large southern state that shall remain nameless (I will, however, say that they sent their governor to the White House, where he still resides as of this writing) when I was asked a similar question. I was speaking to a smart, artful, talented group of teachers who expressed frustration over how "level happy" their districts had become, and I agreed, saying that I fully expected to find the billboards and traffic signs leveled next time I drove the roads of their fine state. "CAUTION! Don't Read This Unless You Are a Level 17!" Not so funny if you're teaching in one of the districts, now liberally sprinkled around the country, in which students are strictly restricted to reading books at their level. Let me say, again somewhat irreverently, that too much of a good thing is too much!

I fully support the need to have a clear idea of each child's current performance level in reading. I understand that if children consistently read texts that are too easy or too difficult for them, they may well become disinterested, frustrated, and disengaged. I understand that, too often, we teachers have not paid close enough attention to the level or quality of the books children read. However, I want to argue for a more moderate approach to book selection and especially to leveling, given its limitations.

Book levels are typically derived from two measurable elements in text—the number of syllables in at least one passage of a hundred words (to ascertain the average length of the words, presuming that longer words are more difficult) and the average number of sentences (to ascertain the syntactic complexity of the sentences—how long are they?). Some count the number of words in the passage that are above, at, and below "grade level," but the lists are, of course, someone's subjective decision about which words are "grade level." By definition, book leveling formulas can not account for a student's background knowledge about the topics addressed in the text, his/her interest in reading it, the level of support the child may receive while reading the text, the size of the print, the presence of graphics or photographs, whether the child has heard any of the text read aloud, the overall length of the text, or the child's familiarity (or lack thereof) with the genres.

You tell Tracy that your staff had concerns about placing so much faith in "accurate" reading levels for kids when the leveling formulas themselves leave so much out of the mix. "We've all known children who, because they were so determined, have read far more challenging pieces of text than their 'level' would indicate possible. And," you continue, "we've also seen kids who cruise along reading texts at their level and become disinterested because the vocabulary is so controlled. There have also been too many children who spend days struggling through books they cannot understand because they lack the surface structure skills to read them fluently."

You tell her that this presented a real dilemma for teachers in your school. As one teacher said (this was during a conversation on teaching the comprehension strategy questioning to young children), "It's pretty tough for kids to ask insightful questions about Mrs. Wishy Washy!" Point taken.

"However," you add, "we know that we don't want kids to flounder in text that is way too difficult or waste their time on text that is too easy for them." Your staff had to ask, What is the proper balance between having kids spend their independent reading time with a leveled text versus a book that they choose (with guidance)?

The What's Essential model (Figure 6.2) may provide a framework for answering this question. In it, I propose that there are several clear reasons for children to work in leveled (instructional or independent-level) text and other reasons for children to work in text of their own choosing, including text in which the ideas and some of the words may be a bit challenging for them. I propose here that, at any given time, students have books in their possession that address at least *two levels of challenge*: First, they have a book that is roughly at their instructional reading level and, second, they have a book they may find challenging, at least with respect to the ideas. Let's take a closer look at the right-hand column:

Use Different Level Texts for Different Purposes
Vary the text difficulty depending on the task

Work in instructional level text for:

- practice in decoding
- practice in word recognition
- practice in oral reading fluency
- practice in word analysis

Work in challenging texts (including read-
alouds, wordless picture books, and texts
that have been read aloud multiple times) for:

- application of comprehension strategies
- study of writer's tools
- analysis of text structures
- book club discussions
- reading with a partner
- learning new content (especially when
  there are text features such as graphs,
  charts, bold print, and/or familiar text structures)

With leveled text, students should practice word identification and oral (and silent) reading fluency. They can spend time (during composing, their independent reading time) identifying word families and spelling patterns and/or working on word analysis tasks such as understanding the role of prefixes and suffixes as well as word derivations. Leveled text (instructional and independent levels) is also appropriate for older students working with content for which they have little schema or an unfamiliar genre or text structure—for example, textbooks that include a great deal of content in a few pages or include few supports such as photographs, graphs, bold print, and so forth. Students in leveled texts are, in other words, exercising the three surface structure systems outlined in Chapter 5—the graphophonic, lexical, and syntactic systems. Leveled texts, generally speaking, are extremely useful for practicing the skills that promote development of the surface structure systems (see Appendix B, "What's Essential").

In addition, I also suggest that students work (during composing time) in a text that may be challenging for them. This *should be* a text that you have read aloud; it *may be* a text that is quite short or an excerpt from a longer piece and it may be challenging in several ways. Typically, when we think of books at children's "frustration" level, we imagine books that have many unfamiliar words, long, complex sentences, and densely packed information. This is not the type of text I have in mind when I suggest that kids should work in challenging text.

Books can be challenging because of the words or the *ideas*, and it is the latter I would like to see kids experience. In books that present interesting, relevant, provocative ideas, kids can work to apply comprehension strategies, engage in discourse with other students through book clubs or other forms of sharing, read more deeply in an area of great interest, and, in general, exercise their deep structure systems (semantic, schematic, and pragmatic). Children can read more challenging books when they have well-developed background knowledge for the topic and/or the genre and text structure.

More challenging texts are often read aloud to students—several times—before they're invited to tackle them. By that time, children are often so excited about the text topic or plot they can hardly wait to get their hands on the book. Moreover, because they are already familiar with the content, they don't have to struggle so much with unfamiliar words and lengthy sentences.

Seven-year-old Maria in Bridgeport, Connecticut, provided one of my earliest insights into this phenomenon and became a memorable example of the powerful use of more challenging text for deep structure purposes—entirely by accident. An English language learner, Maria had listened to her teacher, Delores, read *Our Gracie Aunt* by Jacqueline Woodson and been part of her classmates' demands that it be read again and again. One morning after the crafting session, she approached Delores and shyly asked if she could read *My Gracie Aunt* during composing that day. Delores and I exchanged a doubtful glance, but it was out of character for Maria to ask and I was inclined to trust her judgment. When Delores handed the book to Maria, I suggested that we watch her closely so we could suggest an alternative if she was overwhelmed by it. Delores was convinced that she would struggle with far more words than she did. We hovered around Maria, ostensibly conferring with other kids, but keeping an eye and ear in her direction. She was subvocalizing—reading the words with the exact inflection Delores had used when she read aloud. We smiled and looked back to hear Maria struggling with the word *Roy*, a last name of a character introduced on the first page. She tried the word several ways and then, growing impatient, skipped it and read on—an entirely appropriate move that would not interfere with her subsequent understanding of the story.

She blazed on through several pages, making a few relatively insignificant miscues. Delores was amazed. Then, Maria came upon the word *stiff* in a short sentence several pages into the book. It happens that this word is describing a child's reaction—both physical and emotional—to her aunt, and it's important to understanding the rest of the book. We very nearly intervened, but before we could, Maria turned to another child at her table (interestingly, it wasn't the child who was closest, but one who, according to Delores, was more likely to be able to help) and asked, "What's this?" The boy responded, "Stiff." Maria wasn't getting what she needed and said, "What's *this*?" with more urgency. "Oh, it's that she does that when she isn't sure about something—it looks like this [he demonstrated by making his body go stiff]. In this, she's not sure she's going to like her Gracie Aunt," the classmate told Maria before turning back to his own reading. Maria read on. We marveled at how she had known when to just skip a word she didn't know and when it was important to find out, not only how it was pronounced, but what it meant. Perhaps they are listening to us when we teach!

Not too much later, Maria tired and started to look around the room and thumb through a couple other books. Delores approached her and praised her for her stamina in reading *Our Gracie Aunt* as far as she had. She then redirected her to a text closer to her independent level with the promise that she could read *Our Gracie Aunt* any time she wished.

As we discussed the scenario later, we decided it might make sense to copy short excerpts from some of the books the kids were particularly excited about so that other children might spend some productive composing time in more challenging books. When introducing the idea to the children, we told them we had three governing ideas (we liked that better than rules) about reading "challenging books" and put them up on a chart:

1. Readers must have heard the book read aloud (by the teacher or on tape) at least three times before reading it or an excerpt of it during composing time.

2. Readers must confer with the teacher on the first or second day they spend reading the challenge book and should read in close proximity to another child who might be able to help.

3. Readers can't spend more than a part of two composing periods a week reading challenging texts.

In retrospect, I may have increased the time we designated on the last principle, given that, since Maria, I've seen so many children reading—and by reading, I mean using surface as well as deep structure systems—books their teachers would have thought impossible. Is it because they hear the text read aloud several times first? Is it because they're so motivated to read these tougher books that they're willing to stick with them longer? Is it because the content is intriguing and they are relieved to be reading to learn? I can't say for sure, and believe that these would make great questions for someone (maybe you?!) planning to do graduate-level research. I will say that the morning Maria taught us that kids could read more challenging text turned out to be a most happy accident!

Or maybe not. My husband, who recently taught himself to play the mandolin, said this upon hearing Maria's story: "It's like that in music, too. Sometimes when I'm trying to learn the simplest song on the mandolin, I just can't get it, but then I hear a much harder song and really want to play it and I just find that I can do it because I'm interested in it. Humans naturally set goals. It just seems self-evident to me. That's what people do." To which I replied, "Don't make so much sense; we're talking about schools!"

I've yet to read other theorists or teachers describing this practice, but I can recommend that teachers give it a try for some kids. Which ones? I worry, in particular, about three groups of children: young children who are still learning to decode and read fluently, children who struggle to read fluently at any grade level, and children who are learning English as their second language. Teachers of children who fit any of those descriptions may want to introduce more opportunities to read challenging books, including those significantly above their current performance level, to ensure that those children have variety in their weekly reading fare and a chance to read more interesting books. I suggest that teachers who try this tactic use some governing principles like those offered above. Too often, children in one of those three groups get "more of the same" in terms of the text they read independently day after day. I worry about the missed opportunities to introduce those children to the life of the mind. I am concerned that too many literacy studios may live up to the name only for some children—those we already expect to reach for more challenges.

Numerous books delve into the process of book selection far more comprehensively than I can do here. I try to keep three principles in mind, though, when helping kids make wise choices with respect to the books they read independently during composing.

1. Consider what makes a text truly readable (think beyond sentence length and vocabulary). Text is most readable when children have:

   - Schema for text content and author.
   - Schema for text format, print style, layout, density, illustrations, and graphs.
   - A comprehension strategy to help them extract more meaning from both narrative and expository text.
   - Prereading experiences such as read-alouds and/or discussion about the text content or format.
   - A need or desire to comprehend.
   - A history of and passion for reading.

2. Variety—in genres, authors, themes, and levels of text—is critical. (We want kids to develop a wide range of interests and a capacity to move seamlessly from genre to genre.)

- Children need to read in a variety of genres.
- Children need to read text that challenges them in different ways, in both surface and deep structure learning.
- Children can ensure variety by keeping track of their choices.

3. Teachers should provide explicit instruction to guide children in their book selections throughout the year. Keep in mind:

- High-quality text crossing a variety of genres and levels is essential for each reader.
- Children need to gradually assume responsibility for selecting appropriate texts, with continued teacher input about their selections throughout the year.
- Text sets (groups of related texts) help children make important connections between authors, themes, and genres.
- Modeling is critical—teachers need to model ways in which they select and recommend books.
- Children need to "field test" text—try a page or two, or a section; think aloud; use the five-finger rule (put a finger down if they come to a word they don't know or a confusing idea).

It is 5:30 and you've accomplished almost nothing you had intended to do in your classroom on this particularly steamy summer day, but you feel a curious sense of satisfaction. Having this conversation with Tracy has been stimulating—you've been talking about kids and learning and the ways your school and Nirvana Unified School District are organizing to make learning more likely and more lasting. Your new colleague is grateful, but more important, you realize how much you've enjoyed a conversation that is largely theoretical. You're intellectually engaged, talking about a model that is meant not only to synthesize research, but also to suggest specific instructional moves you and your colleague will make in the coming days, weeks, and months. As you schlep two huge bags of work to the car and drive home, you think about Renaissance kids—what that really means, and how you can create a classroom that promotes Renaissance learning. You wish you had had teachers with that priority when you were young. You think about the Renaissance people you have known.

DWELLING IN THE MIND

My father is a Renaissance man. Growing up with him taught me to value what I have called Renaissance thinking in this chapter. At seventy-seven, he has long since left his original career as an engineer and has thrown himself headlong into more projects and interests and topics than I can remember. A partial list would include skiing (he's thrilled because he can ski nearly free at his age and does, about thirty days a year); creating leaded glass windows (his home is filled with his designs); photography (he gets up at 4:30, heads to Rocky Mountain National Park, and photographs the sunrise); raising, training, and riding Tennessee Walkers (horses); developing commercial properties for start-up businesses; reading (everything from history texts to novels and religious writing to books on photography, Tennessee Walkers, leaded glass, etc.); traveling (last year, China, Hawaii, Mexico, Arizona, Seattle, Kansas, Wyoming, New Mexico; the year before, a four-continents-in-four-months cruise followed by Italy, France, and England); fishing—I could go on forever, and that's just what he's doing these days! Right now he can't decide whether he needs a pontoon boat. His wife thinks not—he nearly drowned fishing off an inner-tube five years ago. He remembers every detail about his childhood and youth and can have a group of twenty-five gasping for air, bent over in hysterical laughter with stories of his wild antics, driving without a license at thirteen—it goes on and on and on.

This list doesn't touch his interests in the last twenty years, including (to my great consternation) riding a motorcycle all over the United States, Mexico, and Europe. He sold that thing when he turned seventy and bought a Vespa that he uses to scoot all over his neighborhood and environs—that's when he's not riding a horse or driving the newest sports car he has decided he *has* to have. His interests aren't always scholarly but they're all-consuming—he gets an idea in his head about something he wants to experience and he'll make it happen, come hell or high water. He's a wild man—he's a Renaissance man, and I can think of no one I've admired more. He doesn't dabble; he dives into each passion as if studying, learning, getting good at each is the last thing he'll ever do.

My husband is also a Renaissance man. It's so troubling to him that small irritations like work get in the way of his other, more important interests. To name a few: coaching soccer (it doesn't matter how old the kids are—this year he has eight-year-olds); kayaking (rapids on the Colorado River and that flipping thing they have to do); learning to play the mandolin (the beginning was painful, but we got through that); traipsing around to bluegrass music festivals and concerts; painting (how he would have liked to earn a living doing that!); remembering with a ferocious accuracy every single sports statistic ever created (or so it seems to me); skiing (our second date was to ski and he left me in the dust—or should I say powder—as he bounced through the moguls at an insane speed); running (he ran his last marathon at forty-five); following politics and writing letters to numerous unsuspecting editors about their coverage; creating political comic books, which he distributes to our friends and family, whether they want them or not (the ones produced during the Bush/Quayle administration were titled *Quayludes*—it's a wonder he wasn't arrested); and of course, reading about all of the above.

I'm drawn to people who have an extraordinary range of interests, but more accurately, an insatiable curiosity. I'm fascinated by people who pursue their questions and interests to a degree others might call extreme, only to move on and follow another question obsessively. I find these people compelling—I'm interested in their lives, in what motivates them, and I wish I were more like them. I've come to believe that true understanding may come chiefly from doggedly pursuing answers to one's own gripping questions. Those questions needn't be the philosophical, scholarly, or artistic quests we think of when we read about Renaissance thinkers; they may just be how to get the best sunrise shot of the elk above timberline, why someone thought to preserve a spot for an urban garden, or how to play the mandolin with aching sweetness.

I worry about people in our profession, including myself, who give so much of their lives to teaching and the vast amount of preparation it requires. I fear we don't allow ourselves to have Renaissance lives, given that so much of our time is devoted to kids. I wonder if we wouldn't be more effective teachers, not to mention more interesting people, if we had a different set of priorities for our time outside of school. I see teachers lugging bags of work out of school at 5:30 each night and hear principals bragging about how early their teachers report to school and how late they stay—as if that were a badge of honor. I can't help but wonder if we might bring more to our children's lives by leaving the bags at school and living more fully in the world.

No one reading this book doubts the power of schema in helping children understand ever more complex ideas. We breathe a sigh of relief when someone raises a hand to share an experience his family had on an Indian reservation or describe what she saw under her home microscope.

We are thrilled when excited students share their discoveries from reading nonfiction, and we ask the child whose parents took her to Williamsburg for spring break to share what it's like to live in colonial times. We work tirelessly to help children who don't have background knowledge for a topic build it through experiences and reading. Have we paused to consider how to build our own schema?

I have no doubt that students' lives would be enriched by interacting with teachers who study art, visit museums, travel, read something other than children's literature and the papers they're grading, attend sporting events, garden, ski, write books, play the piano, act in theater productions, volunteer in their communities, explore genealogy, paint, fish, get involved in politics, quilt, ride motorcycles and bicycles all over the world, hike in the hills and along the beaches, read more broadly and tackle more challenging texts, spend time thinking about all of the aforementioned and, most important, *talk to kids about it.*

I know many teachers who live full lives outside school, and I am concerned about the price they pay. Schools and districts do anything but encourage teachers to be well-rounded people, and I wonder about the ultimate effect on them. We lose colleagues in our profession because they feel too constrained by time and bureaucratic demands, by the amount of effort it takes to meet administrators' and parents' expectations. We create so many school- and district-based professional learning experiences that we are unwittingly robbing people of time to spend observing and learning in the world—observations that could so easily come back to the kids.

I worry too about the effect on children. Do they have an opportunity to learn about Renaissance thinkers by interacting with people who indulge a wide range of interests? Do they have models who inspire them to pursue their passions? Are they encouraged to pose and follow questions, both quirky and profound, by teachers who have sought answers to their own quirky and profound questions?

There are dozens of books about how adults can learn to think like Leonardo or tap into the creative spirit of Mozart (see the bibliography). To me, though, the best guide for our own Renaissance explorations isn't a how-to manual with a list of "try this" activities. The best guide is to turn quietly inward and listen to the questions you've pondered for years. The best guide is to pay attention to what grabs you, what makes your spirit soar, perhaps what makes you cry in a museum, sending your family scurrying away, pretending to speak Swedish.

I wish I could declare that I am such a Renaissance person. I fall into the trap of believing that I will practice the piano more, and take courses in art history and wine tasting when things slow down in my life. The truth is that I hope things don't slow down too much—I thrive on the energy it takes to work with teachers and children. But if I wait, if we all wait to live Renaissance lives, we may wait too long. We may rob the children we serve now of a glimpse into the life of a curious adult who exhibits a bit of the Leonardo.

Tonight, as you wait for sleep to overtake you, take just a moment to listen in the quiet for the questions you would love to follow. Indulge yourself in imagining what you would do if you had two weeks, no restrictions, and a burning question. Then in the more practical light of day, find a way to *really* pursue that question.

And when you do, tell your kids about your journey and ask them about their burning questions. Focus your instruction on what's essential, because that will give you the time to let them explore those questions. When you start to worry that you're not doing what your district demands, think about Michelangelo. Imagine the form of a slave straining away from the stone and feel confident in the knowledge that children need to strain away from the stone as well. If you can't quell the worry, focus on the idea that you may be teaching students who are now infused with the desire to understand, who will give birth to the world's next Renaissance. Not bad, for a day's work.

Chapter 7

Nothing as Certain as Change

It is good, at certain hours of the day and night, to look closely at the world of objects at rest. Wheels that have crossed long, dusty distances with their mineral and vegetable burdens, sacks from the coal bins, barrels, and baskets, handles and hafts for the earth, like a text for all troubled lyricists. The used surfaces of things, the wear that the hands give to things, the air, tragic at times, pathetic at others, of such things—all lend a curious attractiveness to the reality of the world that should not be underprized.

In them one sees the confused impurity of the human condition, the massing of things, the use and disuse of substances, footprints and fingerprints, the abiding presence of the human engulfing all artifacts, inside and out.

Let that be the poetry we search for: worn with the hand's obligations, as by acids, steeped in sweat and in smoke, smelling of lilies and urine, spattered diversely by the trades that we live by, inside the law or beyond it.

A poetry impure as the clothing we wear, or our bodies, soup-stained, soiled with our shameful behavior, our wrinkles and vigils and dreams, observations and prophecies, declarations of loathing and love, idylls and beasts, the shocks of encounter, political loyalties, denials and doubts, affirmations and taxes.

The holy canons of madrigal, the mandates of touch, smell, taste, sight, hearing, the passion for justice, sexual desire, the sea sounding—willfully rejecting and accepting nothing: the deep penetration of things in the transports of love, a consummate poetry soiled by the pigeon's claw, ice-marked and tooth-marked, bitten delicately with our sweatdrops and usage, perhaps. Till the instrument so restlessly played yields us the comfort of its surfaces, and the woods show the knottiest suavities shaped by the pride of the tool. Blossom and water and wheat kernel share on precious consistency: the sumptuous appeal of the tactile.

Let no one forget them. Melancholy, old mawkishness impure and unflawed, fruits of a fabulous species lost to the memory, cast away in a frenzy's abandonment—moonlight, the swan in the gathering darkness, all hackneyed endearments: surely that is the poet's concern, essential and absolute.

Those who shun the "bad taste" of things will fall flat on the ice.

—*Pablo Neruda,* Memoirs

Flying east away from waning light, the sky partitions itself into three distinct layers of blue. We fly into ethereal bands of atmosphere that ascend from the deep gray cast of the earth to azure and indigo; before the song I'm listening to is complete, all three layers lose their contrast to the darkening hemisphere. I always request a window seat and this is why—I never tire of chasing those layers of fading light across this continent. Invariably, that view makes me wonder about similar skies in other times and places. Would a person flying over Western Australia in the last hours of day be witness to a similar demarcation of light thirty-five thousand feet above the barren earth? Did someone making a crossing of the Pacific in 1895 observe the same fading of day into night while crossing the international date line? Might someone bound by gravity on the plains of Tanzania in 1940 have lain on his back, his herd all around him, conscious of the earth and sky, and gazed through those same strata, wondering where the layers end?

I look up from reading the poet Pablo Neruda's *Memoirs* and once again see those layers of light from my airplane window. Tonight I wonder if it was possible that a young Chilean boy in the early part of the twentieth century might have looked skyward into those bands of light, in the newly cloudless sky following a long day of rain. Might he have wondered at the darkening sky above him and felt his first muse surround him in the vastness of the Chilean frontier? Might such a twilight sky have led to sixty-four years of poetry from Pablo Neruda?

Neruda gazed at Southern Hemisphere skies the way I gaze from my Northern Hemispheric perspective, thirty-five thousand feet up, one hundred years later. I have to wonder—is there a child staring today from the window of an airliner, miniscule in the immensity of sky as it makes its way across a continent, capturing in her notebook the contrasts she sees between sky and land, man and machine, word and paper? At this moment, are there children curled up under covers in cozy bedrooms, looking at the "world of objects at rest" and, like Neruda, writing to capture the simple beauty of their stories? Might there be a child huddled in a room with six or seven other family members struggling to hear the voice in her mind over the din of the world as she reads *Bridge to Terabithia* or *Where the Red Fern Grows*?

It was nature that sparked Neruda's earliest work. He writes:

I'll say this about the days and years of my childhood: the rain was the one unforgettable presence for me then. The great, southern rain, coming down like a waterfall from the Pole, from the skies of Cape Horn to the frontier. On this frontier, my country's Wild West, I first opened my eyes to life, the land, poetry and rain. (1977, p. 6)

In his *Memoirs*, trying to remember his first poem, Neruda writes:

I'll try to remember. Once, far back in my childhood, when I had barely learned to read, I felt an intense emotion and set down a few words, half rhymed, but strange to me, different from everyday language. Overcome by a deep anxiety, something I had not experienced before, a kind of anguish and sadness, I wrote them neatly on a piece of paper. (p. 20)

Neruda, whose mother died a month after his birth in 1904, would become a poet; political activist; Chilean consular to Burma, Ceylon, Djakarta, and Singapore; witness to the beginning of the Spanish Civil War; Chilean senator; ambassador to France; and winner of the 1971 Nobel Prize for Literature. He was, many would argue, the greatest poet of the twentieth century. He lived, according to poet and Neruda translator Alistair Reid, in an "entranced absorption in everything around him, natural and human. Neruda left behind him, like shed skins, a whole range of poetic manners, the sea changes in his life reflecting themselves in each new shift in his work" (Poirot 1990). His life was defined by change—both the transformations in his work and the changes he inspired in millions of others.

In 1948 Neruda, then a Chilean senator, published an open letter denouncing Chile's president and was forced into exile, first within Chile and later across the Andes into Argentina. Poems from this era of exile,

entitled "The Heights of Machu Picchu," are among Neruda's most celebrated works. He hoped these poems would give voice to the oppressed
people of Latin America. During this time he was obsessed with trans-
forming his poetry to make it more accessible to the masses. He created a
body of work that enlightened and informed workers and farmers, railroad men and those who lived in poverty in Latin America's sprawling
urban areas. He created what amounts to a new genre within poetry—a
genre sometimes more polemic than poetic that mobilized thousands in
the burgeoning Latin American Communist party. Whether we agree with
the aims of his writing or not, it is remarkable to look back at the power
of poetry in his hands—it was the power to mobilize hundreds of
thousands.

Neruda reinvented his life, his poetry, and his political views dozens of
times, but always anchored himself in the careful observation of the present and the everyday, as the unnamed essay at the beginning of this chapter illustrates. The son of a railroad conductor, he left his hometown in one
of the most remote areas of South America to enter the diplomatic services, but as one critic wrote of his extensive writing, "he has just gone on
exuding [poetry] as he draws breath." The contrasts in his poetry are as
stunning as the contrasts in his life. Neruda wrote the politically provocative and expansive *Spain in the Heart* during the Spanish Civil War, and
twenty years later penned four volumes of odes to ordinary things, including poems like "Ode to the Dog," "Ode to the Bed," and "Ode to the
Artichoke." The one constant in his poetry is his acute attention to
detail—he transforms the ordinary into the profound and, in so doing,
alters our way of seeing the world.

I can't remember how I learned about Neruda or when I first turned to
his poetry, but I do remember its impact on me. I was stunned at his trans-
formation of an object to which I'd never given two seconds' thought—a
spoon—into a vehicle that, in 224 words, instantly transported me from
an image of earliest man scooping water from a fresh stream, to a memory of my own child feeding herself for the first time, and then to a sear-
ing awareness of those the world has left starving.

Ode to the Spoon
    —Pablo Neruda

Spoon,
scoop
formed
by man's

most ancient hand,
in your design
of metal or of wood
we still see
the shape
of the first
palm
to which
water
imparted
coolness
and savage
blood,
the throb
of bonfires and the hunt.

Little
spoon
in an
infant's
tiny hand,
you raise
to his mouth
the earth's
most
ancient
kiss,
silent heritage
of the first water to sing
on lips that later lay
buried beneath the sand.

To this hollow space,
detached from the palm of our hand,
someone
added
a make-believe
arm,
and
spoons
started turning up

all over the world
in ever
more
perfect
form,
spoons made for
moving
between bowl and ruby-red lips
or flying
from thin soups
to hungry men's careless mouths.

Yes,
spoon:
at mankind's side
you have climbed
mountains,
swept down rivers,
populated ships and cities,
castles and kitchens:
but
the hard part of your life's journey
is to plunge
into the poor man's plate,
and into his mouth.

And so the coming
of the new life
that,
fighting and singing,
we preach,
will be a coming of soup bowls,
a perfect panoply
of spoons.
An ocean of steam rising from pots
in a world
without hunger,
and a total mobilization of spoons,
will shed light where once was darkness
shining on plates spread all over the table
like contented flowers.

Reading Neruda makes me pause in my unremarkable day-to-day existence and look out an airplane window—not only to see, but also to experience layers of light in the sky—and ponder others who, in distant places and times, might have done the same. Reading Neruda makes me aware of how much I miss as I run through airports or pick up the cleaning or walk the dogs. Reading Neruda makes me envious of the ability—or is it just a willingness?—to closely observe everything from a common object to a political movement and be changed.

Reading Neruda reminds me how much authors want their readers to be changed by what they pen. I can feel him wanting to define the changing landscape of his life; I can feel him hoping that his acute observations of the world will linger in the reader's mind and heart. I can feel the man who never lost a sense of wonder, who was ever malleable to the world's influences, who allowed himself to be deeply affected by a pair of scissors, a woman, oppression of the poor, or a well-worn banister. For some reason, I let Neruda in. I let him shape me. I let him change me and am glad for the alteration.

Neruda's poems change me, but I also see evidence that Neruda let the world change him—he wove the agony of Chile's political strife and Spain's Civil War into his poetry, adding dimensions and qualities I'm certain he never imagined as a young poet writing *Twenty Love Songs and a Poem of Despair* (1924/1993). When his friend and fellow poet Garcia Lorca was tracked down and murdered in Granada at the dawn of the Spanish Civil War, Neruda began to write of the anguish of oppressed peoples in Spain and Latin America in a way that would lead to his exile. As he aged, Neruda seemed not only to let the world seep into his poetry, but also to use his writing to awaken others—those who might not have been readers of poetry or activists in political conflicts. Change worked both ways with Neruda.

I wonder how much of the world we "let in." We have unprecedented access to information from nearly every corner of the world. When we see a broadcast from the Congo or hear of the oppression of the North Korean people, when we read of another suicide bombing in Iraq or Israel, are we changed? Are the changes visible? Do they incite us to act? When we write a check for earthquake relief in Pakistan, donate used clothes to a shelter, or volunteer in a soup kitchen, is it enough? Or do these actions merely ease our conscience, allowing us to return to our advantaged lives feeling we've made a contribution? Would anything we do ever be adequate? If we did more, would our own families be forced to sacrifice? Really, how much of the world can we bear to let in? Wouldn't it be easier to shut it out and remain unaffected—to tend our gardens, try to raise good kids, and teach well?

And what about invisible changes—the ones that happen within us quietly, in private? When we feel our pulse race while listening to an aria we have loved for years; find a character from a novel lingering in our minds long after we've finished the book; notice our father's hand, dotted with age spots and swollen with arthritis, and realize both his vulnerability and the inevitability of aging—do we let these experiences in? Do we allow them to affect us deeply?

I believe that the ways in which we answer these questions in our own lives affect the choices we make in the classroom. Do we explain to kids how the small, common things in life can affect us deeply? Do we share how we are touched by the world's beauty as well as its horrors? Is it possible to weave these observations into our already hectic school days? If I don't talk to children about how Pablo Neruda's writing impacts me in ways subtle and profound, how can I expect them to be similarly affected by the writers they love? If we neglect to talk to children about how *our feelings, beliefs, and knowledge change* over time and are influenced by forces in the world, how can they gain insight into what it means to understand? If we don't model ways in which our actions can be a force for positive change, how can we reasonably expect our students to mobilize their intellect and act to make changes in their world? Nothing is as certain as change, and nothing so fundamental to understanding.

DIMENSION: CHANGING OUR THINKING

- We manipulate our own thoughts to understand more completely—we *revise our thinking* by incorporating new knowledge, beliefs, and opinions. We can describe how our thinking has evolved over time, how books and other learning experiences have changed us. We *take action* to mitigate or resolve conflicts in our world.

What, then, does it look like, feel like, sound like, when teachers encourage children to consider changes in their thinking and ways in which they can cause others to change? When my coauthor, Susan Zimmermann, and I wrote *Mosaic of Thought* (1997, 2007), we were eager to describe a phenomenon we had observed in dozens of Colorado classrooms. Teachers we knew were deeply involved in providing explicit instruction in comprehension strategies, and we were delighted to see children energetically engaged in discussing books and ideas. Ten years later, we are among many researchers and practitioners (Block & Pressley 2002; Harvey & Goudvis 2000; Tovani 2000; Miller 2002) who have described the effect of explicit comprehension strategy instruction on students' understanding. In *Mosaic of Thought*, we recommended that teachers regularly "think aloud" about the cognitive strategies proficient readers use to leverage better understanding (see Appendix A, "Comprehension Strategies Defined").

I knew the news was good. I heard from teachers around the country and beyond that children are comprehending at a much higher level and are much more enthusiastic about reading when they use the strategies. This, I learned, is especially true for children who have been apathetic about reading and for those who struggle to comprehend. I was thrilled every time I watched the children we weren't used to hearing from—the "unusual suspects"—surprise everyone with insightful and perceptive comments in group discussions. And it wasn't only in the more advantaged schools I observed those unusual suspects rising to the challenge, but also in Cornerstone Initiative classrooms, which serve very low income neighborhoods in rural and urban communities.

I wish I'd recorded the number of times a child arrived at an insight or observation that represented a more far-reaching level of comprehension than I had imagined possible. This happened so many times, I finally realized it wasn't solely the use of comprehension strategies that elevated their understanding—it was defining and describing what the strategies allowed children to understand.

But as more teachers incorporated comprehension strategy instruction and as I encountered children like Jamika (Chapter 1) who pushed my thinking, I came to believe that we did not adequately describe the outcomes of using the strategies—what really happens when someone uses the strategies and achieves greater understanding?

Comprehension Strategies—The Tools to Change and Manipulate Thinking

On a warm February morning in the small Delta town of Greenwood, Mississippi, a group of fifth graders gathered around me as I reread Eve Bunting's extraordinary book *Smoky Night*, a class favorite the teacher had used to teach several comprehension strategies. The book tells the story of a boy driven from his home by fire during one of the Los Angeles riots following the Rodney King verdict and depicts the divisions between Korean and African American families living in the same neighborhood. My lesson was focused on the comprehension strategy determining importance, and initially I was struggling to get the children to say anything. Class sizes are very large in much of the South, particularly in very low income neighborhoods like the one served by this school. The children are often well-behaved and very oriented toward answering teachers' questions correctly, and this class was no exception. I had stopped to think aloud several times and was hoping to turn over some of the responsibility for determining importance to the children as I read further in the book.

In one think-aloud, I said I thought it was important for the reader to know that people in a riot sometimes act against their conscience—that they are swept up in the moment and do things they wouldn't ordinarily do. When I asked the children to share what *they* thought was important, I heard about half a dozen variations on exactly what I had said. I resolved to think aloud a few more times and emphasize how interested I was to hear ideas that differed from mine. After finishing the book, I again asked the children what they felt was important; they still essentially repeated what I had said. I sent them back to their tables to discuss in groups of three and four what they thought was important from the book. I moved around the room in my favorite role—eavesdropper.

I was hovering near LaQuisha's table, trying to appear like I was listening to another group, when I heard her say, "I think it's important to know why the people in the book got mad at each other in the first place. I don't know if they had slavery in California, but here we know why blacks and whites don't get along too good. It goes back to slavery. I think if you're going to get this book, you'd have to know why Koreans and blacks weren't getting along in the first place. Like why were they having fights *before* these riots, really before the book began?"

I must admit that, in the dozens of times I have read this book, I had never considered the *history* of the conflicts between the neighbors depicted in the story, and I couldn't help entering the conversation. I pulled up a chair and said, "LaQuisha, once you decided that it was important to know what led to the conflicts between the African Americans and Koreans in California, what did you understand that you didn't understand before?" She took a long moment to think about that one. Finally, she replied, "I guess it made me think that there are other reasons why races get upset with each other—before that I always thought they was always mad about slavery."

LaQuisha was describing a revision in her thinking. She took what she already knew and revised it to incorporate a new insight—a fundamentally important dimension of understanding. She capitalized on what she thought was important and used it to understand and empathize with the conflict—a fundamentally important outcome of understanding. As teachers, we need to analyze exactly how that happened so we can promote that kind of thinking for the rest of the class more often. If I examine the factors that permitted LaQuisha to change her thinking and understand in a new way, I come to several conclusions.

LaQuisha needed:

- several readings of the same text
- instruction on determining importance, which was provided through the think-aloud
- think-aloud examples that were fairly abstract and/or high level, not just related to the obvious main themes in the book
- time to think
- multiple examples of what a proficient reader believed was important in the text, with an explicit value placed on multiple interpretations and differing ideas about what was important
- time to think
- discussion with her peers, not just about the book, but about their *thinking* (determining importance) about the book
- certain background knowledge—in this case related to strained relations between races
- time to think
- someone to overhear her response and recognize her contribution to the rest of the class so that she and others would know what "a great response" really is
- someone to ask her what the idea she considered important led her to understand
- time to think
- someone to restate and amplify her words, permitting her to think and add more to her own thinking

Interestingly, it isn't only the adults who notice insightful and surprising responses like LaQuisha's. Other kids are watching as well. The students who are accustomed to having the right answers—the usual suspects, those who frequently raise their hands to enlighten everyone in the room—find themselves trying to stay one step ahead of the *un*usual suspects, whose comments may reveal facets in complex books they had never considered in their quest to produce the right answer. I have observed that when children notice this, they rush to join the conversation.

I want to capture and capitalize upon the resulting energy and engagement among students. I want to be able to provoke and promote it. How? It takes me back to the first question I posed in Chapter 1: What does it mean to understand? What are all the things we do when we truly understand, and how can we translate ordinary literacy lessons into those that lead to the kinds of responses we heard from LaQuisha?

I believe we can define, describe, and model what it means to understand—the dimensions and outcomes of understanding—for our students. What was the result of the lesson in the classroom in Greenwood, Mississippi, that morning? When LaQuisha came to understand that African American people were involved in racial conflicts that may have had little to do with the history of slavery in this country, she was using the strategy determining importance to *manipulate and change her thinking*, one of the dimensions of understanding. She used background knowledge to develop empathy for people in a conflict distant from her own experience, one of the outcomes of understanding (see Figure 2.2a). We literally saw her grow new knowledge and revise her beliefs and opinions—we watched her use a comprehension strategy to "let in" books and the world and to manipulate her thinking to accommodate the new information.

During the reflection session later that morning, I brought the kids back to the meeting area and, with LaQuisha, tried to explain that using the strategy wasn't the goal—understanding, in this case exemplified by changed thinking, was the goal. By using what she had been taught about determining importance, LaQuisha changed her thinking, just as Neruda and countless others have manipulated their thinking, changed their beliefs and opinions, incorporated new knowledge, and contributed new ideas to the world.

Pablo Neruda allowed himself to be shaped by everything from the simplest objects to the most complex political scenarios. So, too, the children like LaQuisha who surprise us with their insights are letting themselves be shaped by the books they read and the topics they study. They overcome, with time, preconceived notions about how to respond to books; they gradually stop trying to provide the right answer when it is broader thinking that is called for. By using comprehension strategies, they are actively manipulating their own thinking *in order* to understand more deeply. They are showing that understanding isn't a fixed element—you either get it or you don't—rather, understanding is an outcome that can be manipulated, altered, and improved by using comprehension strategies.

I think I could make a case that the mentors about whom I've written in these chapters used comprehension strategies as tools to understand more deeply, though they don't use those terms. Neruda, for example, *used vivid mental images* to write about a spoon. Van Gogh *questioned* conventional wisdom related to form, color, and light. Hopper *determined importance*, reducing his paintings to an essence from which viewers would need to *infer* far more than they viewed. Reynolds Price *synthesized*—his work evolved continually and was profoundly influenced by other scholars, his teaching, his students, his experience in managing cancer and paralysis, and his faith. The humanists of the Renaissance built on their *prior knowledge* of Greek thinking and philosophy to propose a new conception of human intellectual capacity. We could argue that the mentors used the strategies in order to understand as well as to create new knowledge, new thinking for their fields.

When we hear authors speak, no matter their genre or topic, a common theme emerges: Writers want their readers to be changed by what they have written. I hope, for example, that after reading this book you will walk away with a different perception of children's understanding and intellectual development. I want you to think about the fact that your teaching can actually make it possible for students to think at a higher level, and do so more consistently. I hope that by engaging in conversations with students about what it means to understand, you will all become more cognizant and intentional about demonstrating the characteristics I've called the dimensions and outcomes of understanding. *Of course* I want you to be changed by this book. Otherwise why would I submit myself to the torture—I mean stimulating mental exercise—of writing?!

When Patricia Polacco, Eve Bunting, Sharon Creech, and Gary Paulsen write fiction, they hope that young readers will put down their books deeply affected by the characters and conflicts they've created. When the staff at *Time for Kids* or *National Geographic World* write about current events or endangered species, they hope that kids will be moved to solve problems in their communities and beyond. When Georgia Heard, Ralph Fletcher, and Naomi Shihab Nye write poems for children, they hope kids will be moved to look at the world around them differently and write their own poetry.

I wonder—are we explicit with children about how the books we read change us, causing us to act, to read more, to write, or to change our previously held beliefs? Do we ask, "What happened at the end of Chapter 5?" or questions like these: "In what ways were you changed by this book? How will you approach people in your life differently because you read this book? Are you moved to take action, to make a difference in the world? How have you revised what you thought you believed and understood?" When we teach comprehension strategies, we need to say more than, "What do you think is important?" or "Did you have any connections to that book?" I hope we'll ask, "When you focused on what was important, how did that focus change your thinking? How did your beliefs and opinions change because of this book? What did this author do that you hope you can do as a writer?"

Earlier I listed the elements I believe were important to LaQuisha's process of understanding. Is it possible to design a classroom that is conducive to ongoing revision of thinking? What would characterize a classroom populated by children who discuss change and can describe their evolving beliefs and knowledge? Here's how I envision such a classroom:

- Teachers discuss books that have caused them to question and rethink what they know and believe, and how they act. They encourage children to choose books that will do the same for them.

- Teachers show how to reread selectively and demonstrate the power of rereading to affirm, amplify, or cause them to change their knowledge, beliefs, and opinions. They encourage children to practice rereading.

- Teachers think aloud to show changes in their thinking. They encourage children to use this language—"I used to think . . . but now I think"— in discussions and in written and artistic responses to books.

- Teachers describe circumstances in which books and ideas have caused them to change their thinking or take action to resolve a conflict in their lives; they encourage children to be open to similar changes.

- Children engage in frequent discussions about ideas and are invited to talk about how their thinking changed because of others' perspectives.

- Children use timelines and other written means to track the changes in their thinking between the beginning and end of a project or book.

- Teachers and students continually discuss different ways in which thinking can change over time, including emotions, beliefs and opinions, and background knowledge.

I am cognizant that most of these ideas, as well as many of the suggestions I make in this book, relate to our daily verbal interactions with children rather than the adoption of a new program or curriculum. Is the process of creating a more intellectually rigorous classroom, the process of promoting deeper understanding, merely a matter of what we say to kids? I don't think it's that simple, but what we say to children—our think-alouds, our modeling, the directions we give them to begin independent work—is certainly the most important element when it comes to making deeper understanding a routine occurrence.

Modeling and thinking aloud are the instructional staples, to be sure, but the way in which we send children off to independent work (composing) is critical as well. For example, instead of saying, "Today I want you and your group to decide what is important in this book," we can say, "Deciding what is important is a tool you and your group can use today to help you decide what it is about Eve Bunting's *Smoky Night* that caused you to think differently about people and the conflicts between them," or "Spend some time deciding what your group thought were the most important ideas in this book and then discuss how those important ideas changed things you thought you knew or believed" or "When you read your own books today, keep a double-entry journal and jot some of the important ideas in the left column. Then in the right column, jot some of the ways in which those important ideas changed what you think, feel, or believe about what happened in *Smoky Night*."

With any one of these simple changes, we can promote an entirely different level of insight and understanding. It isn't enough to just tell kids to think about how their thinking has changed, of course. Sending kids off to do that level of independent work is dependent on lots of modeling and thinking aloud in crafting sessions and invitational groups—we teach them how to think at high levels while asking them to do it on their own. But, it is critical to be conscious of and precise in sculpting our verbal expectations for children's independent work. If we want them to let the world in, to manipulate their thinking, to develop flexible and agile minds, we need to be explicit; we can't just tell them to change their ideas, but must show them exactly how proficient thinkers do so. I'll discuss, in much greater detail, the ways in which we can revise our verbal interactions with children in Chapter 8.

When Pablo Neruda wrote the essay with which I began this chapter, he could hardly have been more explicit in describing objects at rest in the waning hours of the day. "Wheels that have crossed long, dusty distances with their mineral and vegetable burdens, sacks from the coal bins, barrels, and baskets, handles and hafts for the earth, like a text for all troubled lyricists." I believe that he was making the mundane and the complex beautiful—giving explicit and lasting meaning to the objects and events of our everyday lives as well as the upheaval of political change. The gradations of sky at the close of day, Neruda's conception of a spoon, the Spanish Civil War, the oppression of the Chilean people—all have the power to change us if we allow it. We should ask ourselves these questions every day: Are we explicit with children about the power of text and ideas to change us? Do we model for them how we manipulate our thinking to reshape our existing ideas and accommodate new ones?

In the next section, I explore another set of tools we can share with children that, along with comprehension strategies, will help them to manipulate their thinking and to revise and reshape their existing knowledge to understand more deeply.

LITERACY ESSENTIALS: TEXT STRUCTURES

Let's return again to the ongoing conversation with your hypothetical new colleague, Tracy, with whom you've discussed the What's Essential model in Chapters 2 through 6. You've told her about your faculty's philosophy related to student learning, which holds that teachers should:

- focus instruction on a few important concepts

- teach them in depth over a long period of time

- permit students to apply those concepts in a variety of texts and contexts

Tracy has given your conversations a great deal of thought, and on the morning before kids return for the new school year, the two of you (who are quite chummy by now; I'm thinking of writing the two of you into the Great American Novel!) are seated next to each other trying to remain conscious during a faculty meeting. Tracy passes you a note. It reads: *Thanks so much for the great conversations the last couple of days. I've studied the What's Essential model and I think things are becoming clearer, but I'm not sure I understand some of the "text structure" objectives—can we talk later?*

Given that the faculty meeting agenda consists of fire safety procedures, new materials request forms, and a calendar for lounge cleaning duties on which you have somehow been assigned to every Friday, you seriously consider passing back a note that says: *How about right now?* Your professional persona takes over and you suggest that you resume your conversation at lunch.

At lunch you are joined by two of your intermediate colleagues, one of whom, Sam, has just returned to teach fifth grade after spending three years in middle school. As you introduce them to Tracy and bring them up to speed about your conversation so far, Sam is eager to share some concerns from his time in middle school.

"One of the reasons I wanted to come back to elementary," he says, "is to focus on kids' writing and try to address some of the problems I saw in seventh grade. The kids in this district really are showing the gains we expected when we started to focus our literacy instruction on the essential elements. But I haven't yet seen those gains transfer to writing as much as I had hoped. The kids' writing is sort of loose and unfocused and, honestly, I think they may be spending too much time at the elementary level on personal narrative and fiction writing. Their expository writing is very, very weak. They are weaker readers in expository text, too, and we spend a lot of time at the middle school trying to just get them excited to read nonfiction. I just have this feeling—and it comes from having a lot of experience in my own elementary teaching—that we're way more focused on narrative reading and writing than expository at the elementary level, and it really becomes apparent by the time they're in seventh and eighth grade."

"I'm sure that's true," you respond, because you've been worried about this issue as well. "The problem has been that we're not sure exactly how to address expository writing—or reading for that matter—at the elementary level. I think we're much more comfortable focusing our instruction on the cognitive strategies—the surface and deep structure systems—that Tracy and I have been talking about [see Chapter 5]. We've had great coaching and professional learning opportunities on the cognitive strategies—those skills and strategies we teach on an *ongoing* basis in our literacy studios—but we haven't talked much about the content we teach on an *intermittent basis,* like text structures."

"I've had another worry," interjects your colleague Jessica, who teaches fourth grade. "I have been astonished at how little the kids seem to retain and reapply from expository texts—even the well-written ones. Last spring, for our study of mammals, I assigned this great reading from *Time for Kids* on whales, and they were totally into it. They were excited and the discussion was great. But when we went back and I tried to get them to use some of the facts they'd learned from the article in their projects, it was like 'light's on, nobody's home'! They didn't retain or reuse any of the material from the article in their projects, and I don't know what to do about that. It's like it didn't get *in* somehow."

"You know, I've noticed the same thing," you tell them, "but I just thought it was about younger kids. It's like they don't change what they already know and believe to accommodate new information—isn't that Piagetian theory? Assimilation and accommodation?" Your colleagues look stunned, again, at your brilliance. "We've got to figure out how to help kids retain and reapply more of what they learn from expository text. It's like they don't manipulate their thinking to understand more and they don't modify their existing knowledge to take new stuff in."

It's time to go to your next meeting, but you see no reason not to linger in this conversation. The afternoon's back-to-school agenda includes a scintillating session on how to complete health care forms, so you and your colleagues decide to ditch that one to continue your discussion. Sometimes, you decide, a little civil disobedience is a healthy thing! You also realize Sam may have more knowledge about expository reading and writing and you are eager to pick his brain.

When the group takes a look at the What's Essential model (Figure 2.3) you realize that the area of concern is the fourth category—Text Structures. You notice aloud that the Cognitive Strategies segment of the model (Figure 2.3b), under the syntactic system, has a cross-reference to text structures. Tracy says, "Perfect! This is what I wanted to ask you all about. Why is that? Why is the Text Structures category related to the syntactic system?" (See discussion of the syntactic system in Chapter 5.) "And, if we're supposed to teach text structures, why aren't they part of the Cognitive Strategies category?" You realize that you've never given that a whole lot of thought and decide this new Tracy is on the ball!

Let's take a closer look at the final category in the model, repeated in Figure 7.1.

Text Structures

In the What's Essential model, I've set text structures as a separate category because they are not necessarily part of everyday instruction, whereas cognitive strategies instruction is ongoing throughout a child's K–12 experience (with the exception of the graphophonic system—see the discussion in Chapter 5). Instead, teachers can provide very effective instruction by setting aside a week or so every quarter to focus modeling and think-aloud lessons on various aspects of text structures, with the clear expectation that children apply their understanding of text structures in composing (independent reading and writing).

Text structure instruction helps children understand the infrastructure of texts across all genres. Imagine walking past a house under construction that has only the framing in place, with its beams and wood slats defining the rooms before the drywall goes in. That image may explain in part the role text structure plays in giving both narrative and expository text form

Fig. 7.1. What's Essential for Literacy Learning
Text Structures

**Students Can Recognize and Use
Narrative Text Structures (whole text)**

Character
Setting
Conflict
Plot structure

- character, setting, conflict, rising action, climax, sequence of events, resolution

Narrative Writing Technique

Develop characters, setting, and conflict through:

- exposition
- action
- dialogue

Create believable characters, settings, conflicts and events through use of writer's tools and voice, including

- foreshadowing
- parallel plot structures
- flashback and fast forward

Effective use of:

- word choice
- diction
- phrasing

**Students Can Recognize and Use
Expository Text Structures (paragraph/section)**

Cause/effect
Compare/contrast
Chronological
Problem/solution
Descriptive
Enumerative

Hurdles for Readers of Expository Texts

Word hurdles

- anaphora
- vocabulary load

Text hurdles

- insufficient schema for content and/or text structures
- inefficient predicting
- naïve conceptions
- staccato reading
- concept load
- pacing demands

Expository Writing Technique

Elaborate/develop and group ideas/themes
Organize ideas with a discernable, but not blatant, structure
Lay out and defend a position based on fact and/or opinion
Write to persuade based on fact and/or opinion
Write compelling leads and conclusions

and shape. The rooms in the house will be shaped and defined by that framing, though eventually you won't be able to see it.

You can't technically "see" text structures as you read, but they form the contours the book will take. Proficient readers sense the shape of a text as they read further into it and are, therefore, able to make efficient predictions based on that sense. In our house construction example, one can guess that if a person is walking from the dining room into another room, it is more likely to be the kitchen than a bedroom, based on a typical home layout. In narrative texts, we can reasonably predict that, following an introduction to the character and setting, we're likely to read about some conflicts. Though the reader doesn't "see" the text structure, he senses, almost "hears" it. Text structure instruction makes the invisible visible so readers can use the content and the structure of the text itself as a tool to enhance understanding, to manipulate their thinking, and revise their existing knowledge, beliefs, and feelings.

To answer Tracy's (very perceptive) question posed earlier: Text structures are a part of the syntactic system because they relate to how we use our "mind's ear" to "hear" when text fits together—when its structure is logical and *predictable*. Text structures are in place at the word, sentence, and whole-text level. Typically, in narrative text, we predict that we'll meet characters in some sort of setting, they'll encounter a conflict, and they'll work through a series of events to some type of resolution. We can predict based on our expectations of what we call "story grammar." But if a writer uses narrative techniques like flashback or fast forward, the changes in time may throw us off for a few moments—we're accustomed to a more chronological sequence of events. More complex plots make predicting just a bit tougher.

Syntax also provides predictable structure at the word and sentence levels. At the word level, for example, when a child says, "We runned around the playground at recess," you correct her because, though her mistake may be logical in terms of how words are typically translated to past tense, you *hear* that she is using the wrong verb form. At the sentence level, you may predict that the blank in this sentence will be filled by a noun: "We invented a new _____ at recess." The word you insert might be *game* because it "sounds like language" (is syntactically predictable) and is meaningful. In this chapter's discussion, we'll focus on structures at the whole-text level. (For a more complete discussion of word- and sentence-level syntax, see Chapter 5 and Appendix B, "What's Essential.")

Figure 7.1 shows the elements writers use to construct narrative and expository text in a way that makes it predictable and otherwise understandable. The first portion of the Narrative Text Structures column lists elements an author uses to create character and setting and to build the action gradually from the beginning of the text, following a plotline through the resolution, which generally is presented in the last pages of the book. That structure, which includes the traditional narrative text elements of character, setting, conflict, sequence of events (including rising action, climax, and denouement), and resolution, evolves over the course of the *whole text*.

Narrative Text Structures

Readers of narrative texts (all fiction genres, memoir, etc.) use their knowledge of these text elements to predict, not only what will occur next in the story, but to predict what *kinds of events and actions* are apt to occur at any particular stage in the story.

In American schools, we do a superb job of teaching children to use narrative text structures in reading and writing. From the earliest stages of their learning experience, children hear about characters and settings, conflicts and resolutions, and they are taught that good stories have a discernable beginning, middle, and end. As children progress through the grades, they are exposed to increasingly difficult examples of narrative text structures, including those with parallel plotlines (two story lines proceeding simultaneously) and flashbacks. Teachers continue to focus instruction on narrative text elements and to demonstrate how authors manipulate these elements for particular reasons and to achieve specific effects. Children are asked to apply what they know about narrative text structures in the stories and narrative pieces they write, which is wonderful practice. High-stakes test scores reflect this strong instruction; narrative text elements and structures show up in every state standards and curriculum document I've ever reviewed and, generally speaking, children perform well in tasks that call for reading (and predicting) narrative texts and for writing (in a cohesive, well-organized manner) in genres like fiction and memoir.

Expository Text Structures

When it comes to expository text, however, the story is much different. We do an inconsistent job, at best, teaching children to identify and predict using the infrastructure of expository text when they're reading, and we provide few experiences in applying their knowledge of expository text structures in writing. To use our housing construction example, when children read and write in expository text, some of the rooms are framed, some are not, some are only partly framed, and some of the framing is crooked! No wonder American students struggle to perform well on class assignments and high-stakes tests that involve expository text structures. I've observed that we teach expository text structures far less consistently and confidently than narrative text elements. With some fairly minor revisions, we could make a huge difference for a lot of kids!

One of the most confounding things for many readers is that expository text structures change frequently. While most narrative text structures evolve over the course of the entire book, expository text structures change at least every section. Expository writers may even change the text structure as frequently as every paragraph in order to address the content appropriately. This is especially true in textbooks, where a committee of writers attempts to squeeze as much content into the book as possible so any potential purchaser is likely to see his or her district's standards addressed. The quality of the writing tends to suffer under these conditions. Authors aren't given the luxury of developing a single idea in great depth over several pages. They find themselves forced to simply list concepts and ideas rather than discuss them, with the result that students have little opportunity to read well-developed passages about complex concepts.

Though it isn't within the scope of this book to synthesize the research on expository text structure instruction, well-known reading researchers Nell Duke and David Pearson (2006) do so and provide several very useful tools that can be used across the grade levels to familiarize students with expository text structures. They emphasize, in particular, that instruction in expository text structures should begin in kindergarten and continue through grades K–12 in progressively more complex text. They have found that students who receive explicit instruction in how expository text structures differ from narrative forms, exactly what those structures are, and how to identify them comprehend more than students who do not receive explicit instruction. Figure 7.2 provides a brief definition for each of the major expository paragraph structures and some "signal words" children can be taught to look for when reading expository text.

The scenario with respect to students' writing isn't any better. When we ask students to write expository pieces, we spend far too little time studying the craft of fine expository writers, looking for clues about how they write in an engaging and informative way. We tend not to teach students the text structures that underlie expository text, and the result is writing that rarely goes beyond a simple chronological summary, revised minimally from the original source the student used. The research is clear—we must incorporate explicit instruction in expository text

Fig. 7.2. Expository Text Structures—Definitions and Signal Words

Paragraph Structure	Definition	Signal Words
Descriptive	This is the most narrative of the expository text structures; it often begins with a key idea, then develops the concept using details, examples, and elaborations.	*For example, for instance, in particular, in addition*
Cause and effect	The text structure shows how one event or a series of events leads to another—sometimes the effect precedes the cause.	*Therefore, because of, led to, as a result of*
Compare/contrast	The text structure lists or describes similarities and differences between one or more objects, events, people, places, or ideas. It may take several paragraphs to list the traits of one idea before contrasting them with the traits of others.	*However, yet, though, although, similar to, different from, unlike, by contrast, like, whereas*
Problem/solution	The text structure defines a problem and lists one or more possible solutions; it may lead into cause and effect text structures.	(See cause and effect.)
Chronological	The text structure lays out the general order of events. These are not always presented in strict chronology, and the reader may be better off inferring the general sequence rather than memorizing the dates or specific order.	*Next, first, last, following, after, later*
Enumerative	The text structure presents a series of tasks to complete, often numbered, similar to a recipe. Science labs and math problems may be presented this way, and it may be critical to complete the tasks in the order listed.	*First, next, then, conclude, step 1*

structures into our literacy and content area courses if we want students to retain and reapply what they read in expository texts.

Children also face difficulties or hurdles unique to nonfiction texts. In Figure 7.3 I list some of the most challenging obstacles children face when reading expository text. Reading researchers refer to text that is laden with these kinds of obstacles "inconsiderate" text. It will be clear from a quick glance at the list, however, that the same text that is inconsiderate for some students (those with little schema, or prior knowledge, about the topic, for example) may be "considerate" for others (those with strong schema for the topic or expertise with this type of text).

Fig. 7.3. Expository Text Hurdles

Hurdle	Description	Example	Instruction
Word Level (hurdles found in words or phrases)			
Anaphora	Any word or phrase that refers to another word, phrase, or concept elsewhere in the text (sometimes as simple as a pronoun and antecedent, but often more subtle and therefore difficult to follow).	*4th grade social studies textbook:* "*Those* early hunters were descendants, or later relatives, of people who had come to North America by land from Asia." *Those* is an example of anaphora. Or, "You could not make *this trip* by land today." *This trip* is anaphoric.	Create transparencies of pages of expository text that contain anaphora, then begin by modeling your own awareness of anaphoric references in simple (pronoun) examples and move to more complex examples. Ask students to work in pairs to identify anaphora in short samples of text. Discuss what happens to comprehension if anaphora is missed. Discuss the need to reread and ensure clarity about anaphora.
Vocabulary load	The rapidity with which vocabulary likely to be new to the reader is introduced and the density of new vocabulary in a given passage.	*High school science textbook:* "Leaves consist of the *petitole*, or leaf stalk and the *blade*, a larger, usually flat part of the leaf. Notice [refers to a figure] that the leaf blade has veins and a midrib. The *midrib* is the large center vein from which all other leaf veins extend." This text defines several of the words in context, making it more *considerate* for readers without schema for this passage. Notice, however, that it does not define	Readers need instruction related to which vocabulary words are essential to remember and which are not—it is nearly impossible to learn all words introduced in a passage like this one. Model, on transparencies, how you decide which words are most important (often those in italics or that refer to a figure, graph, or photo). Discuss how you decide when to look a word up in the glossary or dictionary and when you can infer its meaning.

Fig. 7.3 continues on next page

Fig. 7.3. Expository Text Hurdles *(continued)*			
Hurdle	**Description**	**Example**	**Instruction**
		the word *vein*, which is used differently in this context than most readers would expect. One can imagine students visualizing a vein that carries blood, which would interfere with comprehension.	
Text Level (hurdles that may build over many paragraphs)			
Insufficient schema for text content/text structures	Lack of adequate background knowledge about the content itself and/or lack of adequate background knowledge about expository text structures (see Figure 2.3d)	*8th grade social studies text:* "In the late 1600's and early 1700's, England prized its cluster of colonies on the Atlantic coast of North America for two reasons: the colonies were suppliers of food and raw materials, such as tobacco, rice and lumber, and they were avid buyers of English goods." The reader would need some background knowledge on cause and effect text structures and/or on colonial trade with England in order to fully understand this passage.	Teaching children to identify all text structures is essential to enhance understanding of concept-laden passages such as this. It will also help to think aloud about how you determine what the text structure is in a given passage. If lack of schema for the content itself is the problem, you need to show how to build or create background knowledge through discussion with peers and/or "way-in" texts (see Figure 7.4).
Inefficient predicting	Lack of schema for text structures causes students to predict ineffectively, either because they are predicting as if they were reading narrative texts (looking for characters, settings,	*8th grade social studies text:* "By the late 1960's, the civil rights movement had fragmented into dozens of competing organizations with philosophies for reaching equality."	Thinking aloud is the most effective antidote when dealing with inefficient predicting. Think aloud for students based on the clues you pick up from the text structure itself. In this passage, for example,

Fig. 7.3. Expository Text Hurdles *(continued)*			
Hurdle	**Description**	**Example**	**Instruction**
	etc.) or because they stop predicting altogether.	A reader may predict that the next section will be about the 1970s *or* may imagine that "competing organizations" refer to businesses or sports teams.	you may want to predict based on the verb *fragmented*, which points out the problem in this problem/solution text structure.
Naive conception	A strongly held belief in something that is false, though it usually comes from an authority, either spoken or written.	A child in a class I observed heard an introduction to the phenomenon of a lunar eclipse and, relying on information his grandmother had told him about the four phases of the moon, asked his teacher, "Which moon is eclipsing tonight?" He struggled to understand that there was just one moon with many phases and continued to insist that there were four moons in orbit around the earth—his grandma had told him so!	Often the best person to "erase" a naive conception is not an authority (text or human), but a peer! Though the teacher in this example struggled to convince the child there was only one moon, it was a friend who finally dispelled the naïve conception. However, when text seems to directly contradict what they think is true, you can urge kids to consider the possibility that their belief is incorrect, and to either reread or check with someone to confirm or deny the belief.
Staccato reading	Text that requires the reader to transition rapidly from the text to a graph, figure, chart, or photo and then back to the text. Often children leave the text to refer to the figure, but don't return to the text and lose focus on the meaning.	*4th grade social studies textbook:* "But for millions of years only animals lived in North America. Then, about 12,000 years ago, some hunters arrived in what is now California. The *timeline on the next pages* shows how long ago that was."	Again, modeling is key. Show children, mark a paragraph with a sticky note, refer to something else in the book, then return to the beginning of the paragraph that demanded staccato reading. In that way, they can reread a short portion of the text to regain their focus.

Fig. 7.3 continues on next page

Fig. 7.3. Expository Text Hurdles *(continued)*

Hurdle	Description	Example	Instruction
		Any text that refers the reader to a timeline, graph, chart, figure, or photograph demands "staccato" reading. This example is particularly difficult as the sentences contain anaphora and ask the student to refer to a timeline that isn't on the same page.	
Concept load	The rapidity with which new concepts are introduced and the density of new concepts in a passage or chapter.	*9th grade biology text:* One paragraph from the introduction to a chapter: "Every chemical compound is either an organic compound or an inorganic compound. All organic compounds contain the element carbon. Most organic compounds occur naturally only in living organisms or in their products, although many of them can be produced in chemistry laboratories. In addition to carbon, most organic compounds contain hydrogen, and many contain either oxygen or nitrogen, or both. Less frequently, the elements phosphorus, sulfur, iron, calcium, sodium, chlorine, magnesium, and	In a relatively short paragraph, numerous concepts are introduced with very little exposition on any of them. The next paragraph does the same with inorganic compounds. In passages like these, teachers can use think-alouds to show readers how to focus on the most salient or important concepts— usually those that the reader must understand in order to comprehend the rest of the chapter. In this case, a focus on carbon as the only element found in all organic compounds seems most essential, followed by hydrogen, oxygen, and nitrogen, as

Fig. 7.3. Expository Text Hurdles *(continued)*			
Hurdle	**Description**	**Example**	**Instruction**
		potassium are found in organic compounds. Thus, of the 92 elements found in nature, only a few appear in organic compounds."	they are the next most common elements found in organic compounds.
Pacing demands	Text that, largely because of vocabulary and concept load, requires the reader to slow the pace of reading, reread frequently, take notes, highlight, or otherwise work with the text in order to understand.	Using the preceding passage, the reader may have to reread, subvocalize, discuss with another reader, take notes, or highlight only what's essential. Typically one has to read several sections in a text with dense concept load and then reread in order to know what is most important.	Modeling is key to show students how the pace and need for rereading is very different in expository text. Teachers should think aloud about how they decide what is important and synthesize as they read. These two comprehension strategies are among the most important in reading expository texts.

The solution to these kinds of challenges is very straightforward. We need to give at least as much instructional attention to expository text structures as we give to narrative text structures. A few key principles and a suggested timeline for annual instruction in expository text structures may be helpful, as outlined in Figure 7.4.

The afternoon has flown by and you're still hoping to get some work done. As you walk back to your classroom following the conversation with your colleagues, you resolve to focus at least three times a year for four or five days on expository text structures. It strikes you that, though you and your colleagues have been known to wring your hands over challenges in helping kids understand and write well in nonfiction, the number of crafting sessions you've devoted to expository texts has been very low. You realize that it is hardly fair to ask kids to retain and reapply content without teaching them the tools and the language proficient readers and writers use to manage it.

Fig. 7.4. Attending to the Demands of Expository Text

Key Principles

- Comprehending narrative text is a fundamentally different process than comprehending expository text—the reader must use different tactics and strategies in different types of text.

- Some expository text may be "inconsiderate" for some readers, depending on their schema for text content and structures. It is important for readers to determine which texts are inconsiderate for them.

- There are many different types of expository text—we should use inconsiderate text only after key concepts are understood. We can build a conceptual base from simpler, more narrative (way-in) texts and move to more didactic or textbook-like examples.

- There are far more concepts introduced in expository text than students can understand and remember; we need to help them focus on the most salient ideas and concepts.

Teaching Tactics

- Teach expository text structures explicitly. Use think-alouds to show how you use key words to identify text structures (see Figure 7.2) and how you predict based on the type of structure you are reading.

- Teach expository text hurdles explicitly. Use think-alouds and modeling to show how you identify hurdles and think aloud about two or three ways you can respond to each type of hurdle (see Figure 7.3).

- Activate and/or build schema for text content and structure; help children learn to do this independently.

- Teach children the actual terminology to define text structures and hurdles. We have found it extremely useful to teach children terms like anaphora and staccato reading rather than develop synonyms that may seem "easier" but frequently result in confusion as children progress through the grade levels and encounter other terminology that means the same thing. Teach children to seek their own way-in texts or to talk with more knowledgeable others as needed when they find they lack schema for text content or structure.

- Children should be accountable for showing that they understand expository text structures and hurdles. During composing time, confer and ask them to share examples in independent reading and writing where they have recognized and used expository text structures and hurdles to enhance understanding.

- Use way-in texts whenever possible, moving from narrative to expository selections. Way-in texts help to build schema before moving to more didactic text selections; they provide a "way in" to understanding more difficult text. They are typically shorter, written in a more narrative, considerate (containing fewer hurdles) style, and helpful for building background knowledge for a topic or text structure before students tackle a textbook or more difficult chapter or selection. It's a good idea to develop a library of way-in texts for frequently taught topics in science, math, and social studies.

Fig. 7.4. Attending to the Demands of Expository Text *(continued)*

- Think aloud, demonstrate, and model frequently in expository texts, emphasizing the different tactics you use in different types of texts.

- Help students understand and differentiate between text management strategies (such as rereading, slowing the pace of reading, highlighting, taking notes, etc.) and comprehension strategies. Both are important in comprehending expository text.

- Ask students to generate visual, artistic, spoken, written, and dramatic ways to "hold thinking." (See Appendix E, "Beyond Reporting on the Book."

- Focus strategy instruction on questioning, determining importance, and synthesizing. (See Appendix A, "Comprehension Strategies Defined.")

- Apply comprehension strategies from a variety of points of view; for example, a scientist, a musician, a social scientist, a librarian, a mathematician. (See Appendix F, "Thinking Strategies Proficient Learners Use.")

Frequency of Instruction

Hold crafting sessions focused on text structures and hurdles.

- Allow a week or so of instruction two to three times a year for primary students.

- Allow a week or so of instruction four times a year for intermediate-grade students.

- Allow a week or so of instruction four times a year in each subject area in middle and high school.

When we were students, we had to intuit how to use those tools, and we had little terminology to define and describe them. Many of us didn't really learn how to read complex text until college. Furthermore, many of us as teachers haven't had access to information about expository text structures and hurdles. Much of the relevant information for teachers is reported in research studies and syntheses that classroom teachers don't often read, and too few books have explored teaching implications related to expository reading and writing. We often ask children to use skills and strategies we haven't taught explicitly and forget that we're asking them to absorb far more than we were ever responsible for learning and remembering at their age. The great news is that we can teach children the tools readers use to make content more meaningful and memorable.

Teaching kids to read expository text differently than they read narrative text has staying power—these are tools they'll use long after they have left our classrooms and are called upon to read text and comprehend information we can't yet imagine. Learning expository text structures and hurdles also contributes to the various dimensions of understanding. These tools, like the comprehension strategies, are part of an array of tactics we want kids to carry forward as they absorb new information; change their thinking, beliefs, and behaviors; act on their new knowledge—and let the world in.

DWELLING IN THE MIND

I was in Isla Negra. In the house that was, that is, Pablo's.

All entry is forbidden, by court order. A wooden fence surrounds the house. On it, people write their messages to the poet. There is not a scrap of the wood not written on. They all address him as though he were alive. With pencils or nail-points, each and all of them find a particular way of saying Thank you.

I also, wordlessly found my way. I entered the house without entering. And in silence, we talked over wine, the poet and I, silently speaking of seas, of loves, of some infallible potion to cure baldness. We shared some shrimps in garlic, a huge crayfish pie, and other wonders of the kind that bring joy to the spirit and to the stomach, which are two names for the same thing, as Neruda well knows.

Several times we raised our glasses of good wine, and a sea wind touched our faces. It was all a ceremony to spite the dictatorship, the black shaft in his side, that mother-grief; and it was also a ceremony to celebrate life, beautiful and ephemeral as altars of flowers and passing loves.

—*Eduardo Galeano*

This short piece, written by Uruguayan essayist Eduardo Galeano, is part of a collection of photographs and writings about Neruda entitled *Pablo Neruda: Absence and Presence* (Poirot 2004). The photographs are of Neruda and his home in Isla Negra, Chile, a large, salt-air-worn house surrounded by a rickety white picket fence high above the Pacific. His writings accompany some of the photos, as do remembrances written by Galeano and others who knew him, photographed him, and read and translated his work. Authors like Galeano "knew" Neruda and the places he lived and died; in this piece he invites us into his imaginary, but very believable, conversation with the poet. He asks us along as he runs his fingers over the worn planks of the fence surrounding Neruda's island home, and he permits us to participate in the intimacy he shares with the object of his veneration. He causes us to wonder at the power this poet had to speak to people from every imaginable station in life and to understand how their lives were changed because they read his words.

After reading the essay the first time, years ago, I wrote in a cloth-covered notebook:

> I read this little piece, thinking of a human quality we share—I don't know how to label it, but know how often, from early childhood, we imagine ourselves interacting with those we most revere. As children we may envision ourselves rescuing, from certain disaster, our favorite literary or cartoon hero who thereafter becomes our most devoted companion.
>
> Later, we join fan clubs, read every word written about and go great distances to try to come face to face with our idols. In our most private moments, we allow ourselves to fantasize about interacting with them. We imagine sitting in the most distant seats in the concert arena indulging the wish that the star on the stage will suddenly be stunned by his inability to break the lock between his eyes and our own. Slowly, but with clear purpose, he will move from the stage, ascend the rafters and, as the thousands gathered stare in disbelief, he will finish the song, eyes locked with our own.
>
> Later in life, our minds may wander after someone at a cocktail party poses the question, "If you could have dinner with one person, living or dead, who would it be?" We've just declared that our dream dinner would be with Gandhi and we drift into a reverie about the conversation. We imagine that we are seated on rough benches at a simple wood table with no adornments and lean across the table, look into our dinner companion's eyes, and pose a question elegant in its simplicity. He responds, "I am quite astonished by your query." He pauses, shakes his head and says, "I have never been asked that question and you have caused me to rethink my most fundamental assumptions in life. I suspect your insights will influence my work for the rest of my life."

Isn't it that basic human emotion about which Galeano writes, imagining eating shrimp with the poet Neruda? Doesn't he imagine it with such ferocity that it seems it must, surely it must have happened? He knows himself to be different, a breed apart from those thousands who have scratched and penned messages to the now dead Neruda—killed by the dictator, cancer—in the planks of the fence surrounding his home. He has imagined himself on the literal and symbolic inside of the home on the Isla Negra with the poet engaged in conversation they both will remember for a lifetime.

But the poet is dying. The cancer is spreading, ravaging his frail body, and he knows the conversation with Galeano is among the last he'll have the strength to undertake. The pain, felt by Galeano as acutely as the poet, will separate them at the very birth of their relationship.

I read this piece and wrote the little sequence about it on an evening when I was supposed to be writing a proposal for a large grant. The proposal was due the next day and I knew it needed hours of attention before it would be ready. But the book beckoned, and after reading I was compelled to write about the piece—I didn't want to forget my thinking while I read it. I shoved my responsibility to the back of my mind, turned up the music, and sank into the words—Galeano's and my own. I don't regret it. The grant proposal got written, but I got my time with words and, these six years later, it is the latter I treasure. I go back to reread the essay and my notebook and have a greater understanding of Neruda, a person I had no idea I would be writing about all these years later. Every day we make decisions about how we'll use our time, and I wonder—what is most lasting, what deserves our focus in the few precious moments we spend alone each week? What do we "let in," what truly changes us, calls us to action, helps us to empathize? What kinds of effort will ultimately benefit our students most?

As diligent teachers, we grind on well after dismissal and into the night, completing the myriad tasks that demand our "immediate" attention. These hours are not without their rewards—our principals brag about their wonderful teachers who "stay late and come early," imagining that our tireless work will yield results for children. I long to hear a principal say, "I encourage teachers to leave at a reasonable hour and spend time relaxing with their own families, attending a concert or sporting event, listening to music, reading, writing in their journals, and living full, intellectually interesting lives. Ultimately, those who live interesting lives outside school will bring the most to their students. 'Working hard' for teachers must also mean working to develop their own intellectual passions."

We urge children to read fervently, scrutinizing the most complex and abstract elements of text, and are thrilled when they rise to the occasion. We want them to dwell in ideas, taking time in silence to reflect, reread, and reconsider what they thought they knew. We teach them to manipulate their own thinking, to explore a wide range of topics, interests, genres, and ideas. We teach them to how to study writers they admire for clues about how to write their own pieces more effectively, and celebrate their successes in extrapolating writer's tools to their own work. We teach them that there is value in the struggle itself. But are those dimensions of understanding part of our own lives? Do we walk our talk?

While we struggle to implement the most promising new theories and comply with new mandates, while we organize our lives to respond to the myriad demands teaching presents each week, I wonder—are we forgetting the source of our most innovative, enduring, and powerful ideas? Are we neglecting our own learning?

When we read and write for ourselves and talk to other adults about these experiences, we can seize the opportunity to manipulate our own thinking and to scrutinize the learning process—from within. When we make a conscious decision to read something we know will require our most clear-headed attention, something that will demand focused thought, we are making it possible to understand how children feel when they are similarly challenged. When we pause during reading to jot down a concept from a novel or an essay we believe has altered the way we think and believe, we are sinking into a deeper layer of comprehension than we would if we breezed through the reading without pausing. In these moments of introspection, we have a rare opportunity to consider the learning process—and particularly the dimension of understanding I've discussed in this chapter, how thinking changes over time. If we scrutinize and record our insights about our own learning, we are not only indulging our own intellectual passions, we are also planning for our students' learning. It's hard to imagine a more productive use of time.

In Galeano's imagined conversation with Neruda, I realized that the wish to be recognized and respected by someone we admire is a universal human quality. I became aware that Galeano described the intellectual intimacy he wished for with his colleague through a string of details so precise we feel we can smell the garlic shrimp and feel the salt air. We can hear the laughter of the poet and essayist and in so doing, we understand far greater truths about both—and about ourselves.

Capitalizing on insights from our own reading and writing ultimately permits us to take children on journeys into learning far more relevant to great reading and writing than the standard, prescribed skills. In this book, I've defined and described dimensions and outcomes of understanding I have experienced and observed, but they are not a definitive list, by any means. My fondest hope is that teachers read this book and, through their own intellectual explorations—in and outside of school—begin to develop their own dimensions and outcomes. I envision teachers having conversations with students about what really happens when a person understands. I hope to walk into classrooms around the country to see simple charts hanging on the walls that read, "To understand, we . . ." followed by a list of the ways those children and *their* teacher experience the process of understanding. I imagine that some of the dimensions and outcomes will overlap with mine, and that I will have the joy of learning, long after this book goes to press, about many more.

What am I suggesting in this chapter's Dwelling in the Mind section? We have thousands of demands on our time, but we need to pause and remember that the choices we make in our own learning lives have the potential to lead our children into much more in-depth learning and understanding. We can't always sideline the louder demands in our profession, but I would like to propose a way to gradually reclaim our own learning lives. If each of us were to set aside ninety minutes once a week that would have been spent on "schoolwork" and all that implies, and instead visit an art museum, attend a history lecture or a book signing, or simply sink into a favorite chair, relishing the gift of silence while we read, write, and listen to our own minds think, I imagine we would rediscover the joy of intellectual endeavor.

If we do, not only will we generate a very useful list of crafting sessions, we'll also build a bank of stories from our own learning experiences that, if shared with children, are likely to be remembered long after they leave our care. I believe it was Don Graves, the great writer, educator, and philosopher, who said, "Anything we ask children to do must be for us first." We must experience and analyze what we're asking children to complete in our classrooms and, perhaps more important, we must bring our own intellectual lives vividly into the classroom.

Chapter 8

The Great Conversations

MENTORS: MATISSE AND PICASSO

For someone who is never happier than when I'm in big cities, particularly New York, London, and Paris, this may be a surprising confession—I have a secret love, and it is Fort Worth, Texas. The people are wonderful, of course—it's Texas—but I've discovered that Fort Worth is also a little gem of an arts center. Art, music, beautiful parks—there are places and moments in Fort Worth where you could close your eyes and imagine that you're in Florence! Well, almost! I was invited by my friend Paula Miller to work with Fort Worth teachers in June of 1997 and discovered the Kimbell Art Museum and the Van Cliburn piano competition (held only once every four years).

That June, the Kimbell was hosting an exhibition called Monet and the Mediterranean, in which dozens of Monet's paintings executed in Venice and on the French and Italian Riviera were hung together. As a friend and I wandered through the galleries, the light emanating from Monet's paintings filled me with a kind of longing I found difficult to articulate. I only knew that I wanted everyone I loved to see those paintings, that I longed to watch the most important people in my life react to them, and that I wanted to discuss their reactions. My response baffled me—typically I want to view art alone and react to it in my mind; I am very reluctant to talk about it with others. Usually I cry at some point, and most acquaintances don't want to endure that!

I'm sure part of my reaction is that I don't want to reveal my relative ignorance about art, but I also feel that art museums are a little private gift I give myself, and my thoughts are typically restricted to my notebooks. Not so in this exhibit. When my friend and I left the exhibit, we walked in the park outside the Kimbell and couldn't stop talking about our responses. The conversation that ensued was one of the most intellectually interesting and memorable I've had about art and it enables me, to this day, to recall those paintings in my mind's eye.

Later that evening we attended the Van Cliburn piano competition in downtown Fort Worth and listened as John Nakamatsu took the gold medal. I was startled by the range of very physical reactions I had when listening intently to Rachmaninoff's Piano Concerto no. 2—from tears to a racing pulse to a lump in my throat. The beauty overwhelmed me, and the same kind of longing to talk I had experienced at the Kimbell overtook me.

After the piano competition, we discussed our reactions to the music and the art we had viewed earlier in the day, and I found myself feeling confident that I had something to say that might push our mutual understanding forward. I remember little of what we said, but a great deal about the understanding I had following our conversation. It was the interaction—one response building on another—that brought me to a new level of understanding for the music and for Monet—admittedly not a scholarly level, but one that enabled me to remember them.

At this moment, I can conjure the melodies in my mind. I can still see the light radiating off Monet's paintings. To this day, I can remember the energy and intensity of the discourse. I remember the intoxicating feeling that I was actually adding provocative elements to the dialogue that came, not necessarily from formal training in music or art, but from careful attention to the experience of viewing art and listening to music—of trying to understand it. My observations were breathing life into a spirited conversation. I realized that if I took the time to observe with care, I could discover facets of the art or the music that pushed the conversation forward. I didn't need a doctorate in art history or music theory, I needed to be fully present in the moment and to be willing to bring those observations to bear in subsequent discussions.

Slowly, I realized that these overpowering emotions were the seeds for this book. I began to understand that I wanted to write about teachers finding their own intellectual strength and the importance of communicating it to children. I mention personal intellectual strength because I have long worried that I'm not particularly well educated, and I suspect many others feel the same way. I question whether I have read the "right" books, internalized the principles of scientific thought, or understood the influences of ancient cultures. I began to think about other teachers I have known—beginning with my mother. I believe many of us have gone through periods in our lives where we have not felt particularly smart or adequately educated. In many ways the systems in which we work and the public's responses to us contribute to those feelings.

As I considered the possibility that I may not be alone in feeling less than intellectually powerful, I realized that if other teachers felt similarly, these phenomena could be very destructive in our classrooms. We all understand the power of adult modeling in children's lives. We know how children sense and understand even the most subtle verbal and nonverbal signals from adults. If we feel that our ideas are not powerful or valid, can we pretend that our children don't notice those reactions and begin to internalize them?

The experiences at the Kimbell and the Van Cliburn competition made me begin to feel that, though I might not be able to speak in a manner informed by years of scholarship, my responses were nonetheless legitimate, particularly if they sparked a dialogue that shed new light on the art or music. When we engage in dialogue about ideas, we are creating new knowledge. The volley between two minds with mutual interest isn't limited to sharing the known; when people engage in discourse, they are inventing new meaning, new interpretations that add a layer to earlier ideas.

Two years later I found myself back at the Kimbell in Fort Worth, this time with my friend Stephanie Harvey, author of *Nonfiction Matters* and coauthor of *Strategies That Work* and *The Comprehension Toolkit*. We had completed the first day of a two-day workshop for teachers and stole away to the Kimbell to see the exhibit Matisse and Picasso: A Gentle Rivalry. We learned that for decades, Henri Matisse and Pablo Picasso volleyed ideas back and forth in a dialogue that took several forms—written and oral discussion as well as a conversation that existed through their art. One painting answered another, again and again.

Matisse was the founder of the Fauvist movement, characterized by its vivid domination of color, and Picasso was the Cubist who believed that the essence of a subject could be depicted only by revealing it from multiple angles simultaneously. Though they represented different movements in early twentieth-century art and though Matisse was older than Picasso, they engaged in a dialogue that lasted nearly fifty years.

The dialogue went beyond each artist's influence on the other. In his book, *Matisse and Picasso*, Yves-Alain Bois (1998) argues that to characterize the artists' interactions as merely influencing one another is to limit the scope of their relationship. They were fiercely competitive and, at times, harshly critical of the other's work, but their creative output took on the qualities of a spoken dialogue in the form of paintings. In one of many examples, Matisse, in *Still Life with a Plaster Bust*, experimented with Picasso's Cubist style. Decades later, Picasso answered Matisse's *Still Life* with his own *Still Life: Bust, Bowl and Palette*. Bois argues that "Matisse's 1916 *Still Life with a Plaster Bust* was a move in a sequence of sharp exchanges, in a game of 'tit-for-tat' between the two painters" (p. 11). Theirs was a decades-long chess game in which their conversation spawned paintings that, without the conversation, would surely never have been painted.

There were also years of silence between the two and, as Bois explains, "in works of art as in personal conversations, a non-reply is itself a reply of sorts, if only a negative one: there are several stretches of time where Matisse and Picasso seem to ignore each other completely—even aggressively so" (p. 16). Rivalry fed the silences and competition fueled the conversation, but they always returned to dialogue. When one of the artists heard a critique of the other, he responded defensively—his own criticism was somehow tolerable, but he wouldn't endure critical words coming from someone outside the "dialogue." Matisse said, "Only one person has the right to criticize me, do you hear! It's Picasso."

In another of their conversations beginning with *Woman with Yellow Hair*, Picasso seems to be saying to Matisse, "You are not the first to experiment with bold swaths of color, nor will you be the last." Van Gogh had said, "Instead of trying to render what I see before me, I use color in a completely arbitrary way to express myself powerfully," and both artists build on his ideas. In fact, many art historians argue that it was Van Gogh who led Matisse to reconsider the use of color in the Fauvist movement. In *Woman with Yellow Hair* and in Matisse's response, *The Dream*, then, we experience a three-way dialogue between Van Gogh, Matisse, and Picasso that leads to some of the twentieth century's boldest and most surprising works. Matisse and Picasso frequently discussed their desire to stay away from abstractionism, but seem liberated by their dialogue to experiment with the outer boundaries of realism.

HENRI MATISSE (1869–1954), *STILL LIFE WITH A PLASTER BUST*, 1916.
Oil on canvas, 39³/₈ × 32 in.
Photograph © reproduced with the permission of The Barnes Foundation™. All Rights Reserved.

PABLO PICASSO (1881–1973), *STILL LIFE:*
BUST, BOWL, AND PALETTE, 1932.
Copyright © 2007 Estate of Pablo Picasso/Artists Rights
Society (ARS), New York.

As Matisse neared death, he remarked with a hint of nostalgia, "We must talk to each other as much as we can. When one of us dies, there will be some things the other will never be able to talk of with anyone else" (Bois 1998, p. 16).

As Steph and I meandered through the galleries trying to absorb the visual conversation between Matisse and Picasso, I thought about the implications for children and teachers. In learning, it is so often discourse that leads to understanding. We teachers understand that the more you talk with students about a concept, the better you understand it yourself. Their questions and insights influence how you explain the ideas. Students contribute new perspectives that forever change your point of view. This spirit of revision and rethinking characterized the conversation between Matisse and Picasso, and it continued even after Matisse's death in 1954, just as one child's comments can shape the way we teach long after the child has moved on. In Picasso's work through the late 1950s, according to Bois, "one can read Picasso's growing openness to Matisse's art, as if earlier caution were cast to the winds." (p. 17) Matisse was gone, but Picasso was still listening and the conversation was still playing out on his canvases. Our children move on, but their voices still echo in our minds and hearts.

What does awareness of the dialogue between Matisse and Picasso say to us as teachers? What can we learn from our own potent responses to the experiences we have outside school? I believe we can choose to be more fully aware as we move through the world. I love art, music, and books; you may have other passions. But either way, we can choose to let our passions and our observations outside the classroom influence our work with children.

PABLO PICASSO (1881–1973), *WOMAN WITH YELLOW HAIR*, 1931.
Copyright © 2007 Estate of Pablo Picasso/Artists Rights Society (ARS), New York.

We have a choice: We can stand back in awe at the products of Matisse and Picasso's conversation or we can put the energy of that discourse to work in our classrooms. We can turn over far more of the work of understanding to students, encouraging them to incorporate what they know and what they have closely observed into their daily dialogue. We can choose our words carefully, fully cognizant of the power they have to engender new thinking for children. We can let go of the nagging voices in our own minds that tell us we may not be well-educated enough and gather students around us to talk with them about our reactions to the light coming from a painting or the way a melody made us cry.

DIMENSION: ENGAGING IN DISCOURSE

- We engage in rigorous *discourse about ideas* and find we have more to say than we thought. We consider the perspectives of others and challenge them until we understand our own and others' opinions and principles; we surprise ourselves with the clarity of our own thinking.

Human history can be chronicled by studying discourse—what we accept as truth in the twenty-first century is a by-product of thousands of years of discussion and debate. Great conversations between Socrates, Plato, and Aristotle gave form and definition to thinking and knowing hundreds of years before the common era. These ancient conversations established the processes, such as challenging another's ideas to discover new insights, that countless others would use to more fully understand what they think

HENRI MATISSE (1869–1954), *THE DREAM*, 1940.
Copyright © 2007 Succession H. Matisse,
Paris/Artists Rights Society (ARS), New York.

and believe. Aristotle laid out the Lyceum in Athens in 335 BC so that he could walk through covered paths surrounded by his students, engaged in lectures and arguments. Today, university campuses all over the world have winding paths on which students and professors (at least theoretically!) can walk and converse.

I wonder if we acknowledge the need to discuss as a way to understand in our classrooms today. I have to laugh if I envision a third-grade teacher strolling the grounds of the local elementary school in long robes, pontificating as her students ply her with erudite questions. I am in no way suggesting that we channel Aristotle! But I do want to think about how classrooms might look if we fully acknowledged the role discourse can play in enhancing students' understanding.

Juliana and Sasha, seventh graders when I worked with their class in a suburb west of Chicago, provided a telling example of the power of conversation. I conducted a demonstration lesson focused on using mental images with the book *Elsie's War*, by Frank Dabba Smith. *Elsie's War* tells the story of Elsie Kuhn-Leitz, whose father owned the Leitz camera factory near Frankfurt. Elsie and her family undertook numerous humanitarian efforts throughout their lives and, out of a fierce sense of social justice and a disregard for the consequences for themselves, helped Jews escape Germany in the early years of Nazi power. The extraordinary black-and-white photographs accompanied by Smith's spare prose combine to make *Elsie's War* a book in which the greatest power comes from simplicity.

In the beginning of the lesson, with the students seated on the floor around me, I thought aloud about my own images several times. Then, as it became clear that they were beginning to form images, I asked the students to turn to the person sitting closest to them and share images that helped them better understand the text. Thank goodness for a video camera with a sensitive recording device in the right spot at the right time, or I would have missed Juliana and her partner Sasha's extraordinary conversation. It makes me wonder how many of these conversations I have missed over the years.

Sasha began. "On that last page, in my head, I could hear Elsie whispering to Hedwig—telling her the directions for getting across the border to Switzerland. I could see her lips moving close to Hedwig's ear."

"Cool," Juliana replied. "I couldn't see or hear anything." Sasha resumed talking again about her images. She talked about how she could see Hedwig walking over the Alps just like in *The Sound of Music*.

I read more of the book, thinking aloud several more times, and was delighted to be interrupted by a boy in the back of the group who said, "Ah, sorry, but could we just talk to each other again for a second because I don't want to forget this thing I'm thinking?"

You don't have to ask me twice!

Sasha began again. "When she read that page, I could just hear that big wooden prison door slamming shut with Elsie inside. I could even smell how completely gross the cell was." Here she provided some detail I've chosen to omit.

Juliana said, "Eww," or something to that effect.

There was a relatively long pause before Juliana picked up the ball and ran with it.

"Well, I was trying to figure out how just one woman like Elsie could help enough to really make any difference for, like, millions of Jews. I know this isn't an image. I just couldn't stop thinking about that though, and I knew there probably wouldn't be this whole book, like, written about her if she hadn't really helped a lot of people. So, I had no images."

"Isn't wondering that an image?" Sasha asked.

"I don't know, but then I started to try to picture, like, how many armies it would have taken to get six million Jews out of Germany and around there you know."

"That's an image!"

"Yeah, I know, and I started to see millions of army guys, you know, and then I could hear their boots on the pavement and just as I heard that, I started to hear just as many Nazi army boots, like, moving toward the good army guys."

"Then what?"

"Then I thought more about who all the armies were—I know that's not an image."

"Who cares?" Sasha said, and I couldn't agree with her more.

"I know there were Americans in Europe and stuff. I know they were fighting on the side of France and England and some other people I can't remember."

"Yeah, they were allies."

"Right, exactly, anyway, then I had another image. Here is what I saw. It was like a long, dark tunnel, or maybe more like a cave and just thousands and thousands of Jews were marching down it and instead of hearing big army boots, I sort of hear their feet just shuffling along because they knew they were going down to die. I could hear sighing and groaning and some prayers, you know."

"Cool."

"Yeah, you know I'm just making some of this up right now as I'm telling you, right?"

"Yeah, but that counts!" Sasha reassured her, and she was exactly right.

"Okay, I never would have thought this stuff if I wasn't talking to you, but now that I am I started to picture those army guys again."

"American and Allies or Nazi?" Sasha asked.

"Allies," Juliana replied.

I wish these two had been within the view of the camera, but it picked up only their voices. Here I picture Juliana looking up and away, working to develop her images.

Juliana continued. "Okay, so then in my image all the Allies' armies just get smaller and smaller."

"Like dwarfs or midgets?" Sasha asked.

"Well, not really, just shrinking because they weren't really powerful even though they were supposed to be. The Jews just keep walking into the tunnel-cave thing and these armies just keep shrinking."

"It makes me wonder why American armies didn't try harder to save the Jews, to, like, keep them from walking into that cave," Sasha queried.

"Yeah, like, where were they and why didn't they stop fighting the war and just help the people who were getting killed?" Juliana replied.

"Don't armies have to do that? Aren't they always supposed to help stop stuff like that? Isn't that why America was there in the first place?"

Unfortunately, that was the moment when I pulled the group back together to finish the lesson, which makes me wonder how many times in my career I've cut into a great moment of understanding. Nonetheless, there is enough to learn from. In a short lesson on images from a simple book, Juliana and Sasha built off Sasha's initial images to consider together an issue that has perplexed humankind for thousands of years: What happens when people with a clear understanding of the moral right are unable to stop the onslaught of those with malevolent intent? Juliana and Sasha were able to extrapolate from their images to build a shared understanding that ran much deeper than the book. They were grappling with issues that are woven into millennia of conflict among people. Their conversation led them to insights that would have been unlikely without the discourse.

In Chapter 2, I suggested that, instead of (or in addition to) regaling our friends and family with stories of kids like Juliana and Sasha, we take a moment to analyze and name exactly what is happening when a child understands. I said if we hope to help children think at high levels more often than the occasional "happy accident," we need to define and describe exactly what they are doing in the moment of understanding. I also believe we should analyze the conditions in the classroom at the time and try to replicate them as much as possible.

What conditions made Juliana and Sasha's conversation possible, and how can we recreate them? Figure 8.1 lists some general principles to help teachers create classrooms that encourage discourse.

I don't know this, but I imagine that Picasso's questions wakened Matisse in the middle of the night. I would guess that Matisse's superb integration of Cubism in *Still Life with a Plaster Bust* needled Picasso for years, causing him to consider techniques with brush and canvas he had not imagined. I can't help but speculate that their "gentle rivalry" provoked original thought and a level of productivity that would have been missing without it. They weren't exactly muses for each other—a muse implies a much less equivalent relationship, one in which the artist or writer is dependent on the muse for inspiration. Matisse and Picasso were more like sparring partners, wrangling with ideas that had never been considered by their peers. They provoked each other to express original thought.

Am I wrong to desire that kind of conversation for children in our schools? Is it misguided to believe that we can weave some of the qualities of the artists' fifty-year "gentle rivalry" into our classrooms? If you think I'm wrong, I'd like to discuss it with you—I'd like a chance to make my case, and to be influenced by your thinking and experience. If we don't argue about it a bit, how can we ever hope to understand?

Fig. 8.1. How to Create a Classroom That Encourages Discourse

- Think aloud in crafting sessions and invitational groups to reveal how proficient readers use comprehension strategies to enhance and amplify understanding.

- Use provocative, well-written texts for read-alouds as they lead to richer conversation.

- Model in crafting sessions and invitational groups by describing conversations that led to new insights. What did the dialogue lead the speakers to understand?

- Demonstrate in crafting sessions using a "fish bowl" technique—invite students to observe the conditions present in a conversation that leads to greater understanding.

- Confer with pairs and book clubs occasionally during composing time—help students define and describe how their conversations lead to deeper comprehension.

- Create spaces in the classroom conducive to in-depth discussion—perhaps using soft lighting, a small table, or beanbag chairs on the floor where students can retreat from their independent work spaces to interact in a more intimate atmosphere.

- Create time during crafting sessions for students to briefly share their thinking with each other (turn and talk).

- Create prolonged periods each week during composing time for students to meet in book clubs or literature circles. Encourage them to discuss the content of the books and ways in which they use comprehension strategies to enhance understanding, and to define and describe the outcomes of their new understanding.

- Discuss the difference between arguments born of anger and those constructed to persuade, inform, or provoke thinking. Show how speakers use evidence to build an argument.

- Recognize and discuss occasions in which students engage in argument that leads to new levels of thinking and understanding.

- Ask students to reflect, on paper and in reflecting sessions, on what they are able to understand through discourse that they may not have understood without the benefit of conversation; encourage them to define and describe the role a listener plays in good conversation.

Note: For information on how thinking aloud, modeling, demonstrating, and conferring differ, see Appendix G, "Tactics for Teaching Comprehension."

LITERACY ESSENTIALS: FINE-TUNING OUR INTERACTIONS

In Chapter 1, I suggested that some of the questions we traditionally ask about increasing student engagement might be better answered by studying artists and writers to uncover the dimensions of understanding they exhibited. I suggested that we discuss these dimensions with children and model what more in-depth understanding looks and feels like. But then what? Do we tell them to just start learning fervently or engaging in rigorous discourse? Obviously not.

We need to consider a multitude of ways in which we can make changes, some subtle, some dramatic, in our daily interactions with children. We need to consider ways in which we can make our classrooms more conducive to understanding complex ideas. In addition to studying "intellectual mentors" like Van Gogh, Reynolds Price, Pablo Neruda, Matisse, and Picasso and modeling how we experience understanding in our own lives, what kinds of changes do we make in our teaching if we want children to routinely experience the dimensions and outcomes of understanding?

To answer this question, let's return to Tracy, your hypothetical new colleague. In previous chapters, she has asked you to think through with her which elements of literacy content and practice are essential, according to your experience (and years of research). Before school began, the two of you, along with other colleagues, had some discussions that were stimulating and helped solidify what you know about teaching well.

Now the children have returned and you're both getting to know your new classes. You and Tracy want to keep your dialogue going by creating regular opportunities to observe in each other's classrooms and debriefing afterward to make your observations meaningful for both of you. You have decided that your debriefing sessions can take place after school in a local, shall we say, cocktail establishment, just as easily as in your classrooms. After Tracy's first visit to your classroom, you find yourselves sitting on a sunlit patio, a great day in the classroom behind you and a Pinot Grigio in front of you to spur the conversation. Finally, the kids are starting to get the routines and procedures down. You have passed the "why-didn't-I-go-into-real-estate" phase you experience this time each year.

Tracy's first observation is surprising to you, but she can hardly wait to express it. "You know what I noticed?" She doesn't wait for you to answer. "The way you *talk* to your kids. It's amazing! It's so different from anything I've heard before. At first I thought, 'These kids are only third graders—they're not understanding these words,' but then I realized that you were sort of weaving the definitions of words into the context of what you were saying so that most of them were getting the words just through the discussion. You don't talk down to kids—they feel so respected in your classroom. There is this aura of serious, almost scholarly work, but it's infused with joy and fun! I just never really thought about talking to kids like you do. You really seem to trust them to be able to talk with you about the big, important topics. And the way they respond to you!" She hardly draws a breath. "They are so *intensely* engaged. They aren't paying attention because you tell them to, they're paying attention because they can't bear to miss something important. I love the way they almost mimic—but I don't mean that in a negative way—let's see, what they're really doing is *replicating* the way you speak to them. They're trying to use sophisticated language to define and describe their thinking. They are rising to the occasion!"

It's hard to know how to respond to Tracy's observations. You weren't even fully aware that you talk to kids differently than other teachers. You wonder if that's always a good thing. You remember when you and Tracy first discussed the What's Essential model and reviewed the first category, about bringing a climate of rigor, inquiry, and intimacy to the classroom (see Figure 2.3a on page 32).

You and Tracy spend some time talking about the seen and unseen elements of classroom climate and culture as they are the ones you've been working so hard to build in these early days of the school year. Then your talk returns to one of the cells from the model:

Teach and respond with civility and
respect, modeling sophisticated and
scholarly oral language for children

Tracy's observations relate primarily to this cell—she has picked up on a quality of great teaching that is rare and yet has perhaps the most impact on whether students think at high levels consistently or just as a "happy accident." She has recognized that, because of the way you use language with children, they respond differently—they are more likely to rise to the occasion and stretch the limits of their own language use.

You tell Tracy that your style must have just evolved over the years. You have been concerned, you tell her, with the seeming decrease in the fluency and quality of kids' oral language over the years. You hypothesize that it's because they are so overscheduled; there is no time for thoughtful discussion around the dinner table as there was when you were young. You think it might also relate to the amount of time they spend in front of screens—computer screens, televisions, video games, movies. You have noticed, sadly, a steady decline in your students' use of oral language in recent years. You realize as you're talking to Tracy that you have responded to that decrease in a way that seems counterintuitive. You have responded by *raising* the level and sophistication of your interactions with them. And now that she mentions it, Tracy is right—they have responded in kind. You decide this mutual observation in each other's classrooms is a great idea.

Researchers have calculated that teachers engage in literally thousands of oral interactions with children every day. What we say and the way we say it shapes children's understanding more than any other pedagogical tool we use. Yet we often find ourselves on automatic pilot when talking to children. Are we mindful of our language? Do we take the time to formulate words in a powerful and precise manner? Do we speak in a way that reveals our trust that they will respond at high levels? Do we discuss ways in which we choose words carefully, why we love words, and the power words hold? Are our interactions as potent as they should be if we want to encourage more consistent intellectual growth? By fine-tuning our oral language interactions with children, we can encourage them to live the life of the mind every day.

When I reflect on my own teaching I realize that, like many other teachers I've since observed, I was very enthusiastic in my interactions with children. I welcomed them each day with eager anticipation of the day ahead, I praised them abundantly, I knew how to get kids excited about books and their writing. For example, I could get a group of kids to *want* to read by expressing my enthusiasm about a particular title. When they enjoyed the book and described it to others in book clubs or conferences, I was excited along with them. "That's so cool," I can hear myself saying in response to their ideas. "What an awesome idea!" or "Great, I'm so glad you remembered that part." I was nothing if not enthusiastic.

But was I creating a setting in which students could discuss what it means to read and write fervently, dwell in ideas, think as Renaissance learners, be aware of the changes in their thinking? In retrospect, I realize there wasn't anything about my enthusiastic responses that made a difference for their long-term learning. I wasn't enabling them to gain deeper or more lasting understanding. I wasn't teaching them exactly why what they said was useful and in what additional settings it might apply. It may feel great to a student when we praise an idea in broad terms, but do those kinds of responses lead to anything other than a feel-good moment? What kind of learning impact did I have when I said, "Terrific. I love that. Anyone else?" Did my general praise lead to any greater likelihood that the substantive conversations I sought would occur more often? What conditions had to be part of the daily fabric of the classroom in order to foster more in-depth and lasting understanding? I knew I had to be more thoughtful and systematic about creating such an environment, and I knew that refining my oral interactions with kids was the place to start.

In the hundreds of classrooms I've observed since then, I've come to the conclusion that we should reconsider ways in which our daily interactions with children might be more conducive to in-depth understanding and enable students to routinely demonstrate the dimensions of understanding. I include in this number those classrooms that are already warm and inviting, filled with books and materials for writers, in which the teacher has thoughtfully created spaces that make it possible for children to learn in large groups, small groups, and individually with equal ease. I include in this number classrooms in which the teacher enthusiastically praises children and creates genuine excitement about books. I include in this number classrooms in which the teacher and students have filled the room with evidence of their work. I even include in this number classrooms in which long blocks of time are set aside for independent reading and writing every day, where children have considerable choice about what they read and write. All of those elements described in Chapter 3 as the literacy studio are *necessary, but insufficient* to create lasting learning.

Even with all the accoutrements of a well-organized and inviting classroom, too many children are unable to stay engaged for long periods of time, and they demonstrate too few of the dimensions and outcomes of understanding. They *seem* unable to consistently think at high levels. Why? In my observation, these trends have more to do with their level of discourse—both how we speak with children and how they talk to each other—than their "aptitude" or "ability."

In Figure 8.2 I propose a set of guiding principles for talking with children. It is based on scrutiny of the lives of artists, writers, and other thinkers as well as teachers whose instruction has led to insightful and probing responses from children. It was also inspired by books like *Wondrous Words*, by Katie Wood Ray; *Ways with Words*, by Shirley Brice Heath; and *Choice Words*, by Peter Johnston. If we were to adopt these principles in our everyday interactions with children and use them within a literacy studio, I believe all students would find the support they need to create and sustain a very high level of thinking about text, their topics for writing, and the concepts they learn each day.

What are the teaching implications of these principles? We can apply these principles in the classroom in five key ways (see Appendix G, "Tactics for Teaching Comprehension," for more detail):

1. Thinking aloud
2. Modeling
3. Demonstrating
4. Conferring
5. Informal interactions and sharing

Fig. 8.2. Talk About Thinking: Guiding Principles for Talking with Children

- Speak in the quietest tone appropriate for the situation.

- Use sophisticated words, define them in the context of the discussion, and use them repeatedly.

- Vary the pacing and tone of talk depending on the context and the content.

- Use silence frequently, giving children an opportunity to think about concepts during instruction.

- Provide long periods of time for close scrutiny and discussion of a few ideas, particularly in whole-class groupings.

- Speak with civility and respect, making clear the distinction between settings in which informal language is appropriate and those that call for more formal academic language.

- Create a culture of rigor by focusing on each child's comments for a longer period of time, continually expecting more, pressing the child to probe ideas further, and encouraging the child to explore his ideas orally.

- Create a culture of trust and intimacy by accepting early attempts at thinking deeply, expanding what children are saying into more fully developed sentences without changing the central ideas they are trying to communicate.

- Use discussion and repeated readings of text to amplify children's understanding. Emphasize how understanding evolves and develops with each reading, and help children discover the author's techniques and the subtle ideas nestled below the surface of the text.

- Model what it means to consider the perspectives of others in conversation and to revise one's knowledge and beliefs because of those perspectives.

- Model how one speaker follows on the ideas of the preceding speaker—how a speaker builds upon, extends, or challenges what another speaker has said rather than launching into an unrelated strand of discourse.

- Show children through demonstration what it means to engage in spirited and informed argument using evidence from text; demonstrate engaged and lively discourse with other adults and children, showing passion and clarity about ideas.

- Model ways in which learners restate what they understand during discussions, giving them a chance to further reflect on what they have said and to probe ideas further.

- Describe and model ways in which readers and writers challenge themselves to use more sophisticated and precise language in their writing and with peers.

- Use clear and consistent language to define and describe thinking. When we talk about fervent learning, for example, consistently use that term when describing children's learning efforts or when studying great thinkers.

To get a sense for how a teacher integrates the dimensions and outcomes of understanding and the talk about thinking principles, let's imagine a literacy studio in which a teacher is teaching a comprehension strategy. She takes the next step, however, and emphasizes the behavior associated with a dimension of understanding—fervent learning—and employs the talk about thinking principles. The teacher, Clara, is gathering her second graders, not at their desks, but close to her, on a rug at her feet where she can see their eyes and closely monitor their responses.

Clara pauses for a long moment before beginning. She waits until there is absolutely not a single sound, just the breath of anticipation and eyes riveted on her. This takes several moments, but Clara resists the temptation to begin while children are still squirming into their places. She resists the urge to admonish them to join the group, be quiet, and get ready. She merely smiles and waits; the children know that anyone who breaks the spell will look up to a smile from Clara and silence. They know, because they've repeated this ritual many times; she will not continually remind them to prepare for the lesson. She will wait and smile—at worst, she will cast a worried, not angry, glance at a disruptive child and inquire, "Are you all right? You know how I worry when readers don't have still minds and calm hearts. I worry that something may be terribly wrong." The time it takes to settle grows steadily shorter in the first few weeks of school until the process is firmly established as a classroom habit. At the beginning of the school year, if it takes ten minutes or longer to achieve this moment, Clara is patient, refusing to accept anything less than pin-drop silence and breath-holding anticipation.

Clara is reading *The Story of Ruby Bridges* by Robert Coles and has been working with her second graders on the comprehension strategy asking questions. She has also introduced the children to the idea of concentrating intensively and learning fervently. She wants them to experience the intoxicating feeling of losing themselves in a book so deeply that the world around them disappears. They have had a couple of discussions about what it means to learn fervently at the time of this lesson.

In *The Story of Ruby Bridges*, Coles retells for children the painfully true story of young Ruby Bridges, who was one of the first African American children to attend a white school in New Orleans in the 1960s. The story reveals Ruby's extraordinary strength as she crosses lines of protesters and attends class—alone—each day for months. Clara plans to read the book aloud, pausing to think aloud by posing questions she considers important to understanding the story as a whole and to model fervent learning as she proceeds.

Prior to the lesson, she reread the book to herself, considering places where she might pause to think aloud, but she knows that it is difficult to predict exactly when a question will pop into her mind. She plans to think aloud four or five times, asking her students only to turn and talk in this early stage. She realizes that, if she wants the highest level of thinking possible from these children, she should model for several days at the beginning of the strategy study, fighting her natural inclination to invite the children to share with the whole group. Her experience has told her that if she poses very sophisticated, probing questions during the first two to three days, the children will make contributions that mirror her higher-level insights when they are invited to join the think-aloud process. Let's join the lesson, already in progress. My commentary appears in italics throughout the lesson.

Lesson on Asking Questions with Emphasis on Fervent Learning and the Talk About Thinking Principles

The classroom is completely still, the children gathered at Clara's feet. She begins:

There are books that change the way we think and believe forever.

She speaks slowly, pausing after the word change and again after the sentence for a long moment. How important it is to use silence to punctuate our lessons. The silence gives kids a chance to think about the complexity of the concept Clara is trying to communicate.

There are books that change our opinions and make us want to do something to make the world better. *The Story of Ruby Bridges* is one of those books for me. You have to decide which books, for you, make you think so deeply, you can't get them out of your mind. You are lucky because, in this classroom, you get to begin thinking about books that will change the way you think and believe and even make you want to make the world a better place.

Several hands shoot up at this point, and it is clear these children believe they have already discovered books that make them feel this way. Wisely, Clara declines to call on the children, making this suggestion instead.

I see that some readers already have memorable and powerful books in mind, and I don't want you to forget those titles or how they affected you. Grace, will you please meet with Erica, Tariq, and Raymond immediately following this lesson, and I will help you begin a class chart we can all use to record and recommend those books.

They agree and the hands go down, but Raymond can't resist asking, "When will that be?" Clara smiles at him but returns to the lesson and his hand goes down. She slows her speech and lowers her voice.

Today I will show you what happens in a reader's mind when he or she asks questions as a way to understand more deeply. If a book is going to change the way we think and believe forever, we have to understand it deeply. For several weeks now, we've been discussing how readers understand better when they ask questions while they read. If a book is going to change the way we think and believe forever (*Clara pauses again*), we have to understand it deeply (*another long pause*). We know that questions are tools that can help us understand more deeply. Readers understand better when they ask questions while they read. Readers understand better when they ask questions while they read.

Clara's decision to pause, slow her speech, and repeat the intention of the lesson was very important. She realizes that she is asking seven- and eight-year-old children to simultaneously be aware of their own questions and the plot of the story. This is a complex and challenging charge for them, and while she has no doubt that they will rise to the challenge, she realizes that to teach a lesson of this gravity in the same way she teaches every other lesson is folly.

I want to read a book you haven't heard yet, and I will stop regularly to think aloud about how my questions, the questions my mind creates while I read, help me understand this book more deeply. When you see how well I understand this book, I think you'll see why it is a book that changed the way I think and believe—. *(One of the children spontaneously finishes her sentence by saying "forever!" Everyone laughs.)* Yes, James, forever.

Clara begins to read Ruby Bridges *and pauses on the fourth page.*

Let's see, Ruby was four when they moved—that makes me wonder, how does moving when you're that age change you? Would you be changed? Would you remember moving and how you felt at that age?

Predictably, five or six hands fly into the air and the words being whispered through pursed lips reveal that indeed they do remember what that's like, and several children are ready to tell us all about it! Instead of calling on the children and losing the urgency and focus of the lesson, Clara reminds them of the strategy.

Remember what I told you about letting questions linger? I know that if I can refrain from answering them, the questions will linger in my mind and lead me deeper into the story.

Yes, she used the word refrain *with second graders because it was so clearly defined in the sentence and because she is always cognizant of opportunities to use sophisticated vocabulary, knowing they will follow suit. The hands go down. Clara resumes.*

How would that change you? I mean, she was four. I want to put myself in her heart. I want to use my questions to understand Ruby. I'm going to keep that question in my mind for a while and think about it. I want to know how moving at that age would affect a young child.

Clara continues to read aloud and pauses several pages later to think aloud.

Wait, another question just came into my mind. Do you want to know what it is? It popped into my mind right here where it says that Ruby was going to school and the police didn't help. Here's my question: Why didn't they help her? I can't understand why the police wouldn't have helped this little girl who was just doing what the judge told her to do and going to school. Why wouldn't the police help her?

Clara doesn't stop to think aloud at any predetermined places in the text, though she has previewed it to consider such natural stopping points. But in the lesson, she concentrates on monitoring her own thinking, waiting for questions, while she reads, and when a question comes to her, she carefully considers it before thinking aloud for the children. Clara wants to ensure that the question is sufficiently probing or profound and that it relates to the larger themes and issues in the story, even if those themes have not been revealed at the time she stops to think aloud. The questions Clara poses are genuine and not easily answerable. Clara continues to read aloud and pauses again on the next page.

I just keep having the same question, but because I didn't try to answer and let it linger, my question changed a little bit. Now I'm wondering, did the people who were yelling influence the police and keep them from helping Ruby get through the crowds of protesters and into the school? *(Clara pauses for a long moment, clearly thinking of another question.)* If the police didn't help her—what was in their hearts and minds that would prevent them from upholding the law? I mean, how could they *keep* themselves from helping this little girl? What part of their hearts hardened and kept them from helping?

Clara is demonstrating what proficient readers often do without thinking about it. They may read pages with few or no questions, and then a flurry of questions come to mind in a short space of time. In another lesson Clara may want to speculate with her students why questions come in bunches. At this moment, Chandra raises her hand and can't resist saying aloud, "I have a question, too!" Showing great restraint, Clara smiles and responds.

Chandra, I'm so delighted that your mind is starting to fill with questions because that's how you'll really to be able to understand this book, but I want you to let your question linger for a while. *(To Chandra's disappointed look, Clara responds to the whole class.)* I know how much you want to share at the beginning of a comprehension strategy study, but I have a responsibility to be the best teacher I can, and if I stopped thinking aloud now and let everyone share their questions, I wouldn't be teaching as well as I know how. *(Here Clara whispers.)* But you know what? I want you to share the questions you have so far with the person seated closest to you. Turn your bodies to face each other; ensure that no one around you is left out, and take turns sharing any questions you have about this book now.

For now I'm going to continue reading. Let's see what happens to Ruby. *(Clara reads on, pausing again to think aloud.)* What might those people standing outside Ruby's school be yelling? I am so curious why the author didn't tell us what they were saying to Ruby. Why would Robert Coles, the author, have chosen not to tell us what they were yelling? It's an interesting decision he made . . . and, oh! Once I had that question, it made me think of another. What might the federal police and Ruby be thinking? I can't imagine what a first grader would be thinking when she had guards with guns protecting her. Whew, what is on her mind? Every day she dealt with this.

Clara has purposely inserted a different kind of question into her think-aloud—one that relates to decisions the author made. She may wish to return to questions about what a writer includes and excludes when she is connecting this questioning lesson to the children's writing. Clara continues reading and then pauses to think aloud.

Now I'm thinking of Ruby as an adult, and I'm wondering, how does this kind of experience change her when she's an adult? I wonder if being the first black child in an all-white school has a lasting impact on her. I wonder if she lives her life differently as an adult because of these events. I wonder how these events changed her and how she might be different if she hadn't gone through this experience.

Clara is clearly not bothering with superficial or literal questions. She projects the children forward twenty or thirty years in these questions, causing them to imagine what the adult Ruby Bridges must experience. She knows, of course, that Ms. Bridges has written her own book, Ruby Bridges: My Own Story, *and will bring it to the children for a read-aloud later. Clara finishes the reading with the author's note, briefly describing Ruby as an adult, and promises the children that there will be a time very soon when they will reread* The Story of Ruby Bridges *and be able to pose their own questions about her story.*

The conclusion to Clara's lesson is fascinating and instructive—not only does she return to the point she made earlier about how some books have the power to change the way we think and feel forever, she focuses on how her questions helped her understand the book and also changed what she feels, how she acts.

Now that I've finished the book for today, I want to think about how the questions I asked while I was reading this book helped me understand it better. Let's see, I asked about how having to move when you're that young affected Ruby. When I thought about that question, I think I got to know Ruby a little better, and I realized that making a move like that probably made her a stronger person and better able to handle the challenges she faced when she attended her new school and had to walk through that crowd every morning.

I asked about how the police could ever have resisted helping such a small child in such an overwhelming situation. When I asked that question, it made me realize how strongly white people opposed sending their kids to school with black children. This is so strange to us today it is hard to understand how they possibly could have felt that way, but when I asked the question and thought about the policeman, it made me understand how strongly they felt. I still don't think they were right to feel that way, but to think about an adult who doesn't help a little child helps me know that there was great anger in their hearts.

I know, too, how this book changed the way I think and feel. Every time I read this book I try to imagine that I'm living in New Orleans where this book is set, and it's all those years ago and I'm a white mother considering whether I should continue to send my children to a school in which black and white children are integrated. Reading it now I hope I would have been the very first mother to say, "It's important for children to learn together and to learn *from* each other because they come from different backgrounds." I hope I would have known that children's lives are made better because they live and learn with others who may have different skin color or come from different backgrounds.

But this book also changes the person I am today. I didn't have to make that decision for my children, but I know there are still struggles between African Americans and Anglos—white people—in this country. This book makes me realize that I have a job to do today—I have a responsibility to make sure that my children at home and my children at school understand how important it is to learn alongside others whose lives are different in some way—whether it's the color of their skin or the configuration of their family or the experiences they've had in their lives. I wonder if I remind you often enough how special our different backgrounds and experiences are, and how important it is that we learn from each other about our differences.

This book reminds me to be clear with my children about learning from other kids and celebrating what they bring into the classroom. This really is a book that will change the way I behave as a teacher and as a mom.

Clara returns to the book two days later, having done a similar think-aloud in another book on the intervening day.

Do you remember a couple of days ago when we read Robert Coles' extraordinary book, *The Story of Ruby Bridges*? Do you remember how I told you it was one of those books that changed the way I feel and how I talk with you and my own children? I want you all to notice the chart hanging behind me that Grace and her group began. They titled it "Books That Changed Our Lives," and they made two columns on the chart—one to list the books that had such an impact on them and the other to describe how the books changed their thinking, their beliefs, and their actions. Four other kids have already added to this list, so this is the start of our list of books that are very important to us—these books have such an impact that we remember them for a long time, and we lead our lives differently somehow for having read them.

Today I want to reread *The Story of Ruby Bridges*, and I'll begin by thinking aloud again. Perhaps I'll have different questions than I had two days ago and if I do, I want to pay attention to how those questions help me better understand this book. And today, I want to see if any of you have questions. I'll watch to see if I notice any questions flashing behind your eyes.

Clara's approach is remarkably effective. She creates a sense of tension and suspense leading up to children "getting" to ask their first questions to the group. She makes it clear that questions about superficial aspects of the text are not what she hopes to hear, but she will work with children who share those types of questions. She has circled back to the notion of understanding a book so deeply that you are susceptible to its deepest influences.

You know when I read this part (*pointing at the text*)—I just was wondering why the judge sent only Ruby to this school, while he sent the other black girls to another school together.

Clara gives her silent signal—a gentle lowering of a raised hand— indicating that the children whose hands are raised should lower them. Some of the children gathered before her are about ready to jump out of their skin. Several pages later, Clara pauses and catches Jasmine's eye. Jasmine looks as though she has absolutely no intention of raising her hand to ask a question.

Jasmine, I just noticed something about you when I glanced up. I'm amazed. Even though you were sitting quietly listening to the book, I saw something unmistakable flash behind your eyes. (*Jasmine looks up as if to say, "You did?"*) I saw a question, Jasmine, right here when I was reading this part, I saw a question flash behind your eyes. Do you remember what it was? (*Jasmine shakes her head, astonished, and indicates that she doesn't remember it.*) Oh, that's too bad, but it's not gone forever; do you want to see if, together, we can find it again?

Clara has delivered several clear messages by calling on Jasmine. First, she says without being explicit that the first hands up and waving in front of her face will not be the first to be called upon. Second, she is underscoring the importance of paying attention to your own thinking as well as to the story. Finally, she is injecting a bit of the magic of human thought into the equation. By indicating that she could "see" a question in Jasmine's eyes, she is expressing her belief that Jasmine can generate thoughtful questions.

Jasmine, let me reread the page I just read. It's this one about Ruby and her teacher Mrs. Henry being all alone in her classroom. It was right here on this page that I looked up and saw the question flash behind your eyes. So,

I'll read it again and you see if you can remember the question that you had before. Okay? (*Jasmine shakes her head affirmatively, but looks skeptical.*)

Clara rereads the page and Jasmine shakes her head again, this time negatively. She indicates that she doesn't know and waits for Clara to turn to another child or continue the lesson. No such luck for Jasmine! Clara knows that to turn away from this child now is to deliver a subtle message that Jasmine isn't going to be the kid who comes up with the great question, that she'll probably turn to Keshawn or Grace or one of the other kids who can be counted on to always have the right answer.

You know, Jasmine, I really respect what you're doing right now. You're taking your time to think about the book, remember what your question was, or think of a new one. (*She turns to the rest of the class.*) I love that, in this classroom, we have so many kids like Jasmine who take their time to think. She's the kind of kid who knows that the best questions take the longest time. She's going to take her time to think and not just say something quickly. Yep, I really appreciate that kind of thinker. She'll let us know if she needs me to read the page again.

Silence follows and it is a long silence indeed. Jasmine continues to look at the book. The class squirms. Clara smiles and waits. And waits. And is rewarded.

Jasmine: I wonder how Mrs. Henry gets into the school.
Clara: You wonder how Mrs. Henry gets into the school.

Resisting the urge to sing the "Hallelujah Chorus," Clara merely restates what Jasmine has said and waits. Moments later, Jasmine has more to say.

Jasmine: Yeah, like does she have to go into the school in front of all those people?
Clara: Does she have to enter the building through the crowd of protesters?

Clara uses a subtle, but highly effective strategy here. She repeats what Jasmine has said, but injects slightly more sophisticated vocabulary—the crowd of protesters. She hasn't changed the substance of Jasmine's comment, but she has enhanced the vocabulary. Perhaps next time, Jasmine will use the words crowd *or* protesters.

Jasmine: Yeah, does she have to go in when they're all yelling? And do they yell at her and are they mad at her for teaching Ruby and does she have a guard with a gun, too, and is she scared?

Clara (her voice, loud, filled with excitement and pride and a bit of relief!): Whoa, Jasmine, I thought you didn't have any more questions! Yikes, I think that was four new questions. That was amazing. Look what happened when Jasmine took her time to think of questions. Each one of those questions can really help us understand this book better.

Hands are up all over the room. Some children want to answer Jasmine's questions, others want to pose their own. The energy is high and getting higher. There is an intensity to the children's engagement that reminds me of Van Gogh's fervency. Nothing, no one could have interrupted the thinking these children are engaged in right now. I honestly believe if a fire alarm sounded, they would maintain their focus on the book. I notice that children begin to look at Jasmine with a fresh perspective. Maybe Jasmine is the kind of kid who can ask a lot of questions and get everyone thinking. But instead of beginning to call on other kids, Clara returns her focus to Jasmine.

Clara (her voice very low, almost a whisper and speaking very slowly): Okay, Jasmine. I want to stop and really think about your questions. Your questions really made me think about Mrs. Henry for the first time. I realize I've been thinking so much about how Ruby felt and what she was thinking that I had totally forgotten about Mrs. Henry. Sometimes when a reader like you, Jasmine, asks a question about a character other than the main character, it makes you understand the book in a whole new way.

Now, just a second, Jasmine, I want to think about your questions again. Here's what you asked. Did Mrs. Henry have to enter the school through the crowd of protesters? Are they mad and yelling at Mrs. Henry too? How do they feel about Mrs. Henry when she is teaching Ruby? Does she have a guard? Is she frightened?

Clara lets silence sink in around the children.

Jasmine: I asked all that? I know the answers!

Clara is beaming with pride, but resists the temptation to praise Jasmine in general terms and let her spill out the "answers" to all her questions.

Clara: Jasmine, you taught all of us something so important here today. I think every reader in the room can remember what you taught us and can use it in their reading. I'm going to say and write on this chart, what you taught us about using questions to understand more deeply. Okay? And, if I get something wrong, I want you to tell me right away.

Jasmine (with great gravity): I'll make sure.

Clara pauses to write, not Jasmine's questions, but the following state-ments on a blank piece of chart paper hanging on a nearby easel.

Some questions take a lot of thinking before you can share them.

**When one person asks a question, it helps everyone
to think about the text in a new way.**

**Sometimes it's better not to try to answer the question
right away—let it float in your mind for awhile.**

The "float in your mind for awhile" was offered by Mikhail, one of the students, when Clara paused and talked about how she was searching for just the right words to capture what Jasmine taught the class. I was delighted to hear that, at least for Mikhail, the care Clara took in choos-ing words was reflected in his contribution to the chart: "You have to let a question float around in your mind for awhile." Mikhail seems to know that it's not only okay to experiment with words in this classroom; it's what everyone, including the teacher, is trying to do.

> *Clara:* I'm going to close the book right here (*audible groans and expres-sions of disappointment*) and we'll finish our rereading at another time. Share any questions you have right now with a partner sitting close to you. (*After the turn and talk, Clara pauses for a long moment and nearly whispers.*) I noticed something very important about the readers in this classroom today. (*Here, Clara's voice rises in volume and increases in pace and intensity.*) Every single one of you was totally caught up in what Jasmine was asking. I know this because you were leaning in toward me; I know this because I could hear and see you longing to answer Jasmine's questions or to offer your own. I know this because I could see and feel and almost *hear* the thinking about this book. It was fervent learning, just like we've been talking about. You showed how deeply you are beginning to understand this book by learning with such fervency today!
>
> Now (*here Clara pauses for a long moment and lowers her voice again*), wait till you hear what we're going to do. I'm going to give the class a wonderful gift. Instead of finishing this book right now, I'm going to let you read while Jasmine's lessons are fresh in your mind. That way, you will be able to see what questions pop into your mind while you're reading, and you can write them down on a sticky note so that when I come around to confer, you and I will be able to discuss them.

Clara uses a gesture that begins with each hand resting on the oppo-site shoulder and sweeps outward—a silent signal that the time for inde-pendent reading has begun.

❧

When I consider these interactions with respect to the talk about thinking principles, it is clear that Clara seamlessly wove many of the principles into her lessons on questioning, never losing sight of the fact that the goal was gaining a deeper understanding of the text.

Clara used silence, varied her pacing and volume, created a culture of rigor, and restated what Jasmine said, enabling her to probe the subtleties of the meaning more deeply. She modeled civility and respect throughout and reread the text to show the children how new understandings emerge each time one reads a book. She showed trust and intimacy in turning to Jasmine and waiting until she had a chance to formulate a question, never giving in to the temptation to call on one of the children who may have answered more quickly. She used consistent terms to define and describe their thinking, focusing on fervent learning and ways in which books change our lives (both dimensions of understanding) and on questioning (the comprehension strategy the children were studying at the time).

Perhaps most important, Clara was teaching for long-term retention and reapplication. What the children learned in these lessons can inform them, not just in their immediate reading tasks, but when they read independently from now on. These were not simple, one-day, teach-it-and-move-on kinds of lessons. They were meant to have staying power, and I believe they will. They were meant to matter to children over the long haul.

In my own practice with children, I keep the talk about thinking principles close at hand. I refer to the list before I begin a lesson, just to remind myself to be careful and precise in the words I use; to give the children time to think and to reward them, verbally, for doing so; to vary the pace and tone of my words, building excitement with quicker, louder talk and encouraging reflection with slow words uttered almost in a whisper. I often ask children if they will indulge me for a moment while I think of the right word to use, and then I pause and think. I tell them I want to be careful not to use sloppy words like *stuff* and *things*. I'm trying to be precise and civil. I'm trying to show them my respect for them through the words I choose, just as Van Gogh, Matisse, and Picasso were precise in their selection of color, shape, and composition. If I am to help children dramatically improve their use of oral language, I know that the words I use and the artistry with which I use them matters immensely.

I have created a tool I call, creatively enough, "Best Practices in Oral Language Teaching and Learning" (see Appendix H). It is designed to be used by teachers observing in each other's classrooms, as Tracy did in yours or as a checklist you can use to reflect on your own use of oral language with children. I've included several additional examples of thoughtful teaching based on the talk about thinking principles and the instrument itself, which is in the form of a short checklist with space to jot observations.

DWELLING IN THE MIND

My own history is dense with discussion. Holidays when I was growing up were never the Norman Rockwell scenes we envision when we think about Thanksgiving. There was nothing calm or soothing about them because I grew up in the same town where my parents were born and where their parents still lived. My grandfathers, both Colorado natives, served as state senators—on opposite sides of the aisle. Grandpa Bain was a conservative in the work-ethic, Goldwater tradition who thought Franklin Roosevelt had nearly been the undoing of this country. My grandpa Oliver had a framed black-and-white photograph of FDR on the mantel alongside photos of his children and grandchildren, cousins, aunts, and uncles. A visitor to his home would have been forgiven for assuming FDR was just another Oliver. I knew that Grampy Bain had been president pro tempore of the Senate and that Gramps Oliver had met with Lyndon Johnson. Both were points of enormous pride on both sides of my family, and I grew up listening to my two grandpas—whom I revered—engage in, shall we say, very energetic debate over Thanksgiving turkey and Christmas prime rib. Particularly in the late autumn and early winter, when they were in the process of informing themselves about the issues of the forthcoming legislative session, they rehearsed their arguments to each other over protests from my Republican mother, who begged them to postpone the debate until "everyone has had a nice dinner." They never did.

I clearly remember the tone those arguments took. Grampy and Gramps were close friends and held each other in highest esteem—they spoke with gravity and civility about the matters of the state. They took their responsibilities very seriously and were resolute in defending their positions. But, as they lobbed the issues back and forth like a tennis ball, it was not unusual to hear them acquiesce a point or to be influenced by each other's ideas. They graciously acknowledged when the other scored. When the grandpas argued, I knew it was conflict about ideas, not disdain for each other, that contributed to the intensity I heard. I learned *from and because of* the arguments. I understood the give and take and never doubted their true affection and respect for one another. Their conversations were, above all, civil.

As an innocent bystander, I got to learn about housing and migrant workers' issues, education (Grampy was also on the Greeley, Colorado, School Board), health care, roads, prisons, and compromise. When my school classes went to Denver to see the Senate in session, I got to run back and forth across the aisle to sit on two laps and hear both of them take the podium to speak about issues I'd first heard debated at my dining room table. I remember the day I told the grandpas I registered as a Democrat; Grampy put all his energy into changing my mind as Gramps leaned back in his chair and grinned. I realize now how lucky I was, and how rare my experience.

My parents had what they called a "mixed marriage," but my mother voted for some Democrats and my Democrat father eventually became a Republican who now votes for candidates in both parties. I thought that spirited debate was the norm in families and was surprised to learn how peaceful (boring?!) the talk was around my friends' dining room tables.

It wasn't terribly surprising that I married someone whose great-grandfather had been a Republican U.S. senator from Colorado and whose father was head of the Colorado Republican Party for many years. The debate started before we were married and continues to this day. Election day is a very big deal at our house, and we always take Elizabeth with us into the voting booth to watch us cast our votes. She has heard the debate and she has watched us cancel each other out time and again. When she was about eight, she emerged from behind the curtain with her dad, took me aside and said, "Mommy, Daddy did it all wrong." It was, to quote another great political leader, my "finest hour." Elizabeth has grown up listening to spirited debate from parents who (usually) keep it civil and within a year, she'll be casting her first ballot. I have a feeling I'm going to be the one leaning back in the chair grinning, but I have no doubt that both sides of the arguments she heard will play in her mind throughout her life, and for that, I have no regrets.

I wonder if you have thought about the role of discourse in your intellectual life. When you attend your monthly book club, do you walk away with a head so full of new ideas that you have a completely new understanding of the book? Do others' experiences bring a dramatically different perspective to complement your understanding of the books you read? Do you find yourself, at dinner parties, arguing a point about politics or education policy and almost surprise yourself with the clarity of your own thinking? "Wow," you think, "I sound goooood." Do you relish conversations with a certain friend or family member because he or she always finds a way to make you think about old issues in new ways? Do you have a friend who can describe with clarity and precision an idea you've been struggling to articulate? Do you have a colleague whose remarks at faculty meetings irritate you until you realize that you are merely wishing you had those ideas first?

A decades-long conversation conducted though talk, letters, and paintings defined Henri Matisse and Pablo Picasso's thinking in a way we can now study on behalf of our students. But similar conversations are at work in our own lives—if we pause long enough to pay attention. I have proposed, in this chapter, that we take time, as I am now, in the quiet of a spot we love, to analyze such conversations with an eye to improving the discourse in our classrooms. Somehow it is easier for me to think about talking (and talk about thinking!) when I am alone, with Yo Yo Ma playing the cello in the background, a fire burning on this late autumn day, Elizabeth at school, and the dogs at my feet. I have become acutely aware of the role discourse plays in my life and in the lives of mentors and friends I admire, but sometimes it's nice to be alone while I play back all that gorgeous dialogue.

Chapter 9

To Feel, to Remember, to Understand

MENTOR: EDWIDGE DANTICAT

Tante Atie . . . picked up a broom and began to sweep the mosaic floor.

"My angel," she said, "I would like to know that by word or by example I have taught you love. I must tell you that I do love your mother. Everything I love about you, I loved in her first. That is why I could never fight her about keeping you here. I do not want you to go and fight with her either. In this country, there are many good reasons for mothers to abandon their children. . . . But you were never abandoned. You were with me. . . . When my father died, my mother had to dig a hole and just drop him in it. . . .

"If we can live here, if you have this door open to you, it is because of your mother. Promise me that you are not going to fight with your mother when you get there."

"I am not going to fight," I said.

"Good," she said. "It would be a shame if the two of you got into battles because you share a lot more than you know."

She reached over and touched the collar of my lemon-toned dress.

"Everything you own is yellow," she said, "wildflower yellow, like dandelions, sunflowers."

"And daffodils," I added.

"That is right," she said, "your mother, she loved daffodils." Tante Atie told me that my mother loved daffodils because they grew in a place that they were not supposed to. . . .

Tante Atie took the card from under her pillow and put it on the night table, next to the plane ticket. She said that it would be nice for me to give the card to my mother personally, even though the daffodil was gone.

—*Edwidge Danticat*, Breath, Eyes, Memory

Elizabeth has just been accepted to Barnard College, the women's college at Columbia University in New York City. When I began *Mosaic of Thought*, she was in kindergarten, and as I finish *To Understand*, she is off to college. As I write these words, we sit side by side, laptops whirring under our fingers; Elizabeth is working on a paper for one of her last classes in high school. When she was little, we had "side-by-side reading" time. This was the diversion I invented when (I'm not proud of this) I wanted to read my own book rather than read aloud to her. I reasoned that we could still be together reading side by side and I could forgo reading *Miss Rumphius* for the seven thousandth time. She bought it. Now we write side-by-side the way we used to read side by side. A year from now she'll be reading and writing side by side with someone in a dorm room. I'm not sure how I'll endure her departure.

Elizabeth wants to be a writer. When we looked at Barnard, we discovered that it was the intellectual birthplace of some rather well-known scientists, journalists, and writers. When we first toured the campus, I think she felt the presence of Barnard alumnae Zora Neale Hurston, Anna Quindlen, Erica Jong, Margaret Mead, Mary Gordon, Maria Hinojosa, Ann Brashares, Jhumpa Lahiri, and Edwidge Danticat, the author of *Breath, Eyes, Memory*, from which the opening excerpt was taken. It was the first college we visited, and she immediately declared it "the one." I encouraged her to wait and look at the dozen or so other colleges on her list, which she did, but she had the same remark after each visit—it's not Barnard. She wants to walk in the same halls and study in the same classrooms where these and thousands of other women developed their writing style, formulated ideas, invented, fought stereotypes and prejudices, imagined a more just world, and bolstered their courage to swim upstream in a world that was, and in some places still is, hostile to women. She wants to be in New York City, a quick subway ride from Lincoln Center and the American Ballet Theatre she loves so much. She wants to take advantage of $12 standing room tickets to the New York Philharmonic and the Metropolitan Opera. With her Columbia ID, she tells me, she can get into any museum in the city—for free. She is wild with joy and anticipation.

Mom and Dad's emotions are a bit more complex. They run the gamut from dread to pride to anticipation of great things to come for our little girl. One moment I'm so excited for her I can hardly stand it; the next I can't imagine the loneliness we'll feel as we walk by her unoccupied bedroom; then I feel confident and certain that she is ready to tackle college and the city; an hour later I wonder if we'll ever again have our long talks where she shares every detail of her life; the next hour I know we will. I'm experiencing the typical how-did-it-go-so-fast and did-we-do-all-we-should-for-her emotions most parents feel, balanced by the knowledge that she set her sights on particular goals and worked tirelessly to get there. We actually had very little to do with it.

When I read the preceding passage from Edwidge Danticat's stunning little book, *Breath, Eyes, Memory*, I almost choke with the pain that this child's aunt must have felt sending her from the only home she has ever known in Haiti to meet her parents in New York City. My child will be three hours away by plane and I can and will (to her chagrin) get on that plane and take my little girl to the theater if I so choose. Tante Atie raised the child and then sent her away, not knowing when or if she would see her again. Yet the pain of separation Tante Atie anticipates is, to me, poignantly familiar as I reread *Breath, Eyes, Memory*. I feel new bolts of emotion, new levels of empathy for this character as I anticipate the separation that is now only months away. I can picture the flight itinerary on my own kitchen counter—round trip for us, one way for her. I flash back to the moment my parents left me in the dorm parking lot (a mere sixty miles from home) and I saw my father cry for the first time. The memory of my own departure for college is overlaid with a piercing sadness. Those would be the last four years of my mother's life and I would not be home.

All these emotions swirl around a few short paragraphs in a book written about people and places absolutely unlike my own experience. I've come to realize that in this and in so many other books, when I close the cover, it is the emotional content I remember. As I read, the emotions of characters become woven with my own, inextricably tied. This is the gift of a great writer like Danticat; when we read her words, we're not sure if the emotions are the characters' or our own. The apparent differences between an island in the Caribbean and a dorm parking lot in Denver fade. Any differences between my circumstances and the characters' are swept away by the gentle touch of an aunt's fingers brushing against the collar of a daffodil-colored dress. In my mind, those fingers become my own, my mother's, Tante Atie's, Elizabeth's. It is the gentleness of the touch that remains. I realize that, so often, I read to be touched in just this way. I realize that when I am so touched, I remember and I understand.

I reread the first paragraphs of this chapter and sit down to continue writing it from the rooftop deck of a hotel in Barcelona, Spain. We are drinking in life along the Mediterranean during Elizabeth's graduation trip to Europe. Her departure for college is now only weeks away, and Danticat's words strike even closer to home. The emotions I experience in rereading are more acute, the likelihood that I'll remember Danticat's book far higher.

When I reread what I wrote several months ago, I realize that I wrote about only one kind of emotional reaction: responses based on shared emotion and empathy with characters in fiction. But thinking back over my reading, just in the past few days, I realize that I experience many different types of emotion when I read. When I travel, for example, I devour books about the area I visit. We have never been to Barcelona, and I find myself reading almost obsessively. David and Elizabeth occasionally have to remind me to put the book about Barcelona down to actually look at Barcelona. I want to know the history of the place, understand the people and the conflicts upon which their experience rests. I want to understand the late nineteenth/early twentieth-century architect Gaudi and his surprising facades sprinkled all over Barcelona, including the one directly in my view as I write these words. I want to understand the role Barcelona played in Pablo Picasso's life, how the city's fragrances and breezes flow in and around the canvases I viewed yesterday at the Museu de Picasso. I want to be able to navigate the city confidently, explore areas other tourists might not find, pop on and off the trains and find the undiscovered narrow, winding streets and the cafes where Barcelonans drink *café con leche*.

To know these things, I read with urgency and a very different set of emotions. I am driven to know more, to feel the city rather than to merely traipse through it—I want to remember the particular pulse of this city and its people. I want to recall the intensity of a conversation I observed this morning between two elderly women, perched on a bench at a bus stop, dressed formally as if they were off to church (perhaps they were) in the middle of a weekday. I could feel, without understanding a single word, that they had known each other for decades and could anticipate each other's thoughts before they were uttered. How universal that scene, yet how particularly Spanish. Their interaction, their intimacy—that's what I want to remember.

The knowledge I amass from reading about this city and some of its most famous residents is the foundation on which I stand when I go out to experience it, to feel it. For example, reading about Picasso's evolution from more realistic paintings to the abstraction of Cubism allowed me the insight and emotion I felt as I stood before his paintings, and it's that emotion I'll remember. I am not likely to remember the exact years Picasso lived here, nor will I recall which paintings he created here and which in Paris, but I am very likely to recall the movement and light within his paintings. In one, for example, I could actually see the subjects move and watch as the light shifted and highlighted different aspects of the painting. How could he make a canvas move like that? I was riveted. The need to stay planted in front of a painting, watching to see it move again and again—that, I'll remember.

Without the knowledge I gained from reading about the genesis of Picasso's Blue Period, I wouldn't have felt the melancholy of those paintings engulf me. I wouldn't have known about his friend's suicide or why Picasso might have placed these subjects in overwhelming desolation. I wouldn't have taken in the hopelessness of those subjects, and I wouldn't have felt transfixed as I stood before his paintings from that era. I realize now that when I read to inform myself, I am still reading to feel, to remember.

When we leave here tomorrow, it is the emotion that will remain. I read to inform myself; I read to experience my own emotions through characters. But in both cases, I know that the reading, the learning, leads to something more lasting—insight about myself and the promise of remembering details that might otherwise be fleeting. Emotion and memory, it seems, are integrally tied.

Dimension: Emotion and Memory

- Our understanding is enriched when we have *emotional connections*. We love to reexperience what we find beautiful, and we understand better when learning includes aesthetic journeys. In our own creative endeavors, we seek to craft something luminous and memorable, something that matters to others. Ultimately, our insights become potent and lasting—and *we remember*.

When we recall the most profound and memorable learning experiences of our lives, they are laden with a range of emotion. I wonder how often we articulate those experiences to our students, how we talk with them about the potent role of emotion in understanding.

Bruce Morgan, author of *Writing Through the Tween Years* (2005) is a dear friend. It is primarily in his classroom that I have studied and recorded how emotion affects understanding. Bruce is simply fearless in the face of a wide range of human emotion. He is a masterful teacher in many ways, but his great gift is the ability to articulate how emotions affect what he understands, the way he studies the world, and the ways in which he writes. Emotions that make others cringe or retreat into a cozy state of denial are fodder for daily discussion in his classroom.

Bruce is relentless. Always brimming with humor and unconditional love for kids, he can look a fourth grader in the eye and challenge him to face his fears and overcome the negative judgment and doubt that plague him. When children skim the surface or try to slide by with a shrug and an "I dunno," Bruce reminds them that the reason they aren't attending to deeper levels of meaning in a book may have something to do with a reluctance to face the same emotions in their own lives. He is intrepid in the face of preadolescent angst and indecision, prodding, encouraging, and probing until kids are honest with themselves and each other.

Bruce is honest. When he makes a mistake in an approach to a lesson, he admits it and encourages children to do the same. He shows children what it means to be responsible for one's own actions and honest in facing one's feelings. He is an avid reader of books for tweens and young adults and can match a kid to a book, not only based on the level or topic, but also on the emotional territory that matches the challenges or joys a particular child is facing at that moment. When the child wades into the text, Bruce is right there, sharing his own experiences and emotions, laughing and crying.

Bruce is passionately curious. He notices everything, wonders about everything, and opines at length (and at high volume) about everything he notices and wonders. "I can't believe a writer of her caliber would use such a lame phrase, it's a throwaway phrase, it doesn't push the plot forward, it's filling space, and worst of all, it sounds so eighties. Doesn't she know she's writing for twenty-first-century kids!?" He questions constantly. "Now why would this writer just gloss over the mother's reaction to that? If you were writing it, how would you have been more honest about her feelings?"

Bruce is a Renaissance man. He brings his love of architecture, city planning, the outdoors, the environment, politics, and social justice right into the classroom. At a time when school districts live in fear of litigation and ask teachers to sterilize their interactions with children, Bruce treads where others dare not go, and children thrive (and he's never faced a lawsuit!). He brings his passions into the classroom with an infectious fervor that children reflect right back to him. He questions constantly. "Did you notice that amazing sunrise this morning? Did you see the way the clouds just shimmered from purple to pink to orange to yellow? Did anybody in this classroom get up early enough to watch it? You did! Did you write what you saw in your notebook? What are you going to do with that entry? Will it become part of a piece you're already working on? A new piece? Oh, I'm so jazzed about that. I can't wait to see it!"

Bruce's passion carries over to his life outside of school. When we take a walk he has a thousand new observations to share. "Have you noticed that they're doing midcentury modern there (inevitably, no), what do you think is going to go there, why would they paint that green color (I have no earthly idea), what do you think of that facade, why didn't they incorporate that building more carefully with the others around it, did you ever wonder why no one planned open space in this area, isn't this just a *killer* city?" He never stops. Believe me, he never stops. When we visit other cities, he just unleashes the whole string of questions again. A ninety-minute architecture tour we took in Chicago morphed into three hours— the rest of the tour participants gradually slipped away somewhere until it was just me, Bruce, and the exhausted guide.

Can you imagine being a fourth grader in Bruce's classroom? Imagine breathing that energy all day! Would you be more likely to pose your own questions and to explore the answers? Might you be more likely to face your own fears, express emotions, and use those feelings to leverage deeper understanding from what you read?

It's tough to describe what Bruce does, and it would be even tougher to measure it. The true barometer of his impact lies in the confidence of kids who didn't believe in themselves and the willingness to feel among kids who used to hide from emotion. But the outcomes are academic as well: enhanced empathy for characters and conflicts in books, exquisite voice in writing, passion for ideas, curiosity about the world, bold questioning of the status quo, breadth and depth of vocabulary to talk about books, and the ability to overcome negative self-esteem in the face of new academic challenges. I also sense that many know there may never be another Mr. Morgan in their lives.

I want them to have another Mr. Morgan. I want all of our children to have access to teachers with his passion and fearlessness in defining and describing human emotion. The reason kids thrive in Bruce's classroom, the reason they actually retain and reapply what they have learned, is that often—not always, of course, but often—they have an emotional connection to the concept they've learned. I am not suggesting that the way Bruce teaches should necessarily be replicated by the rest of us—his style is uniquely his own. I am suggesting, however, that we open ourselves to what we feel when we learn and allow ourselves to express it to children. I am suggesting that we release more of ourselves into our interactions with children. I am suggesting that we tackle controversial issues with children and, without trying to influence their opinions, model what it is to be a passionately curious person in the world. I am suggesting that we be honest and forthright with kids—they don't need us to sugarcoat, dumb down, sterilize, and homogenize our emotions. They do need us to *teach* how emotion plays a role in human understanding.

We know that people understand, retain, and reapply what they have learned when they have an emotional connection to it. When teachers lament the fact that children don't seem to remember and reapply what they've been taught, I worry that we have sterilized our teaching approaches and removed so much of the emotional component from our daily conversation that children have little to anchor the concepts they've been taught. Recall my emotional reaction when I reread *Breath, Eyes, Memory* in the context of Elizabeth's impending departure, and how different it was from what I experienced in Barcelona. I'll probably not remember the dates Picasso lived in that city, but I will remember the movement and light, the way his paintings caused my heart to pound, how they held my undivided attention. That kind of deeply emotional experience has staying power.

I also know that what Bruce (and thousands of other teachers) does for his students is difficult, if not impossible, to measure directly. This creates a contradiction of sorts in my professional thinking. As I mentioned earlier, I have long advocated that teachers read the research and original theory on learning and develop teaching tactics that reflect the latest findings. My goal in creating the What's Essential model was to make a vast amount of research more manageable and organized. I want the model to help teachers focus instructional attention on what research indicates is the most important content in literacy learning. I believe that research and theory provide a critically important barometer for making decisions about curriculum and instruction at the classroom and district levels, and I am in awe of the meticulous process researchers undertake to study and analyze effective teaching practices and student outcomes. Their findings are invaluable—but how do you quantify a Bruce?

Given the respect I have for the research community and its contributions to teaching and learning, the questions I am about to propose may seem incongruous, but then this book is about posing tough questions. I have to wonder—is it even possible to (scientifically) study human comprehension processes, including those I've called the dimensions of understanding? Can the best researcher design a study to examine fervent learning or to analyze the standardized test results among students who use silence to develop deeper understanding? Is it possible to describe the long-term effects on children who are encouraged to be Renaissance learners, or to analyze the impact on a child's scores when he effectively uses discourse to enhance his understanding of books? Must everything we value and teach in our classrooms be research based? What about, for example, the role of emotion in understanding? Can we measure the degree to which a child understands more deeply because she connects emotionally to a piece of literature?

Is it possible to have a large body of peer-reviewed research to "prove" that teaching children to pause and reflect on ideas from books is a good idea? Can we benchmark the subtle changes in language and diction a teacher makes to inspire? Does a teacher's seamless modeling of any one dimension of understanding have measurable results? How do you measure a teacher's artistry, passion, and world knowledge? All of the dimensions of understanding I've explored in this book to some degree defy scientific analysis, but does that mean they're not worth teaching?

In the final pages of this book, I want to call for equilibrium between the need for research to guide our practice and an acknowledgment that much of what matters most may never be measured scientifically. Both matter. Our children need and deserve to be riveted with emotion to the books they read from the earliest ages; they need to be *taught* to believe that struggle is the way to build intellectual muscle; they need to understand that to be influenced, to change one's thinking, is a gift, not a deviation from the "right" answer. And they deserve to have teachers who focus instruction on a few important, research-based concepts, teach them over a long period of time, and give students an opportunity to apply their learning in a wide variety of texts and contexts.

I want to add mine to the growing chorus of voices in our field who recognize the need for that equilibrium, who understand the role research should play in classroom and policy decisions *and* the need for each teacher to bring the depth and breadth of his personal experience, style, and artistry into the classroom. Teaching should be joyful work. Learning should be joyful work. Isn't there a place for joie de vivre in schools?

LITERACY ESSENTIALS: THE OUTCOMES OF UNDERSTANDING

I suspect that we all might express a bit more joie de vivre if our days were less harried and frenetic. In these pages, I've tried to articulate some ideas about how we can incorporate the most basic instructional principles: focus instruction on a few key concepts, teach them over a long period of time, and have students apply those concepts in a wide variety of texts and contexts. This statement has become the maxim to which I return over and over to remind myself what's most important and how people learn most effectively. If we can focus on what matters most, we *do* have the flexibility to dwell for long periods of time in discussion of ideas, allow kids to be fervent learners with a wide range of passionate interests, encourage rigorous discourse about ideas, teach kids how to manipulate their own thinking in order to understand more deeply, and show them how emotional connections make concepts more memorable. In other words, we can teach the concepts that matter most and still have time to explore and practice what it means to understand.

In each chapter of *To Understand*, I've investigated four key questions:

1. What does it mean to understand? (Mentors section)

2. How do we define and teach toward high expectations and high levels of understanding? (Dimension section)

3. What matters most in literacy learning? (Literacy Essentials section)

4. In what ways can we live our adult lives as intellectually curious models for our students and our colleagues? (Dwelling in the Mind section)

I've used three theoretical models—Dimensions and Outcomes of Understanding, What's Essential for Literacy Learning, and Literacy Studio—to help explore those questions. Beginning in Chapter 3, I've described one of the dimensions of understanding and one of the categories in the What's Essential model in each chapter. I have not, as yet, fully elaborated the outcomes of understanding. It is perhaps the most self-explanatory of the models. Here's how it came about.

When Jamika asked the profound question about what "make sense" means, I began to explore new qualities and characteristics of comprehension. As I explained in Chapter 2, the dimensions and outcomes of understanding evolved from observations of adults (including myself) and children in the act of understanding as well as discussion with adults and children about their comprehension processes. But Jamika's question caused me to wonder—what else? In addition to thinking aloud about various comprehension strategies and querying children about their application of the strategies, I wanted to take the next step. It is one thing to question or determine importance or infer, it's entirely another to be able to articulate what you came to understand *because* you used the strategy. I began to ask myself, colleagues, and children this question: "What did your use of the strategy help you understand? What do you understand about this text that you might not have understood without the strategy?" I carefully gathered notes about children's and adults' responses and, gradually, the outcomes of understanding emerged (repeated here as Figure 9.1). The comprehension strategies listed at the top of the chart may lead to one or more different outcomes in reading narrative (left column) or expository (right column) text. In some cases, the outcome on the narrative side correlates to the outcome on the expository side; in other cases they are not related.

Teachers can use the Outcomes of Understanding model in several ways. Each of the outcomes can be taught explicitly by modeling and thinking aloud. When teaching a comprehension strategy, for example, a teacher might think aloud about her inferences *and* go to the next step to think aloud about how inferring helped her to (for example) empathize with the character—to feel things the character felt even though their life situations differ significantly. Gradually we can ask students to share, not only the inferences they make, but what those inferences lead them to understand that they may not have understood had they not used the strategy (or any strategy). Over time the class can add to the model if new outcomes become evident. An example from a classroom may illuminate this a bit further.

One steamy spring morning in a Spartanburg, South Carolina, third-grade classroom, I used Robert Coles' *The Story of Ruby Bridges* as part of a series of crafting sessions focused on using schema. Samantha, a tiny African American girl, could hardly contain herself as I read aloud

Fig. 9.1. The Outcomes of Understanding

What Happens in Our Minds

We gain deeper understanding of text through the use of cognitive strategies:

- Monitoring
- Asking questions
- Determining importance
- Synthesizing
- Using prior knowledge (schema)
- Inferring
- Creating sensory and emotional images

Cognitive strategies may lead us to experience the following outcomes:

In Fiction/Narrative/Poetry:	In Expository Text:
Insights for writing—the ability to learn from great narrative writers, to read their work with a writer's eye and to incorporate writer's tools into our own writing	**Insights for writing**—the ability to learn from great expository writers, to read their work with a writer's eye and to incorporate writer's tools into our own writing
General empathy—a belief that the reader is actually a part of the setting, knows the characters, stands alongside them in their trials, brings something of himself to the events and resolution; emotions are aroused	**A sense of importance**—a clear idea of what matters most, what is worth remembering
Character empathy—the sense that we are feeling and believing what the character feels and believes	**New applications**—the ability to retain and reapply newly learned concepts in new settings and circumstances
Setting empathy—a feeling of actually being there, of experiencing the time, place, and conditions	**Connections**—the realization that newly learned concepts "fit" with and extend existing background knowledge, and make sense in relation to what is already known; they affirm our existing knowledge
Conflict empathy—a sense of experiencing a similar conflict such that the reader can relate to the internal and/or external struggle the characters endure	**Clarity about the problem and possible solution(s)**—a sense of the elements that make a situation problematic and what steps might be taken to solve the problem, perhaps in a particular order
Author empathy—understanding why/how one's interpretations have been shaped in the way they have and what literary tools (diction, foreshadowing, imagery, voice, plot structures) the author used to shape the reader's interpretation	**Author's intent**—understanding what the author thinks is important and is trying to communicate; an ability to cull key ideas from interesting details or long descriptions

Fig. 9.1 continues on next page

Fig. 9.1. The Outcomes of Understanding *(continued)*

Cognitive strategies may lead us to experience the following outcomes:

In Fiction/Narrative/Poetry:	In Expository Text:
A sense of what's next—the ability to anticipate what might be forthcoming and to predict events	**A sense of the general order or chronology**—understanding the order or progression of a series of events; the ability to predict with some accuracy what is likely to occur or be described next
A sense of what makes a text distinct—understanding how this text is similar to and different from others, perhaps those by the same author or in the same genre	**The ability to compare and contrast**—developing a sense of how concepts presented in text are alike or different and why that contrast matters to the overall text
Confidence—the ability and propensity to discuss and contribute to others' ideas about the narrative	**Confidence**—the ability and propensity to discuss and contribute to others' knowledge about a concept
A sense of the aesthetic—a desire to linger with portions of the text we find beautiful or moving; the desire to experience it again	**A sense of the aesthetic**—a developing sense of wonder about the complexities and inherent subtleties related to a concept
A need to pause and ponder—the desire to reread or pause to consider new facets and twists in the text, and to discuss or share ideas in some way	**A need to reread and revise thinking**—the desire to revisit, reread, or explore other texts in order to learn more about a concept
A desire to advocate—the feeling of being "behind" the character(s) or narrator, wanting events to evolve in a particular way, believing it is right that the plot moves in a certain way	**A desire to advocate**—a growing conviction of what is "right" related to a concept; a desire to support, learn more about, and convince others of an idea
Believability—a sense that "this is real and I believe it"; a sense of satisfaction with the way the events evolved	**Fascination**—a growing sense of wanting to know more, a developing passionate interest in a particular topic or idea
A gradual recognition of patterns and symbols—the ability to use literary tools to recognize motifs, themes, and patterns; the ability to examine one facet of the text and extrapolate to a larger meaning	**A sense of cause and effect**—knowledge of how events relate to each other and how new events are likely to relate; a sense of the effect or impact of one force, factor, or event on another
A revision of one's thinking—changing one's mind, revising, rethinking, and reshaping understanding	**A revision of one's knowledge**—forgoing previously held knowledge/beliefs in favor of updated factual information

Fig. 9.1. The Outcomes of Understanding *(continued)*

Cognitive strategies may lead us to experience the following outcomes:

In Fiction/Narrative/Poetry:	In Expository Text:
An affirmation of beliefs/values/opinions— reaffirmation of existing beliefs/values/ opinions and/or developing new ones because of what we've read	**An affirmation of beliefs/values/opinions**— reaffirmation of existing beliefs/values/ opinions and/or developing new ones because of what we've read
An increase in cognitive stamina—the willingness to sustain interest and attention and to exclude competing or distracting interests	**An increase in cognitive stamina**—the willingness to sustain interest and attention and to exclude competing or distracting interests
Clear recollection—the sense of permanence that comes with deeply understanding something; the ability to reapply that understanding in a new situation	**Clear recollection**—the sense of permanence that comes with deeply understanding something; the ability to reapply that understanding in a new situation

and paused to think aloud about my schematic connections. Her eyes were brilliantly alive and eager. When I asked her if she would like to share her schema, she compared Ruby Bridges' second day of school in Mrs. Henry's classroom with her own first day in her present school, earlier in the spring.

"It was just like that in my comin' to this school. My mama walked me here to this school that first day but she couldn't the second day and I was scared, boy was I scared." With that comment, she had said what she wanted to say, but I've learned that there is always more. The depth of thought often doesn't emerge until the second, third, or fourth comment, so I pressed her, "What else, Samantha?"

"Well," she said, taking the book from my hands, "this last part— it made me feel sad when Ruby's mother went with her one day but then the next she said she couldn't go with her and that reminds me that my momma went with me at first and then she couldn't go." Essentially, she repeated what she had already said, so I reflected her words back to her. "So, you're saying that you really know how Ruby felt in the new school, especially on the second day when her mom couldn't go with her?"

"Yeah, I know that feeling and I was scared and she was scared too. But, you know that here there is lots of kids."

I wasn't sure where she was going with the last comment and said, "There are lots of kids here?"

"Yep, and Ruby was scared in her heart but there weren't other kids to make her forget the scared."

"Oh, I see—wait a second, Samantha, you're saying something really new and different here. You're saying that you could understand how Ruby felt about being new at school because you too have been scared when you were new here, but now you're saying that she faced a kind of fear you didn't have to face—she wasn't surrounded by other kids who distracted her and played with her and made her feel at home in her new school. Because she was attending a school that had previously served only white students, she was alone when all the white parents pulled their kids out of school. Did I get that right?"

This unleashed a torrent of new information. "Yeah, and it was different for her because, see, the white kids and those parents really hated her, and now I have to go to a new school, but I don't have to have it like that. White people don't keep their kids out of school because I'm here." She paused a long time and other kids' hands flew into the air. I gave them a signal to lower their hands and said, "I love the way Samantha takes her time to think."

Finally, Samantha said, "Except I know that in some places, white people still don't want black people there."

Best to let that comment rest in the air for a few moments, I thought. The rest of the class—about half African American students—seemed to lose themselves in thought.

Samantha spoke again. "I guess I do know more about Ruby than I thought." It sounded as if her thoughts had escaped her lips unintentionally.

The comments that followed from Samantha's classmates were respectful and very specific.

"My papa told us that when he was little, black children couldn't go to school with white children."

"In my old school, white kids always got the new stuff—books, balls for the playground, the best seats on the bus, and that shouldn't be true after Rosa Parks sat in the front for all black people."

"My papa says he still doesn't like black people and I do, and I get so mad at him but I still love him, but my mom says with some older folks, it's just that way, but I don't want him to still think that, but I try, but he says that's how he grew up and he ain't changin', but I don't know if that means I shouldn't love him, but I do."

It went on. Some comments I can't bring myself to write.

Sadly, the comments were real, close to home, and recent. The civil rights struggle is far from won in this country.

As the children shared their schematic connections, I grabbed a marker and recorded them on chart paper. When the talk dwindled, I rejoined the conversation.

"I want you to understand that the stories you have shared are so important that I'm thinking I'll teach you something I hadn't planned to teach today. Scholars have words to describe what you have been sharing today and I think you're ready—even though you're only in third grade and some kids don't get to learn about this kind of thing until they're in high school—I think you're ready to learn about what scholars call . . ." I paused for a long time, ensuring that I had everyone's undivided attention, and even interjected, "Are you sure you're ready to learn this?" They assured me that they were.

"Okay, I'm going to write this word on the right side of this chart alongside the schematic connections you've made. The word is *empathy*." I wrote it slowly, letting the children voice each phoneme as I wrote. "Empathy means that you not only understand someone else's experience, you actually share it. You have felt and known, for yourself, what another person is talking about. Your heart pounds with the clarity of remembering and your mind flies right to the moment in your own life when you felt the exact same way. When you read, it's one of the most important things you can experience. When you feel this way in your heart and mind, you can be pretty sure that you understand the book. It's an extraordinary and important experience. Did I explain what empathy is enough that any of you can tell me what empathy feels like?"

Immediately, the children responded. Raymond exploded, "I know, I know, I know. It's when you feel like you're right there in the book and you're the kid and you're already in the book and the author wrote it about *you*!"

I was completely caught up in their energy. They got it—they knew what it meant to empathize! They were eight and they got it.

"Absolutely, Raymond, that's empathy!"

DeVonte said, "I had empathy in another book. It was that book about those two girls a long time ago and it was about a fence and no white kid was s'posed to cross it and no black kid was s'posed to cross it, but these two girls, they sat on top—"

"*The Other Side*, by Jacqueline Woodson," I said.

"Yeah, *That Other Side*," he said, "I was empathy."

"Empathic," I added.

"Empathic, yeah, I was that when I was trying to make friends with some white kids at Big Brothers. So, it felt like maybe we wasn't s'posed to make friends, but I thought maybe I will and we played and fixed a bike together and stuff."

"So, DeVonte," I said, "you're empathic, you can really understand what the girls in *The Other Side* felt because you have felt the same thing. Can you tell me how that connection helped you understand *The Story of Ruby Bridges*?"

"I'm not sure."

I waited. "I know you're not sure, DeVonte, but if you were sure, what would you say?"

Long pause.

"Well, I think I know. Maybe I don't, because I didn't live in those days."

I waited. And hoped. I was not disappointed. I never am, if I have the discipline to wait.

"I think it felt like the people around her hated her for just being black."

Wait, I said to myself, don't let yourself speak.

"I think even though I live in the future, I think that people I still know, like my brother, still know what Ruby felt—like when the white people hated her—I think sometimes black people still, ahhh, don't know, wonder, I think, whether people, um, white people, like us at all or, umm, enough, you know?"

I don't know. I can't know. As a white person, I can never know. It breaks my heart, but this is an empathy I will never know. As much as I may wish to empathize, as much as I can work to imagine what they feel, I can never understand as deeply as Raymond or DeVonte or Samantha.

"DeVonte, I can never know, I can never fully empathize," I told him, "but I can feel in my heart just how much you do."

Though the lesson could have followed a number of different paths—we could have discussed the civil rights movement, we could have focused on how much schema their families' stories contributed to their understanding— ultimately, I chose to teach them about empathy. I have learned from kids like those in South Carolina that teaching them where a strategy can lead—empathy or any of the other outcomes—can help build an important shared language for talking about what they come to understand. And, in this case, focusing on empathy may have been more lasting than focusing on some of the events in this book or in their families' lives. Comprehension instruction should focus far more on how a strategy or an outcome can help them as readers in *any* reading situation than on recalling or describing events specific to a particular text. Comprehension instruction reaches into the future, equipping children with tools they can use—in this case schema and empathy—in many reading contexts.

DWELLING IN THE MIND

Jamika entered high school in the fall of 2007. We still communicate via text messaging and an occasional phone call. Her mom faxes assignments Jamika has been asked to complete and we laugh over and occasionally celebrate the way that Jamika's teachers have defined what "make sense" means. When asked to complete a worksheet called a "narrative pyramid," Jamika couldn't understand why she had been asked to put the name of a character on one line, two words describing the character on the lines just below, three words describing the conflict below that, four words describing the setting below that, and so on. She asked, in her ever-direct way, "Do you have to only use two words to describe the character because if you used more it would wreck the pyramid? I don't really get why it has to be in the shape of a pyramid, anyway, do you?" No, I don't, Jamika. To ask children to complete assignments like this isn't teaching comprehension—it's testing comprehension, and it isn't even a very authentic assessment of real comprehension. Why do we persist in doing it?

If I could rewind to the fall of 2000 when Jamika was an adorable second grader who looked up at me and said, "None of y'all ever say what make sense means," what would I say? I might just say, "Jamika, to understand means to remember. To understand means that you take your time to think about an idea for a long time; you hold it up to the light of your mind, turning it over and over until it becomes a part of you. It means you're willing to work hard to understand an idea, that even though you don't get it at first, you want to know with all your heart, so you talk to other people and read more and reread, and you ask people whose wisdom you trust and you keep thinking and thinking until you realize that you do understand. Sometimes understanding might feel like a tiny second when everything becomes clear—what adults call an 'aha' moment—other times it may dawn on you so slowly that without even noticing it, you have begun to understand. To understand, Jamika, means that you love thinking about an idea so much that you give your entire mind's attention to it; the whole world around you may seem not to matter. It may mean that you can hardly wait to talk to someone else so you build on what you know with their ideas. It also means that you're not interested in just one book, one genre, or one author; you feel an urge to explore a lot of different ideas. They might be very different, but you can fit them all into your capacious mind. To understand means you change your mind, Jamika; you realize that the more you read or study an idea, the more you want to know and the more you change your first thoughts. Authors want their readers to be changed, not just in what they know, but how they feel, what they value, and how they act to make the world a better place. When you understand, you may feel that everything you ever knew or believed or felt is changing—or you might feel even more secure and strong in your feelings, values, beliefs, and knowledge than you ever have before. If you understand, you see how things fit together, how one thing is the same as or different from another—you see patterns in ideas and can predict based on those patterns. When you understand, it means that you get to decide which ideas matter most and add those ideas to all the things you already know. Jamika, if you understand something, you get to feel your heart pound a little harder, you get the same emotions in your own heart that the characters in the book feel. When you understand, you may start to feel like you could read or learn for a really long time—you have what we call stamina for reading and learning—and at that moment you just can't imagine wanting to do anything else. To understand means that you get to feel what characters feel, you even know enough about their problems to think of your own ways to solve them. 'Make sense,' Jamika, means that you can use strategies like schema and questioning and inferring and determining importance to understand even more than the author and illustrator of the book wove into its pages—imagine knowing *more* than the author, Jamika! To understand is to decide to remember. To understand is to know that your mind holds important ideas, and you are the lucky one who gets to savor those ideas—you are the one who gets to try to make them last in your mind, just like you want to make a great cup of hot chocolate last on a cold day."

I wish I could have responded to Jamika in a more thoughtful way that day in Jackson, but it took the better part of six years for me to figure out at least a beginning response to her profound question. My hope for the readers of this book is that, alongside the children you teach, you build your own answers to Jamika's question. I hope that your thinking about the depth and breadth of children's thinking changes, that you come to understand how children's capacity for thinking is nearly limitless if we create the learning conditions to support it, if we provide a language to define and describe thinking, and if we simply ask, "What else?" or "I know you don't know, but what would you say if you did know?" There is always a deeper idea, an idea well beyond the superficial, if we have the patience to ask and the faith that they will answer. And to support you as you understand Jamika, means that we grownups must trust the vastness of your intellect and know that you will share your exquisite insight into the world. To help you understand, Jamika, we promise that we will not only ask, but listen.

Appendix A

Comprehension Strategies Defined

MONITORING MEANING

- Proficient readers monitor their comprehension during reading—they know when the text they are reading or listening to makes sense, when it does not, what does not make sense, and whether the unclear portions are critical to overall understanding of the piece.
- Proficient readers can identify when text is comprehensible and the degree to which they understand it. They can identify ways in which a text becomes gradually more understandable by reading past an unclear portion and/or by rereading parts or the whole text.
- Proficient readers know what they need to comprehend from a text—they are aware of their purpose for reading and what will be required of them with respect to reporting on their reading.
- Proficient readers are aware of the purpose for their reading and direct special attention to the parts of the text they most need to comprehend for that purpose.
- Proficient readers are able to assume different "stances" toward a text. For example, a child can read a book from the point of view of different characters, of a book reviewer, or of a writer seeking new techniques for his/her work.
- Proficient readers identify difficulties they have in comprehending at the word, sentence, and whole-text levels. They are flexible in their use of tactics to solve different types of comprehension problems.
    - Proficient readers solve word- and sentence-level problems with surface structure strategies such as decoding strategies and/or word analysis.
    - Proficient readers solve text-level problems by monitoring, evaluating, and making revisions to their evolving interpretation of the text while reading. They then compare the emerging meaning to their background

knowledge and make adjustments to incorporate new information into existing memory stores.

- Proficient readers can "think aloud" about their reading process. They are aware of and can articulate the surface and deep structure strategies they use to identify words, read fluently, and comprehend and can create solutions to reading and learning problems.
- Proficient readers can identify confusing ideas, themes, and/or surface elements (words, sentence or text structures, graphs, tables, etc.) and can suggest a variety of different means to solve the problems they encounter.
- Proficient readers are independent, flexible, and adaptive:
  - They show independence by using surface and deep structure strategies to solve reading problems and enhance understanding on their own.
  - They demonstrate flexibility by using a particular strategy (such as determining importance) to a greater or lesser degree depending on the demands of the text.
  - They are adaptive in their ability to "turn up (or turn down) the volume" on a particular strategy or use all comprehension strategies in concert.
- Proficient readers use text management strategies. They pause, reread, skim, scan, consider the meaning of the text, and reflect on their understanding with other readers.

Using Relevant Prior Knowledge, or Schema

- Proficient readers spontaneously and purposefully recall their relevant prior knowledge (schema) before, during, and after they read and learn (text-to-self connections).
- Proficient readers use their schema to make sense of new information as they read and to store that new information with related information in memory.
- Proficient readers assimilate information from text and other learning experiences into their relevant prior knowledge and make changes in that schema to accommodate the new information. Linking new understandings to other stored knowledge makes it easier to remember and reapply the new information.
- Proficient readers adapt their schema as they read, converse with others, and learn—they delete inaccurate information (naive conceptions), add to existing schema, and connect chunks of knowledge to other related knowledge, opinions, and ideas.
- Proficient readers can articulate how they use schema to enhance their comprehension in all forms of text and in all learning situations.

- Proficient readers capitalize on six types of schema when comprehending text and learning new material:
  - memories from particular experiences that shed light on the events, characters, and so on in a book (text-to-self connections)
  - specific knowledge about the topic; general world knowledge (text-to-world connections)
  - specific knowledge about text topics, themes, content, structure and organization (text-to-text connections)
  - their knowledge of potential obstacles to comprehension (particularly in nonfiction text or text with completely unfamiliar content)
  - knowledge about their own reading tendencies, preferences, and styles
  - specific knowledge about the author/illustrator and the tools he or she uses to create meaning
- Each type of schema permits students to monitor for meaning, pose questions, make predictions, draw conclusions, create mental images, synthesize, and determine importance as they read and learn.
- Teachers assist readers in activating their schema (giving students the necessary tools to recall relevant prior knowledge).
- Teachers help readers build schema (actually create background knowledge on a given topic, author, text structure, etc.) if they lack adequate schema for a particular reading situation.
- Students can articulate ways in which using schema enhances their comprehension.

ASKING QUESTIONS

- Proficient readers spontaneously and purposefully generate questions before, during, and after reading, depending on their purpose in reading.
- Proficient readers ask questions to:
  - clarify meaning
  - speculate about text yet to be read
  - show skepticism or a critical stance
  - determine an author's intent, style, content, or format
  - locate a specific answer in text
  - consider rhetorical questions inspired by the text

The types of questions differ based on the type of text (genre) and the reader's purpose.

- Proficient readers use questions to focus their attention on ideas, events, or other text elements they want to remember.

- Proficient readers understand that many of the most intriguing questions are not answered explicitly in the text but are left to the reader's interpretation.
- However, when an answer is needed, proficient readers determine whether it can be answered by the text or whether they will need to infer the answer from the text, their background knowledge, and/or other text.
- Proficient readers understand how the process of questioning is used in other areas of their lives, academic and personal.
- Proficient readers understand and can describe how asking questions deepens their comprehension.
- Proficient readers are aware that as they hear others' questions, new ones—called generative questions—are inspired in their own minds. In some cases, a reader's own question causes him or her to generate more questions.

INFERRING

- Inferring is the process of creating a personal and unique meaning from text. It involves a mental process that combines what is read with relevant prior knowledge (schema). The reader's unique interpretation of text is the product of this blending.
- When proficient readers infer, they create a meaning that is not explicitly stated in the text. The process implies that they actively search for or become aware of implicit meaning.
- Inferring may cause the reader to read more slowly, reread sections, converse, write, or draw to better understand the content.
- Inferences may be more thoroughly developed if the reader pauses to reflect and consider multiple interpretations and perspectives.
- When they infer, proficient readers:
  - draw conclusions from text
  - make reasonable predictions as they read, then test and revise those predictions as they read further
  - create dynamic interpretations of text that they adapt both while they read and after they read
  - use the combination of background knowledge and explicitly stated information from the text to answer questions they have as they read
  - make connections between conclusions they draw and other beliefs or knowledge, and use the inferences to extend and adapt existing knowledge
  - arrive at insight after struggling to understand complex concepts
  - make critical or analytical judgments about what they read
- When proficient readers infer, they are more able to remember and reapply what they have read, create new and revise existing background knowledge,

discriminate between and critically analyze text and authors, and engage in conversation and/or other analytical or reflective responses to what they read.

- Proficient readers revised their inferences based on the inferences and interpretations of other readers.
- A wide variety of interpretation is appropriate for fiction and poetry; a narrower range of interpretation is typical for nonfiction text. Teachers should allow great latitude for inferences, provided that the readers can defend their inferences with a description of relevant, prior knowledge and specific text they have read.

EVOKING IMAGES

- Proficient readers spontaneously and purposefully create images while and after they read. The images emerge from all five senses and the emotions and are anchored in a reader's prior knowledge.
- Proficient readers create images to immerse themselves in rich detail as they read. The detail gives depth and dimension to the reading, engaging the reader and making the text more memorable.
- Proficient readers use images to draw conclusions, to create distinct and unique interpretations of the text, to recall significant details, and to recall a text long after it was read.
- Images from reading frequently become part of the reader's writing.
- Images from personal experience frequently become part of a reader's comprehension.
- Proficient readers adjust their images as they continue to read. Images are revised to incorporate new information revealed through the text and new interpretations they develop while reading.
- Proficient readers understand and can articulate how creating images enhances their comprehension.
- Proficient readers adjust their images in response to the shared images of other readers.

DETERMINING IMPORTANCE IN TEXT

- Proficient learners make purposeful and spontaneous decisions about what is important in text at each level.
  - *Word level:* Words that carry the meaning are contentives; words that connect are functors. Contentives tend to be more important to the overall meaning of a passage than functors.
  - *Sentence level:* There are usually key sentences that carry the weight of meaning for a paragraph, passage, or section. Often, especially in

nonfiction, they may contain bold print, begin or end the passage, or refer to a table or graph.

- ○ *Text level:* The text contains key ideas, concepts, and themes; our opinions about which ideas are most important change as we read the passage. We typically make final conclusions about the most important themes after reading the passage, perhaps several times, and/or after conversing or writing about the passage. Clues, such as repetition for emphasis, illustrations or diagrams, symbolism, foreshadowing, character and setting prominence, and conflict all point to importance at the text level.

- • Decisions about importance in text are made based on:
  - ○ the reader's purpose
  - ○ the reader's schema for the text content—ideas most closely connected to the reader's prior knowledge will be considered most important
  - ○ the reader's sense of the aesthetic—what he or she values, considers worthy or beautiful
  - ○ language that surprises or otherwise captures the reader's sustained focus
  - ○ the reader's beliefs, opinions, and experiences related to the text
  - ○ the reader's schema for text format—text that stands out visually and/or ideas that are repeated are often considered most important
  - ○ the reader's understanding of text structures—for example, in a cause-and-effect text structure, the reader should direct her attention to those elements
  - ○ concepts another reader mentions prior to, during, or after reading

- • Frequently, pointing out nonexamples (what is unimportant) helps students to distinguish importance more clearly.
- • Interesting discussion emanates from dispute about what is most important. Children need to work toward defending their positions, but there is rarely one "right" set of important ideas.
- • Students should be able to articulate how they make decisions about what is important in a given context and how those decisions enhance their overall comprehension of the piece.

Synthesizing

The process of synthesizing occurs during reading.

- • Proficient readers are aware of changes in their ideas and conclusions about text as they read further into the text. They can articulate orally or in writing how their thinking about a given text evolves.
- • Proficient readers maintain a cognitive synthesis as they read. They monitor the overall meaning and themes (there is often more than one theme in the text). Proficient readers actively revise their cognitive synthesis as they read.

New information is assimilated into the reader's evolving ideas about the text, rendering some earlier decisions obsolete.

- Proficient readers are aware of the ways text elements (in fiction, character, setting, conflict, sequence of events, and resolution) "fit together" to create that overall meaning. They focus purposely on and use their knowledge of these elements to predict and synthesize as they build a sense of the overall meaning.

- Proficient readers are aware of text structures in nonfiction (cause and effect, compare/contrast, problem/solution, description, enumeration, and chronological paragraph structures). They focus purposefully on and use those structures to predict and synthesize as they build a sense of the overall meaning.

The process of synthesizing occurs after reading.

- Proficient readers are able to express, through a variety of means (written, oral, artistic, or dramatic), a cogent, succinct synthesis of what they have read that includes ideas and themes relevant to the overall meaning of the text.

- A synthesis is the sum of information from the text, other relevant texts, and the reader's background knowledge, ideas, and opinions, produced in an original way.

- Proficient readers use syntheses to share, recommend, and critically review books they have read.

- Proficient readers can articulate how using synthesis helps them better understand what they have read.

Appendix B

What's Essential?
Literacy Content K–12

SURFACE STRUCTURE SYSTEMS

Independent word use in which children use print knowledge to identify and write words, read fluently, both orally and silently, and write fluently.

What should we teach children to do within each system?

Graphophonic (K–2)

Recognize letters and features of letters.

Form both upper and lowercase letters.

Recognize all sounds associated with each letter.

Understand that there is a consistent relationship between letters and corresponding sounds—an alphabetic principle.

Isolate sounds in a word by pronouncing them separately.

Recognize patterns in words, such as spelling patterns or word families, and pronounce new words based on pattern.

Use the preceding strategies to pronounce unknown words in context and make early attempts at writing unknown words.

Lexical (K–12)

Recognize words instantly by sight (without sounding them out).

Recognize words as the same despite graphic differences (upper and lowercase, bold, italic, etc.) in different contexts.

Understand features of words (e.g., vowels in each syllable).

Write words in a graphically similar way consistently.

Continue to build a bank of words that can be spelled conventionally through all writing experiences.

Continue to build a bank of words that can be instantly recognized through all reading experiences.

Store all newly learned words in visual memory so they can be read fluently when next encountered.

Use the preceding strategies to identify words and write them rapidly and fluently.

Syntactic (K–12)

Recognize when language is constructed in a grammatically correct manner, whether spoken or written. Be aware when language sounds like language.

Recognize which words carry the weight of the meaning when spoken or written in a particular context.

Recognize and write acceptable word, sentence, paragraph, and text structure; understand and use increasingly complex text structures in reading and writing, speaking and listening.

Use knowledge of text structure and conventions of language to read and write fluently and comprehensively.

What do children need to know and be able to do to show us they can use each surface structure system independently?

Graphophonic (K–2)

Recognize spelling patterns and word families and generate new words from patterns already known.

Point and slide—gradually pronounce the letters in a word as they are revealed.

Use invented spelling during daily writing to practice phonics (encoding).

Isolate sounds within words and pronounce the sounds correctly.

Pronounce sounds based on recognition of letters and blends out of context.

Find graphophonically similar words in context.

Substitute a graphophonetically similar word when unsure how to pronounce a word in or out of context. Double check to make sure it is correct.

Search for words within words that are familiar; use them to pronounce and write unknown words.

Represent all syllables when attempting to pronounce an unknown word.

Lexical (K–12)

Demonstrate (write or show) various graphic representations (e.g., use larger/smaller letters, upper/lowercase) of a word, knowing that they are the same word.

Use words one can recognize visually in daily writing, gradually build a large bank of conventionally spelled words, and use them consistently in daily writing.

Demonstrate how to purposefully remember what a word looks like (closing eyes and picturing a word); find known words and pronounce them by sight.

Build a word bank of frequently used words (sight words and words associated with content being studied).

Practice increasingly fluent reading, both orally and silently, in increasingly difficult text,

Read with reasonable speed given the demands of the text.

Syntactic (K–12)

Become familiar with the "architecture" of language and discover how the syntactic system provides the structure and predictability of language.

Recognize (hear) increasingly subtle examples and nonexamples of syntax.

Predict accurately and/or substitute a grammatically correct form when unsure about a word (e.g., substitute a noun for a noun, a verb for a verb).

Predict based on text structures (beginning, middle, end, chronological, cause/effect, etc.).

Use increasingly complex sentence and text structure forms in writing.

Practice fluent oral reading with appropriate inflection and expression; account for varying punctuation.

Recognize author style in relation to flexible use of syntax.

Use word analysis strategies—look for recognized words within words, root words, compound words, prefixes, and suffixes.

Experiment with syntactical forms for various stylistic effects in writing.

Understand various text and paragraph structures from the word level (root words, prefixes, and suffixes) to the text level in narrative (character, setting, conflict, sequence of events, resolution) and expository (cause and effect, compare/contrast, chronological, enumerative, descriptive, and problem/solution) text.

DEEP STRUCTURE SYSTEMS

Independent construction of meaning and interpretation during reading and independent construction of meaning during writing

What should we teach children to do within each system?

Semantic (K–12)

Develop knowledge of a growing number of word meanings and use them in reading and content area study.

Reveal understanding of concepts that relate to words and phrases.

Generate a wide variety of associations (from personal experience as well as background knowledge) for word meanings.

Understand connections and relationships among many words.

Select words with care and precision when writing, closely matching meaning to purpose and audience, and showing nuanced understanding of the potency of particular words in particular contexts.

Schematic (K–12)

Know when they understand, when they don't, what they need to understand, and what they might do to repair comprehension when it breaks down.

Use personal experiences that relate to the text to enhance understanding.

Use world knowledge that relates to the text to enhance understanding.

Create background knowledge through reading and speaking to more knowledgeable others when needed to understand more challenging material.

Use knowledge of text types, elements, structures, genres, and formats to enhance understanding.

Use knowledge of the author's style to better understand text.

Use knowledge of related texts to better understand a given text.

Ask questions to clarify and probe meaning more deeply.

Create detailed images from the emotions and all five senses in order to understand more deeply.

Change their thinking, incorporating new information during reading; create a cogent synthesis, incorporating information from other sources as well as values, beliefs, and opinions after reading.

Understand the whole text and draw conclusions about it that may include inferences, opinions, and judgments.

Understand key themes and ideas in a text.

Build greater background knowledge than is actually used when writing fiction, nonfiction, or poetry.

Use knowledge of writer's tools to make writing more meaningful.

Pragmatic (K–12)

Interact with others or write to better understand the ideas in a given text.

Set and/or use a particular purpose for reading and writing.

Adapt written form and content for a specific audience.

Understand the social mores and needs of readers and writers in general and oneself in particular.

Enhance comprehension because of and in conjunction with the interpretations of others.

Use others' opinions and recommendations to revise one's writing.

Assume a stance toward the author, the text, and other readers.

Create models (oral, written, artistic, and dramatic) to show thinking about a text.

Make decisions about what is important to remember.

Recall and reapply concepts in new texts and contexts.

What do children need to know and be able to do to show us they can use each deep structure system independently?

Use Cognitive Strategies

Determine Importance

Infer

Ask questions

Activate and create schema

Use sensory and emotional images

Monitor for meaning

Synthesize

Understand Key Differences Among Narrative and Expository Text Genres, Structures, and Features

Recognize and use key types of expository paragraph structures (chronological, cause and effect, compare/contrast, problem/solution, enumerative, descriptive).

Recognize and overcome hurdles presented by expository text (anaphora, vocabulary load, inefficient predicting, insufficient background knowledge for text content and/or format, naive conceptions).

Recognize and use key features of expository text (bold print, captions, heading, italicized print, graphs, figures, photographs, and charts).

Recognize and use a variety of narrative text structures (leads, endings, character, setting, conflict, sequence of events, building action, creating suspense).

Recognize and use exposition, action, and dialogue in narrative text to develop character and plot.

Recognize and use key features and structures of other types of text such as poetry, persuasive text, journalism, opinion/editorial, biography, etc.

Understand the differing demands for comprehending a wide range of text types; use different text management strategies depending on the demands of the text (rereading, writing about text, taking notes, adjusting the pace of reading).

Write persuasively and meaningfully in a wide range of genres.

Recognize and use characteristics and qualities of a wide variety of genres.

Use Increasingly Sophisticated Vocabulary in Writing and Speaking

Reveal an understanding of subtle differences in word meanings.

Read books with increasingly difficult vocabulary.

Live a Literate Life

Use the rituals and routines that characterize a serious reader's and writer's life.

Know how readers select material to read, choosing to challenge themselves in increasingly more difficult texts and writing tasks.

Use a variety of approaches to select writing topics wisely and write for particular audiences and purposes.

Seek others' opinions and feedback; use that feedback to shape their own opinions, writing, and interpretations of text.

Understand that readers and writers are changed because of what they read and write; articulate those changes in themselves.

Engage fervently in reading and writing every day.

Dwell and focus on certain ideas in order to understand and/or articulate them with more depth and insight.

Struggle and persevere to understand a concept or to articulate it in writing.

Manipulate their thinking (use comprehension strategies) during a particular reading in order to understand more effectively.

Create oral, written, artistic, and/or dramatic models of their thinking about a text.

Build increasing stamina for reading and writing.

Engage in rigorous discourse about text and others' writing.

Appendix C

Conditions for Success in Reader's and Writer's Workshops

- Teachers create a climate of respect and civility using rituals, a predictable schedule, and well-defined procedures for meeting routine needs. They trust children to become increasingly independent and to work together to solve problems

- Teachers create a warm, inviting environment with soft lighting, work areas defined by rugs and bookshelves, readily available materials, and an abundance of children's work and records of their thinking on display.

- Teachers ensure that the classroom includes a variety of work spaces— comfortable places for children to work independently and talk with each other, an area for the whole group to gather, and a space for the teacher to meet with small groups.

- Teachers create a culture of rigor, inquiry, and intimacy by continually expecting more, probing ideas further, and pressing children to explore their intellect.

- Teachers create a culture conducive to in-depth study of books, genres, topics, authors, and comprehension strategies.

- Teachers provide equal access for all to the materials and expertise that readers and writers need.

- Teachers serve as learning models by living literate lives and modeling how literacy plays an important role in their lives.

- Teachers model what readers who comprehend think about and how they create a literate life.

- Teachers model what writers who write convincingly think about and how they observe the world to feed their writing.

- Teachers think aloud to reveal the thinking strategies proficient readers and writers use and to show how to use comprehension strategies and writer's tools.

- Children have at least three opportunities per week to participate in large-group, heterogeneous lessons (crafting sessions) focused on comprehension and writer's tools.
- Children choose most books and topics and the ways in which they share thinking and knowledge.
- Children confer with their teachers individually about their work as readers and writers. Teachers use conferences to understand children's present performance level and to suggest new directions for their reading and writing.
- Children have daily opportunities to read and write for long periods of time and to apply what has been taught in small- and large-group settings.
- Children have opportunities, as needed, to participate in more focused and intensive small-group instruction (invitational groups) to meet specific learning needs.
- Children engage in in-depth discourse about books, writers, and ideas every day.
- Children have regular opportunities to share ways they have applied what they learned in new contexts. Often children take responsibility for teaching each other (reflection sessions).

Appendix D

Conference Record

Name _____ Date _____

Surface Structure Systems

Text title _____

First reading? _____

Graphophonic

Evidence/patterns of strength and need: The student can identify words within a larger word, isolate and blend sounds to pronounce a word, use word families or physical strategies such as point and slide to identify unknown words, and so on.

Lexical

Evidence/patterns of strength and need: The child can immediately pronounce words upon seeing them in print without decoding them. The child recognizes words with graphic differences.

Syntactic

Evidence/patterns of strength and need: The child replaces unfamiliar words with words that make sense and sound like language (nouns with nouns, verbs with verbs); the child can identify which words hold the bulk of the meaning in a given sentence; the child can tell when language (spoken or written) sounds syntactically correct when pronounced out loud or read silently.

Deep Structure Systems

   Text title _____ First reading?_____
   Was text read aloud to child or did child read aloud? _____
   Did child read silently? _____
   Report on previously read material? _____

Semantic

Evidence/patterns of strength and need: The student is willing/able to speculate and elaborate on word meanings when unsure of definitions; the student is able to generate several associations with challenging, but known words; the student is able to make connections between known words and the words being discussed; the student is able to talk about how/why the word is important to the text.

Schematic

Evidence/patterns of strength and need: The student speaks of key themes in narrative text, ideas or concepts in expository text, relevant personal connections, inferences, probing questions, extending the text, through the use of sensory and emotional images, and synthesis of meaning before reading (changing thinking appropriately as he/she reads) and after reading (producing a cogent synthesis incorporating other sources of information and background knowledge).

Pragmatic

Evidence/patterns of need and strength: The student understands a variety of ways to interact with others in order to better understand the text, knows that his/her interpretations may enhance others' knowledge and vice versa, and understands how readers interact with one another.

Appendix E

Beyond Reporting on the Book

How Children Can Record Their Thinking About Books

Written Means to Share Thinking About a Book

Thinking notebooks—children record their strategy use in a notebook and comment on how the strategy helped them better understand the text.

Sticky notes to show strategy use in the text. These may be lifted so the teacher or other students can review them.

Double-entry journals containing quotes from the text followed by the child's thinking about the quote.

Fluency responses—writing everything the child thinks while reading a short text or excerpt.

Venn diagrams to show inference or how thinking overlaps (the intersecting area is the inference; the outer circles show the background knowledge and text sources for the inference).

Column charts to compare thinking for several rereadings of an excerpt. Children may use two, three, or four columns so their thinking on two, three, or four consecutive readings can be recorded adjacent to one another.

Letters to other readers and authors about a child's thinking/use of a strategy and how that strategy helped the child better understand a book.

Highlighting text to show where strategy was used.

Story maps/webs to show thinking about important themes/topics. The theme may be reported on one "branch" and the child's use of the strategy on "subbranches."

Transferring a text excerpt to a transparency. A teacher or child can use a wipe-off marker to show strategy use. This can be done in crafting or reflection sessions.

Coding text to show use of one or more strategies in the text—for example, DI = Determining Importance, ? = Question, IN = Inference.

Timelines to show how a child's thinking changes over time.

Bar and line graphs to show changes in frequency of strategy use over time.

Artistic Means to Share Thinking About a Book

Sketching images and other manifestations of thinking during reading.

Group depictions of text concepts and use of strategies during reading.

Artistic metaphors—creating a visual metaphor for thinking during reading.

Artistic timelines to show changes in thinking over time.

Photographs of the mind—quick images from particular moments in a text.

Oral Means to Share Thinking About a Book

Four-way share (clockwise share), typically at a table or desk grouping.

Think-pair-share—begin with pairs, refine thinking in fours, eights, and so on.

Book clubs and literature circles to focus on strategy use.

Turn and talk—a brief oral interchange on a focused topic, usually in the middle of a crafting session or during a composing session.

Large- and small-group sharing—learning to take time to think in front of a group.

Notice and share—observing demonstrations, fish bowl, and so forth.

Strategy study groups in which children gather to experiment with a strategy in a shared text.

Dramatic Means to Share Thinking About a Book

Any student-created dramatic representations of students' use of a strategy, their thinking about a book, or an excerpt from a book.

Appendix F

Thinking Strategies Proficient Learners Use

MONITORING MEANING

Readers

- Readers monitor their comprehension during reading. They know when the text they are reading or listening to makes sense, when it does not, what does not make sense, and whether the unclear portions are critical to overall understanding of the piece.

- Readers can identify ways in which a text gradually becomes more understandable by reading past an unclear portion and/or by rereading parts or the whole text.

- Readers are aware of the processes they can use to make meaning clear. They check, evaluate, and make revisions to their evolving interpretation of the text while reading.

- Readers can identify confusing ideas, themes, and/or surface elements (words, sentence or text structures, graphs, tables, etc.) and can suggest a variety of different means to solve the problems they have.

- Readers are aware of what they need to comprehend in relation to their purpose for reading.

- Readers must learn how to pause, consider the meanings in text, reflect on their understandings, and use different strategies to enhance their understanding. This process is best learned by watching proficient models "think aloud" and gradually taking responsibility for monitoring their own comprehension as they read independently.

Writers

- Writers monitor during their composition process to ensure that their text makes sense for their intended audience at the word, sentence, and text levels.

- Writers read their work aloud to find and hear their voice.

- Writers share their work so others can help them monitor the clarity and impact of the work.
- Writers pay attention to their style and purpose. They purposefully write with clarity and honesty. They strive to write boldly, simply, and concisely by keeping those standards alive in their minds during the writing process.
- Writers pause to consider the impact of their work and make conscious decisions about when to turn a small piece into a larger project, when revisions are complete, or when to abandon a piece.

Mathematicians

- Mathematicians check to make sure answers are reasonable.
- Mathematicians use manipulatives/charts/diagrams to help make sense of the problem.
- Mathematicians understand that others will build meaning in different ways and solve problems with different problem-solving strategies.
- Mathematicians write in order to better understand.
- Mathematicians check their work in many ways: working backwards, redoing problems, and so on.
- Mathematicians agree/disagree with solutions and ideas.
- Mathematicians express in think-alouds what's going on in their head as they work through a problem. They are metacognitive.
- Mathematicians continually ask themselves if each step makes sense.
- Mathematicians discuss problems with others and write about their problem-solving processes to clarify their thinking and make problems clearer.
- Mathematicians use accurate math vocabulary and show their work in clear, concise forms so others can follow their thinking without asking questions.

Researchers

- Researchers are aware of what they need to find out and learn about.
- Researchers can identify when they comprehend and take steps to repair comprehension when they don't.
- Researchers pause to reflect and evaluate information.
- Researchers choose effective ways of organizing information—taking notes, webbing, outlining, and so forth.
- Researchers use several sources to validate information and check for accuracy.
- Researchers revise and edit for clarity, accuracy, and interest.
- Researchers check sources for appropriate references and copyrights.

USING PRIOR KNOWLEDGE—SCHEMA

Readers

- Readers spontaneously activate relevant, prior knowledge before, during, and after reading text.
- Readers assimilate information from text into their schema and make changes in that schema to accommodate the new information.
- Readers use schema to relate text to their world knowledge, text knowledge, and personal experience.
- Readers use their schema to enhance their understanding of text and to store text information in long-term memory.
- Readers use their schema for specific authors and their styles to better understand text.
- Readers recognize when they have inadequate background information and know how to create it—to build schema—to get the information they need.

Writers

- Writers frequently choose their own topics and write about subjects they care about.
- A writer's content comes from and builds on his or her experiences.
- Writers think about and use what they know about genre, text structure, and conventions as they write.
- Writers seek to better recognize and capitalize on their own voice for specific effects in their compositions.
- Writers know when their schema for a topic or text format is inadequate and they create the necessary background knowledge.
- Writers use knowledge of their audience to make decisions about content inclusions/exclusions.

Mathematicians

- Mathematicians use current understandings as first steps in the problem-solving process.
- Mathematicians use their number sense to understand a problem.
- Mathematicians add to schema by trying more challenging problems and hearing from others about different problem-solving methods.
- Mathematicians build understanding based on prior knowledge of math concepts.
- Mathematicians develop purpose based on prior knowledge.
- Mathematicians use their prior knowledge to generalize about similar problems and to choose problem-solving strategies.
- Mathematicians develop their own problems.

Researchers

- Researchers frequently choose topics they know and care about.
- Researchers use their prior knowledge and experience to launch investigations and ask questions.
- Researchers consider what they already know to decide what they need to find out; they self-evaluate according to background knowledge of what constitutes high-quality products/presentations.

QUESTIONING

Readers

- Readers spontaneously generate questions before, during, and after reading.
- Readers ask questions for different purposes, including to clarify meaning, make predictions, determine an author's style, content, or format, locate a specific answer in text, or consider rhetorical questions inspired by the text.
- Readers use questions to focus their attention on important components of the text.
- Readers are aware that other readers' questions may inspire new questions for them.

Writers

- Writers compose in a way that causes the reader to form question as they read.
- Writers monitor their progress by asking questions about their choices as they write.
- Writers ask questions of other writers in order to confirm their choices and make revisions.
- Writers' questions lead to revision in their own work and in the pieces to which they respond for other writers.

Mathematicians

- Mathematicians ask questions before, during, and after doing a math problem.

  Could it be this?

  What happens if?

  How else could I do this?

  Have I seen this problem before?

  What does this mean?

- Mathematicians test theories/answers/a hypothesis by using different approaches to a problem.

- Mathematicians question others to understand their own processes and to clarify problems.
- Mathematicians extend their thinking by asking themselves questions they don't have answers to.

Researchers

- Researchers ask questions to narrow a search and find a topic.
- Researchers ask questions to clarify meaning and purpose.
- Researchers ask themselves:

  What are the most effective resources and how will I access them?

  Do I have enough information?

  Have I used a variety of sources?

  What more do I need?

  Does the concept make sense?

  Have I told enough?

  Is my thinking interesting and original and does my writing have voice?

INFERRING

Readers

- Readers use their schema and textual information to draw conclusions and form unique interpretations from text.
- Readers make predictions about text, confirm their predictions, and test their developing meaning as they read on.
- Readers know when and how to use text in combination with their own background knowledge to seek answers to questions.
- Readers create interpretations to enrich and deepen their experience in a text.

Writers

- Writers make decisions about content inclusions/exclusions and genre/text structure that permit or encourage inference on the part of the reader.
- Writers carefully consider their audience in making decisions about what to describe explicitly and what to leave to the reader's interpretation.
- Writers, particularly fiction and poetry writers, are aware of far more detail than they reveal in the texts they compose. This encourages inferences such as drawing conclusions, making critical judgments, predictions, and connections to other texts and experiences possible for their readers.

Mathematicians

- Mathematicians predict, generalize, and estimate.
- As mathematicians read a problem, they make problem-solving decisions based on their conceptual understanding of math concepts (e.g., operations, fractions).
- Mathematicians compose (like a writer) by drawing pictures, using charts, and creating equations.
- Mathematicians solve problems in different ways and support their methods through proof, number sentences, pictures, charts, and graphs.
- Mathematicians use reasoning and make connections throughout the problem-solving process.
- Mathematicians conjecture (infer based on evidence).
- Mathematicians use patterns (consistencies) and relationships to generalize and infer what comes next in the problem-solving process.

Researchers

- Researchers think about the value and reliability of their sources.
- Researchers consider what is important to a reader or audience.

USING SENSORY AND EMOTIONAL IMAGES

Readers

- Readers create sensory images during and after reading. These may include visual, auditory, and other sensory images as well as emotional connections to the text and are rooted in prior knowledge.
- Readers use images to draw conclusions and to create unique interpretations of the text. Images from reading frequently become part of the reader's writing. Images from personal experience frequently become part of the reader's comprehension.
- Readers use their images to clarify and enhance comprehension.
- Readers use images to immerse themselves in rich detail as they read. The detail gives depth and dimension to the reading, engaging the reader more deeply and making the text more memorable.
- Readers adapt their images in response to the shared images of other readers.
- Readers adapt their images as they read to incorporate new information revealed through the text and new interpretations they develop.

Writers

- Writers consciously attempt to create strong images in their compositions using strategically placed detail.
- Writers create impact through the use of strong nouns and verbs whenever possible.
- Writers use images to explore their own ideas. They consciously study their mental images for direction in their pieces.
- Writers learn from the images created in their minds as they read. They study other authors' use of images as a way to improve their own.

Mathematicians

- Mathematicians use mental pictures and models of shapes, numbers, and processes to build understanding of concepts and problems and to experiment with ideas.
- Mathematicians use concrete models and manipulatives to build understanding and visualize problems.
- Mathematicians visually represent thinking through drawings, pictures, graphs, and charts.
- Mathematicians picture story problems like a movie in the mind to help understand the problem.
- Mathematicians visualize concepts (parallel lines, fractions, etc.).

Researchers

- Researchers create rich mental pictures to better understand text.
- Researchers interweave written images with multisensory (auditory, visual, kinesthetic) components to enhance comprehension.
- Researchers use words, visual images, sounds, and other sensory experiences to communicate understanding of a topic (which can lead to further questions for research).

DETERMINING IMPORTANCE

Readers

- Readers identify key ideas or themes as they read.
- Readers distinguish important from unimportant information in relation to key ideas or themes in text. They can distinguish important information at the word, sentence, and text levels.

- Readers utilize text structure and text features (such as bold or italicized print, figures, and photographs) to help them distinguish important from unimportant information.
- Readers use their knowledge of important and relevant parts of text to prioritize in long-term memory and synthesize text for others.

Writers

- Writers observe their world and record what they believe is significant.
- Writers make decisions about the most important ideas to include in the pieces they write. They make decisions about the best genre and structure to communicate their ideas.
- Writers reveal their biases by emphasizing some elements over others.
- Writers provide only essential details to reveal the meaning and produce the effect desired.
- Writers delete information irrelevant to their larger purpose.

Mathematicians

- Mathematicians look for patterns and relationships.
- Mathematicians identify and use key words to build an understanding of the problem.
- Mathematicians gather text information from graphs, charts, and tables.
- Mathematicians decide what information is relevant to a problem and what is irrelevant.

Researchers

- Researchers evaluate and think critically about information.
- Researchers sort and analyze information to better understand it.
- Researchers make decisions about the quality and usefulness of information.
- Researchers decide what's important to remember and what isn't.
- Researchers choose the most effective reporting platform.

Synthesizing Information

Readers

- Readers maintain a cognitive synthesis as they read. They monitor the overall meaning, important concepts, and themes in the text and are aware of ways text elements "fit together" to create the overarching ideas. They use their knowledge of the text elements to make decisions about the overall meaning of a passage, chapter, or book.

- Readers retell or synthesize in order to better understand what they have read. They attend to the most important information and to the clarity of the synthesis itself.
- Readers capitalize on opportunities to share, recommend, and critique books they have read.
- Readers may respond to text in a variety of ways, independently or in groups of other readers. These include written, oral, dramatic, and artistic responses and interpretations of text.
- A proficient reader's synthesis is likely to extend the literal meaning of a text to the inferential level.

Writers

- Writers make global and focal plans for their writing before and during the drafting process. They use their knowledge of text elements such as character, setting, conflict, sequence of events, and resolution to create a structure for their writing.
- Writers study other writers and draw conclusions about what makes good writing. They work to replicate the style of authors they find compelling.
- Writers reveal themes in a way that suggests their importance to readers. Readers can create a cogent synthesis from well-written material.

Mathematicians

- Mathematicians generalize from patterns they observe.
- Mathematicians generalize in words, equations, charts, and graphs to retell or synthesize.
- Mathematicians synthesize math concepts when they use them in real-life applications.
- Mathematicians use deductive reasoning (e.g., reach conclusions based on knowns).

Researchers

- Researchers develop insight about a topic to create new knowledge or understanding.
- Researchers utilize information from a variety of resources.
- Researchers enhance their understanding of a topic by considering different perspectives, opinions, and sources.

Appendix G

Tactics for Teaching Comprehension

Effective Strategies for Teaching Deep Structure Systems

THINKING ALOUD

How do readers and writers think?

Teachers read aloud, pausing to make their thinking explicit.

Teachers are clear about how the strategy they're using helps them comprehend more than they would have comprehended without the strategy.

Teachers work to ensure precision in their think-alouds, focusing on the most far-reaching use of the strategy, resisting the urge to think aloud about the most obvious content or new vocabulary in the text.

MODELING

How do readers and writers behave?

Teachers describe their lives as readers and writers—where and when they like to read, how they choose books, what they prefer in relation to author's style, content, and genre

Teachers help students develop and describe their own preferences.

Teachers create a classroom environment conducive to in-depth learning. There are spaces conducive to group work, independent work, and small-group discussion; books are accessible; records of children's thinking and group ideas line the walls.

Teachers ensure that learning experiences are authentic—that what they ask students to do in class is something readers actually might choose to do outside of school.

DEMONSTRATION

How do readers and writers interact?

Teachers demonstrate or help students show how readers deepen comprehension via oral, written, artistic, or dramatic means.

Teachers set up "walk-through" demonstrations in which students enact the processes of obtaining resources and materials (e.g., select books) in the classroom or transition from one activity to another.

Teachers walk students through demonstrations showing how book clubs, think-pair-share, turn and talk, and other interactive sequences work in the classroom.

Teachers show through "fish bowl" types of demonstrations how students can build on other students' thoughts in discussion and how they can use "open forum," in which the whole group converses about a book or idea.

CONFERRING

How do readers and writers reach beyond their current work?

Teachers ensure ample time every day to confer with students during composing (independent work) time.

Teachers make decisions about which children need shorter, more frequent conferences and which will benefit from less frequent, more in-depth conferences.

Teachers ask each student to reflect on his or her growth as a reader in each conference.

Teachers build on each child's strengths and progress; they make clear, well-documented decisions about what to teach next in the context of the conference.

Teachers are explicit about how the strategy or skill discussed in a conference can be generalized beyond the current context.

Teachers invite students to share new insights during reflection sessions.

Managing Sharing Opportunities

How do readers and writers teach others?

Teachers encourage students not only to share, but also to teach others what they have attempted in their reading. These sessions can involve pairs, trios, or small or large groups and are often called reflection sessions.

Students who wish to share actually prepare a lesson and consider ways to teach that will meet all learners' needs.

Students reflect on their own learning and set new goals in the context of reflection sessions.

Students use a wide variety of learning strategies to share and focus not on retelling or summarizing a text, but on making their thinking about that text public.

Students may use written, oral, artistic, or dramatic means to share their thinking.

Appendix H

Best Practices in Oral Language Teaching and Learning

Suggested uses for this tool:

1. Review the goals (in bold print) as a summary of the research on best practices that relate to oral language learning. Then review the examples listed below the goals and generate your own examples of children's work from your classroom. By examining what your children are doing, you may be able to draw conclusions about areas in which you'd like to concentrate further instruction.

2. If, as a teacher, you would like feedback on your use of best practices in oral language, you might ask a colleague to observe in your classroom, taking notes on the reflection checklist that follows the examples.

3. Use video and/or tape recording to review your own teaching practice in relation to the criteria listed below.

4. Use the tool in faculty study groups in which you and your colleagues discuss ways you can continually stretch children's use of sophisticated oral language.

5. Share these goals directly with your students. You can tell them that you have goals in your use of language with students and that they should have goals in increasing the efficacy of their spoken language as well. The checklist can help you and your students keep track of evidence that you are meeting your goals.

Note: Teaching and learning goals are printed in ***bold***. Examples follow.

BEST PRACTICES: TEACHING

1. Teachers define sophisticated vocabulary parenthetically during discussion.

Example

Teacher: These people were descendants (or later relatives) of people who had come to North America by land from Asia.

2. Teachers explicitly teach the language of thought.

Example*

Teacher: When you're reading and you create images, those images help you understand books better. I'm going to describe some of my images as I read this book, *When I Was Young in the Mountains*, by Cynthia Rylant. When I stop reading to make myself hear the sounds of the crickets as she walks through the darkness to the 'johnny house,' I can better imagine how she feels being alone, listening to the sounds of the night around her. I almost feel, in my heart, how she might have felt *both* lonely and exhilarated by being alone in the dark.

3. Teachers purposefully use silence in their interactions with children.

Example

Teacher: Let me take just a moment to formulate my thinking. I am trying to use the best possible words to describe how my mental images help me better understand this book, *When I Was Young in the Mountains*. But I need time in silence to choose those words carefully. *(The teacher pauses and, with children looking on, takes time to think.)*

or

Teacher: Marcus, thanks for sharing your image with us. I wonder if you are thinking of any more images.

Marcus: Nope.

Teacher: I know you're not thinking of an image right now, but if you were, what would it be?

Marcus: Uhh.

Teacher: I know that what Marcus most needs now is time in silence to think of other images that will help him better understand the book. I so respect kids like Marcus who take their time to think. Look at Marcus; now that's the face of a thinker. Let's all give Marcus some time in silence to consider other images that will help him better understand this book.

4. Teachers generate anchor charts to capture and celebrate increasing sophistication in oral language use.

Example

Teacher: Let's add Jamal's comment to our list of ways in which writers try to write interesting leads. Jamal, how did you say it?

Jamal: I said we're trying to write breathtaking leads.

Teacher: Great, Jamal, I love the word *breathtaking* and we can add it to this chart, but I'd love to hear what you mean by breathtaking leads.

5. Teachers amplify simple syntax into more complex sentences.

Example

Chris: I thought that, too.

Teacher: So Chris, you agree with Jamal that part of a writer's job is to write in a way that causes readers to pay such close attention when they begin to read your piece that they don't want to put it down.

Chris: Yeah.

Teacher: I'd like to hear you amplify your comments. Can you tell Jamal exactly what you think about his comments?

Chris: I don't know what I said.

Teacher: You might want to start with this phrase: "Jamal, I agree that we need to write breathtaking leads, because . . . ."

6. Teachers generate spontaneous and planned opportunities for purposeful interaction between and among students.

Example

Teacher (spontaneous): I'm so sorry to interrupt your writing, but I wanted to call your attention to something I just heard in this conference with Tiffany. Tiffany has written a piece in which she leads with an image she had while reading yesterday. Though the image came to her when she was reading another book, she has decided to adapt it for her lead in a piece she's working on in her writing. Please turn to the person sitting closest to you and talk about how what Tiffany did might apply to you as a writer.

Teacher (planned): In your book clubs this week, please bring a book you've been reading at home, a book you're *not* reading with your group. Then, talk about how you use the strategy you're working on right now—creating images—to help you understand the book you're reading more deeply. You might want to start with words such as "The image I created was . . . ; it helped me understand this book more deeply because . . . ."

7. Teachers probe ("what else?") rather than immediately accept responses from children, helping them go deeper to discover the more complex and abstract insights that lie below the their initial responses.

Example

Kayla (raising her hand): I have a connection! I made a text-to-self connection when she walked to the johnny house outside—once when my dad and I went camping, we had to use an outhouse!

Teacher: I understand that you have a text-to-self connection, Kayla. Can you tell me how it helped you understand *When I Was Young in the Mountains* better?

Kayla: Nope.

Teacher: I know you're not sure, Kayla, but if you were sure, what would you say?

Kayla (waiting a long time): Uh, I think I got it that she had to go outside to go to the bathroom.

Teacher: What else?

Kayla: Well, really what I thought was that I was worried that an animal might get me when I got up and I was wondering if she got worried about animals getting her and then I thought, are her mountains like my mountains and do they have the same animals and . . . .

8. *Teachers explicitly teach and promote civility in oral language interaction.*

Example

Children are taught to be more formal in their academic language interactions than they might be in less formal settings. For example, when they are sharing in a large group, they invite each other to share by using the child's name and saying something like this:

Jessica: Jamal, would you like to share?

Jamal: Yes, thank you, Jessica.

After Jamal shares, he invites the next child to share in the same way.

Children are taught to enter the conversation with words such as, "Pardon me, Chris, I have something to say about your comment."

9. *Teachers model what it means to consider the perspectives of others.*

Example

Children observe instances in which their teacher demonstrates how his or her thinking was changed or influenced by another person. The teacher discusses ways in which his/her thinking changed and what another person said that caused him/her to pause and rethink an opinion or belief.

10. *Teachers demonstrate spirited and informed argument about ideas from text.*

Example

The teacher shows under what circumstances and in what ways readers and writers disagree about topics in text or their writing. He/she demonstrates how a well-reasoned argument can lead to deeper understanding of a topic.

11. Teachers restate and amplify what children share, allowing them to correct their restatement if necessary and to take additional time to elaborate their thinking.

> **Example**
>
> *Rachel:* I just think if I was that girl and I had to go outside in the night I'd be scared, and I can just feel like what the cold, wet grass would feel like on my bare feet and I think I wouldn't want to do that.
>
> *Teacher:* Rachel, tell me if I am restating this correctly, but I believe what you said is that when you imagine what it is like to feel the cold, wet grass on your feet as you creep through the darkness to the johnny house, you better understand this book because it allows you to imagine what the character's life is like and how different it is from your own.
>
> *Rachel:* Yeah, and all the things they do like taking a bath only once a week in water that would make me have goose bumps and ewww, I wouldn't want to share my water with my brother and the way she writes, you just feel like you're in the water. Ewww.

12. Teachers describe ways in which learning is a struggle.

> **Example**
>
> Teachers discuss times in which they read or wrote something that didn't make sense and how they reread and rewrote, talked with others, and incorporated their points of view until, gradually, they began to understand what they were writing or began to write more cogently.

BEST PRACTICES: LEARNING

1. Children seek to use recently introduced vocabulary, more sophisticated syntax, and formal academic language in their interactions with other children and their teacher.

> **Example**
>
> *Student:* I read *When I Was Young in the Mountains*, and stopped to create images that went beyond the pictures. I tried to stop and hear what the girl heard on her way to the johnny house. I tried to use emotional images to imagine what she might have felt. I wondered if she was scared, I wondered if she longed to have an indoor bathroom.

2. Children determine when to use colloquial/informal language and when to use more formal/academic language in settings, differentiating which is most appropriate in which settings.

Example

Children are taught that informal, dialectical, colloquial, and slang uses of language are acceptable in some settings and not in others. They can describe which settings require more formal academic language. These may include

- crafting sessions
- invitational groups
- reflecting sessions
- book clubs
- asking another child or the teacher for clarification
- speaking with other adults or visitors in the classroom and around the school

3. Children revise the content and delivery of oral language to suit different audiences.

Example

Children are taught to vary the vocabulary, pacing, and content of their ideas for different audiences in the classroom and around the school. For instance, language should vary when

- working with or presenting material to younger children
- sharing familiar content with other children in the classroom
- sharing unfamiliar content with other children in the classroom
- making a request of an adult
- making a request of another child
- sharing learning with other adults who may be unfamiliar with the material being shared
- speaking to the teacher in order to prove, defend, or exemplify recent learning

4. Children actively work to perfect oral language and know that they must be accountable for such improvements.

Example

Children use composing time to practice oral language presentations, continually seeking greater clarity and persuasiveness.

5. Children take the time they need (even if it means long periods of silence in the presence of others) to fully formulate and develop their thinking before they speak.

Example

Children grow increasingly comfortable with taking prolonged periods of time in silence to think about their comments before sharing them.

6. Children show evidence of listening intently when others are speaking, probing others to develop their thoughts. Children permit themselves to be influenced by others' thinking.

Example

Children ask relevant, probing questions to amplify their understanding of what others are sharing. They may probe in the same ways they have seen their teachers probe.

Chris: Jessica, I like the way you stopped reading and created images to help you understand more. Can you tell me more about the emotional images?

Jessica: I'm not sure.

Chris: I know you're not sure, but if you were sure, what would you say?

Jessica: Well, I just knew that if you were in that kitchen with that family you could smell all kinds of smells. It would probably smell like bacon and maybe like what it smells like at my house on Sunday mornings, and I just knew that I smelled what Cynthia Rylant smelled when she wrote it.

Chris: I never thought of smelling bacon on that page, but now I can too!

7. Children appropriately initiate and sustain conversation with other children and adults, including times when they express disagreement and defend their positions with evidence from text and/or background knowledge.

Example

Children can choose to engage in sustained conversation with others. They respond to their conversation partners' contributions rather than continually introducing their own topics into the conversation. They show genuine interest in their partners' contributions to the conversation and ask questions to help the partner further develop his/her thinking.

8. Children use oral language to show curiosity and to seek information about topics of interest.

Example

Children ask questions of adults and others knowledgeable about topics of interest to them. They can create formal interviews to pursue research topics when appropriate. They view others as sources of information and take pleasure from oral inquiry.

9. Children openly share what they are struggling most to learn, inviting support and celebrating insights that occur as a result of the struggle.

Example

Kenneth: "I was thinking I didn't get this *When I Was Young in the Mountains* book at all. I just kept wondering why an author who is as good as writing *The Relatives Came* would just put down all this stuff about these people a long time ago. But then I thought, wait a minute! This is like the book *Little by Little*. It's one of those memer [memoir] books, just shorter, and then I understood why she'd want to put in all that stuff about the mountains and those people a long time ago.

---

* All oral language excerpts from November 10, 2003, transcribed second-grade demonstration lesson in Guilford, CT. Text: *When I Was Young in the Mountains,* by Cynthia Rylant.

Oral Language Reflection Tool		
Oral Language Behavior	**Examples of Evidence**	**Evidence Observed**
Teaching		
Define sophisticated vocabulary parenthetically during discussion.	Rename vocabulary to define it.	
Explicitly teach the language of thought.	Model own thinking; use words like *schema, infer, I wonder, hear, imagine, feel*, etc.	
Purposefully use silence in interactions with children.	Model by taking time in silence to think about your own responses; give time for children to think in silence.	
Generate anchor charts to capture and celebrate increasing sophistication in oral language use.	Chart what the children say as a history of thinking and learning; put the child's name with his thoughts.	
Amplify simple syntax into more complex sentences.	Use complex sentences; encourage and/or help child to amplify (add to) his thinking.	
Generate spontaneous and planned opportunities for purposeful interaction between and among	Encourage children to converse and discuss. Turn and talk: • planned • spontaneous	
Probe—ask "what else?"—rather than immediately accept responses from children; help them to discover the more complex and abstract insightsthat lie below their initial responses.	Delve deeper; ask, "What else?"	
Explicitly teach and promote civility in oral language interaction.	Instruct and provide practice for children as they engage in independent discourse, showing respect for others in speaking.	
Model what it means to consider the perspectives of others.	Speak about ways in which you have been influenced by others' ideas.	

Figure continues on next page

Oral Language Reflection Tool *(continued)*

Oral Language Behavior	Examples of Evidence	Evidence Observed
Demonstrate spirited and informed argument about ideas from text.	Demonstrate how a speaker defends his/her opinions with support from the text, other factual sources, and/or background knowledge and experience.	
Restate and amplify what children share, allowing them to correct your restatement if necessary and to take additional time to elaborate their thinking.	Rephrase and restate, giving children an opportunity to elaborate their thinking.	
Describe ways in which learning is a struggle.	Show how the most important insights may come after a difficult intellectual struggle.	
Learning		
Children seek to use recently introduced vocabulary, more sophisticated syntax, and formal academic language in their interactions.	Do children use the vocabulary they have learned? Are their spoken sentences sophisticated?	
Children determine when to use colloquial/informal language and when to use more formal/academic language appropriately, in different situations.	Do they know when to use slang/home language and when to use formal/academic language? (What they say)	
Children revise the content and delivery of oral language to suit different situations.	Do they use appropriate content and tone of voice for different audiences? (How they say it)	
Children actively work to perfect oral language and know that they must be accountable for such improvements.	Do they practice oral language during composing sessions? Does it seem they know they should speak correctly?	
Children take the time they need (even if it includes long periods of silence in the presence of others) to fully formulate and develop their thinking before they speak.	Do they give themselves the gift of silence in order to develop their thinking?	

© 2008 by Ellin Oliver Keene, from *To Understand* (Heinemann: Portsmouth, NH).

Oral Language Reflection Tool *(continued)*

Oral Language Behavior	Examples of Evidence	Evidence Observed
Children intently listen when others are speaking, probe others to develop their thoughts, and describe when they are influenced by others' thinking.	Do they listen and respond appropriately?	
Children appropriately initiate and sustain conversation with other children and adults, including well-informed arguments about texts, ideas, and opinions	Do they start conversations? Are they at ease conversing with others?	
Children use oral language to show curiosity and to seek information about topics of interest.	Do they ask questions of adults and other children to gain knowledge?	
Children openly share what they are struggling most to learn, inviting support and celebrating insights that occur as a result of the struggle.	Do children trust others enough to share struggles and insights?	

Bibliography

Children's Literature

Balian, Lorna, and Lecia Balian. 1972. *The Aminal*. New York: Star Bright Books.

Bridges, Ruby. 1999. *Through My Eyes*. New York: Scholastic.

Bunting, Eve. 1996. *Going Home*. New York. HarperCollins.

———. 2001. *Gleam and Glow*. New York: Harcourt.

Cleary, Beverly, 1978. *The Great Gilly Hopkins*. New York: HarperCollins.

Coles, Robert. 1995. *The Story of Ruby Bridges*. New York: Scholastic.

George, Jean Craighead. 1972. *Julie of the Wolves*. New York: HarperCollins.

Hoestlandt, Jo. 1993. *Star of Fear, Star of Hope*. Paris: Editions Syros.

Kraus, Robert, and Jose Aruego. 1971. *Leo the Late Bloomer*. New York: Windmill Books.

Kraus, Robert, Jose Aruego, and Ariane Dewey. 1974. *Herman the Helper*. New York: Simon & Schuster.

Lewis, C. S. 1950. *The Lion, the Witch and the Wardrobe*. London: C. S. Lewis Pte. Limited.

Muth, Jon. 2002. *The Three Questions*. New York: Scholastic.

Paterson, Katherine. 1977. *Bridge to Terabithia*. New York: HarperCollins.

Rawls, Wilson. 1961. *Where the Red Fern Grows*. New York: Doubleday.

Rylant, Cynthia. 1996. *An Angel for Soloman Singer*. New York: Scholastic.

Say, Allen. 1993. *Grandfather's Journey*. New York: Scholastic.

Smith, Frank Dabba. 2005. *Elsie's War*. London: Frances Lincoln.

Van Allsburg, Chris. 1986. *The Stranger*. New York: Houghton Mifflin.

Woodson, Jacqueline. 2001. *The Other Side*. New York: G. P. Putnam's Sons.

———. 2002. *Our Gracie Aunt*. New York: Hyperion.

References from the Mentors Sections

Bois, Yves-Alain. 1998. *Matisse and Picasso*. Paris: Flammarion.

Cisneros, Sandra. 1984. *The House on Mango Street*. New York: Alfred Knopf.

Danticat, Edwidge. 1994. *Breath, Eyes, Memory*. New York: Soho Press.

Frankel, Viktor. 1988. *Man's Search for Meaning*. New York: Pocket Books.

Jin, Ha. 1999. *Waiting*. New York: Random House.

Kushner, Harold. 1981. *When Bad Things Happen to Good People*. New York: Schocken.

Levin, Gail. 1995. *The Poetry of Solitude: A Tribute to Edward Hopper*. New York: Universe.

Manchester, William. 1992. *A World Lit Only by Fire: The Medieval Mind and the Renaissance*. Boston: Little, Brown.

Neruda, Pablo. 1937. *Spain in the Heart*. Santiago, Chile: Fundación Pablo Neruda.

———.1970. *Neruda: Selected Poems*. Translated by Anthony Kerrigan. New York: Houghton Mifflin.

———. 1974. *Memoirs*. New York: Penguin.

———. 1994. *Odes to Common Things*. New York: Bullfinch Press.

———. 1995. *Love: Ten Poems by Pablo Neruda*. New York: Hyperion.

Poirot, Luis. 1990. *Absence and Presence*. New York: W. W. Norton.

Price, Reynolds. 1982. *A Whole New Life*. New York: Scribner.

———. 1999. *Letter to a Man in the Fire*. New York. Simon & Schuster.

———. 2000. *Feasting the Heart*. New York: Simon & Schuster.

Schmied, Wieland. 1999. *Edward Hopper: Portraits of America*. Munich/New York: Prestel-Verlag.

Stone, Irving. 1934. *Lust for Life*. New York: Doubleday.

Professional Resources

Beck, Isabel. 2006. *Making Sense of Phonics*. New York: The Guilford Press.

Block, C., and M. Pressley, eds. 2002. *Comprehension Instruction: Research-based Best Practices*. New York: The Guilford Press.

Calkins, Lucy. 1989. *The Art of Teaching Writing*. Portsmouth, NH: Heinemann.

Changeaux, Jean-Pierre, and Paul Ricoeur. 2000. *What Makes Us Think? A Neuroscientist and a Philosopher Argue About Ethics, Human Nature and the Brain*. Princeton, NJ: Princeton University Press.

Dymock, S. 2005. "Teaching Expository Text Structure Awareness." *The Reading Teacher* 59(2): 177–182.

Egan, Kiernan. 1997. *The Educated Mind: How Cognitive Tools Shape Our Understanding*. Chicago, IL: University of Chicago Press.

Gardner, Howard. 1997. *Extraordinary Minds*. New York: Basic Books.

Graves, Donald. 2003. *Writing: Teachers and Children at Work*. 2nd ed. Portsmouth, NH: Heinemann.

Hall, K. M., B. L. Sabey, and M. McClellan. 2005. "Expository Text Comprehension: Helping Primary-grade Teachers Use Expository Texts to Full Advantage." *Reading Psychology* 26: 211–234.

Hansen, Jane. 2001. *When Writers Read*. 2nd ed. Portsmouth, NH: Heinemann.

Harvey, Stephanie, and Anne Goudvis. 2000. *Strategies That Work*. Portland, ME: Stenhouse.

———. 2005. *The Comprehension Toolkit*. Portsmouth, NH: Heinemann.

Heath, Shirley Brice. 1983. *Ways with Words*. Cambridge, UK: Cambridge University Press.

Hindley, Joanne. 1996. *In the Company of Children*. Portland, ME: Stenhouse.

John-Steiner, Vera. 1997. *Notebooks of the Mind*. Oxford, UK. Oxford University Press.

Johnston, Peter. 2004. *Choice Words*. Portland, ME: Stenhouse.

Keene, Ellin Oliver. 2006. *Assessing Comprehension Thinking Strategies*. Huntington Beach, CA: Shell Educational Publishing.

Keene, Ellin Oliver, and Susan Zimmermann. 2007. *Mosaic of Thought: The Power of Comprehension Strategy Instruction*. 2nd ed. Portsmouth, NH: Heinemann.

Langer, Ellen. 1989. *Mindfulness*. New York: Perseus.

———. 1997. *The Power of Mindful Learning*. New York: Perseus.

Miller, Debbie. 2002a. *Reading with Meaning*. Portland, ME: Stenhouse.

———. 2002b. *Happy Reading* (videotape). Portland, ME: Stenhouse.

Morgan, Bruce. 2005. *Writing with Tweens*. Portland, ME: Stenhouse.

Moss, B. 2004. "Teaching Expository Text Structures Through Information Trade Book Retellings." *The Reading Teacher* 57(8): 710–718.

National Reading Panel. 2000. *Teaching Children to Read*. Report of the National Reading Panel. Bethesda, MD: National Reading Panel.

Newkirk, Thomas. 2002. *Misreading Masculinity*. Portsmouth, NH: Heinemann.

Pearson, P. D., and Nell Duke. www.itrc.ucf.edu/forpd/strategies/strattextstructure.html (accessed April 2006).

Pinker, Steven. 1997. *How the Mind Works*. New York: Norton.

Ray, Katie Wood. 1999. *Wondrous Words*. Champaign/Urbana, IL: National Council for Teachers of English.

Ritchhart, Ron. 2002. *Intellectual Character: What It Is, Why It Matters, and How to Get It*. Hoboken, NJ: Jossey-Bass.

Rumelhart, D. E. 1976. "Toward an Interactive Model of Reading." In *Attention and Performance, VI*, edited by S. Dornic. Hillsdale, NJ: Erlbaum.

———. 1981. "Schemata: The Building Blocks of Cognition." In *Comprehension and Teaching, Research Reviews*, edited by J. T. Guthrie. Newark, DE: International Reading Association.

Singer, Harry, and Robert Ruddell. 1985. "The Interactive Reading Process: A Model." In *Theoretical Models and the Processes of Reading*. 3rd ed. Newark, DE: International Reading Association.

Smith, Frank. 1991. *To Think*. New York: Teacher's College Press.

Sweet, A. P., and C. E. Snow, eds. 2003. *Rethinking Reading Comprehension*. New York: The Guilford Press.

Tovani, Cris. 2000. *I Read It, But I Don't Get It*. Portland, ME: Stenhouse.

——. 2004. *Do I Really Have to Teach Reading?* Portland, ME: Stenhouse.

Vacca, R. T., and J. L. Vacca. 1999. *Content Area Reading: Literacy and Learning Across the Curriculum*. 6th ed. New York: Longman.

Williams, J. P. 2005. "Instruction in Reading Comprehension for Primary-grade Students: A Focus on Text Structure." *The Journal of Special Education* 39(1): 6–18.

Zemelman, Steve, Harvey Daniels, and Arthur Hyde. 2005. *Best Practice: Today's Standards for Teaching and Learning in America's Schools*. 3rd ed. Portsmouth, NH: Heinemann.

Index